The Life-Threatened Elderly

The Life-Threatened Elderly

EDITED BY

Margot Tallmer, Elizabeth R. Prichard, Austin H. Kutscher,
Robert DeBellis, Mahlon S. Hale, and Ivan K. Goldberg

With the Editorial Assistance of Lillian G. Kutscher

New York   Columbia University Press   1984

Columbia University Press
New York   Guildford, Surrey
Copyright © 1984 Columbia University Press
All rights reserved

Printed in the United States of America

Clothbound editions of Columbia University Press Books are Smyth-
sewn and printed on permanent and durable acid-free paper

Library of Congress Cataloging in Publication Data
Main entry under title:

Thanatologic issues of old age.

  (Foundation of Thanatology series)
  Bibliography.
  Includes index.
  1. Terminal care. 2. Aged—Psychology. 3. Death—
Psychological aspects. I. Tallmer, Margot.
II. Series: Foundation of Thanatology series
(Columbia University Press)
R726.8.T466 1984   362.1'75   83-14263
ISBN 0-231-04966-8

Contents

Preface

MARGOT TALLMER

CURRENT INTEREST in the field of gerontology has been generated in part by the numerical growth of our older population, in part by the frightening fragility of their economic security, and in part by their social isolation as a result of the separating effects of the geographic mobility of younger kin. In general, the issues of retirement, correlates of widowhood, intergenerational relationships, and the effects of institutionalization have engaged the research efforts of social scientists in gerontology.

Concomitantly, we have witnessed a surge in popular concern with the topic of dying—with a proliferation of studies and speculations on all aspects of death among many population groups. Unfortunately, aging and dying have often been treated as parts of a single equation: to be old is to be dying.

One theory of aging, the disengagement theory, reflects the supposed linkage between senescence and death. According to this theory, psychological and social disengagement, broadly defined in terms of "withdrawal," are dress rehearsals for the final drama which is the scene of death: we all begin to disengage in middle age or thereabouts so that we can comfortably depart in old age, gratified because our dropping out will not upset our already loosened connections with the social network. Disengagement, seen in this light as a natural, voluntary, circular, and inevitable process of withdrawal, leaves both the disengaged and society happier. In this theory, there is a clear association between aging and death, with the ultimate in disengagement being death itself. Other theorists, emanating from Freud and his followers, go further, proposing a death instinct which is present from birth.

Disengagement theory is a sociological explanation of the need for society and the individual to deal with the physical fact of impending death in middle age. Some of the studies that have resulted from the theoretical propositions include the Freudians' ideas of diminished ego energy.

We do not agree with the disengagement theory, and its notions have not been validated empirically. The fact is that we do not observe that most elderly are, or desire to be, persistently and purposefully concerned with death. Many gerontologists specifically press for continued, sustained involvement with life throughout the life span. They urge a resistance to the narrowing of social roles and opportunities by substituting new activities for those one is forced to surrender and by denying the association of being old with being dead; in short, by devoting oneself to life, not death.

This act of resistance on the part of the elderly becomes more difficult when they are faced by life-threatening events. At these times, those who care about the elderly can help them to survive rather than to lose hope. When death becomes a sudden and imminent reality, the process of dying, with all the implied psychological and physical changes, is then a paramount problem. Older persons naturally worry about the process of dying, not death itself. That process may involve having their personal decisions taken out of their hands. Indeed, severe illness does often preclude personal choices, with decisions being geared to medical exigencies and made by authorities. Solutions emerge as hasty compromises, imperfect and only temporary, but in the meantime the geront may experience a loss of autonomy that those same authorities may never take steps to reverse, contain, or even acknowledge.

Any imposed decision, no matter how well considered, is less easily accepted than a self-made, voluntary choice. Furthermore, some issues are so affect-laden that any reasoned acceptance of a solution may be impossible. For example, institutionalization evokes such anger and fear, such negative images, that although it may be the most reasonable choice, it cannot be rationally considered by the older person. The same may be true when an ailing older person is forced to stay in a hospital, though preferring to die at home, because the support system necessary for home care is not available.

Society is not conspicuously helpful here. When a young person is in danger of dying, societal efforts are mobilized to prolong or sustain life. The nature of any such extended efforts is questioned when the patient is old, and the issue of choice in extending life by mechanical means, so important today, may not even exist as a possibility for the elderly. Many nursing homes have no advanced technological equipment at all, thus institutionalizing a sense of hopelessness and the inevitability of imminent death.

The interplay between normal aging and life-threatening events morally and psychologically should be understood by the persons involved—in this case the elderly and their families or social network. The elderly themselves, the caregivers, and the professionals must be aware of and alert to the information, findings, and resources now available. Humaneness and fairness in services and treatment emerge only from an informed awareness of the multiple problems to be solved and the experiences of others in finding solutions. We need education about aging, about the human needs of the elderly, and the issues inherent in old age in both habitual and life-threatening situations. Then, when the elderly confront crisis, activities and energies supportive of hope and function can be mobilized to accomplish the tasks of living.

Acknowledgment

THE EDITORS WISH to acknowledge the support and encouragement of the Foundation of Thanatology in the preparation of this volume. All royalties from the sale of this book are assigned to the Foundation of Thanatology, a tax exempt, not for profit, public scientific and educational foundation.

Thanatology, a new subspecialty of medicine, is involved in scientific and humanistic inquiries and the application of the knowledge derived therefrom to the subjects of the psychological aspects of dying; reactions to loss, death, and grief; and recovery from bereavement.

The Foundation of Thanatology is dedicated to promoting enlightened health care for life-threatened or terminally ill patients and their families. The Foundation's orientation is a positive one based on the philosophy of fostering a more mature understanding of life-threatening illness, the problems of grief, and the more effective and humane management and treatment of patients and family members in times of crisis.

Part
One

The Meaning of Aging

On Thanatology

ANONYMOUS

I KNOW NOW that I am going to die relatively soon. The team of doctors who made the diagnosis and prognosis are all specialists on the staff of the four-year medical school at the University of North Carolina at Chapel Hill, which includes the North Carolina Memorial Hospital, a teaching institution.

The prognosis, based on statistical data and their judgment, is that I may live from six to eighteen months, barring an accident, with not more than a one in one hundred chance that I might have a remission that would change this judgment.

More than three years ago, after excising the upper right lobe of my lung, where he had discovered a large carcinoma with squamous type cells, the surgeon told my family that I would not live more than one year. Later, after he discharged me from his care, he told me that statistically he believed that I would be dead within five years. Two years later, the head of the team of physicians at Chapel Hill examined me and told me that he believed my basic good health had overcome this original tumor and that I was completely free from its influence.

A little more than a year later, with the use of his team of specialists and the most sophisticated equipment, he found a second large tumor of the same type, which was the size of an orange, practically closing one of the twin bronchi, pressing on the other, and also pushing my trachea to one side. Without urgent therapy, this threatened to completely cut off my respiration. After this diagnosis was confirmed, cobalt radiation and a variety of palliative medicines were immediately begun.

After I had received the permissible lifetime limit of cobalt radiation, based on their calculations, an x-ray showed that the cobalt had shrunk the tumor, and they predicted it would continue to shrink in the weeks and months ahead. Nevertheless, they predicted that, even if this tumor did not revive immediately or continue to block my respiration, other pockets of malignant cells undoubtedly existed in various parts of my body and would break out somewhere in succession and in the near future.

I was, therefore, put on a 60-day schedule for examinations, which might find new symptoms, and for decisions on palliative therapy, if any, during the time remaining to me. Both my local internist and my radiologist were to continue to monitor me between these periodic examinations by the original team in Chapel Hill.

Unsurprised, I was ready for this event and the conclusions reached, for I had been given this knowledge frankly by my surgeon who had removed the first tumor three years and four months previously. I had, therefore, been able to think through and arrive at a conclusion about reordering the priorities of my life and the remaining time left to me. I attempt here to briefly state what these are:

1. I intend to spend this period in cultivating my family and my closest friends.

2. I will stay at my home, except for trips to Chapel Hill for examination, so long as I am conscious and also until my bodily functions begin to break down.

3. I have then requested, and have agreement with my wife, my son, and my personal internist, that I may be taken to the local hospital but only to receive palliative treatment. I wish to die a natural death without the use either of medicine or of machinery and equipment that would keep me alive beyond this point. This means, I hope, that I may be able to retain some dignity in the process of dying, as opposed to having my life extended mechanically and medically when it no longer means anything to me and can serve no purpose for my family and friends.

This is not a sudden change in attitude. I have been acquainted with death all my life. As a little boy, from age six onward, I shared with the family in looking at the open casket and heard their outspoken grief. And then again I would share with the family, or with friends if the deceased was not a member of the family, the open coffin with its occupant lying in state in the church, the short trip to the deep and narrow grave, watching the coffin lowered, and hearing the quick thuds of earth shoveled into the grave by volunteer teams of family and friends, who gave a final shape to the mound and then placed flowers on it. These experiences were continued throughout my teenage and adult life at frequent intervals, so that I can carefully say that I am acquainted with and unafraid of death. I do have a human fear, which I can tolerate, of the ordeal of the last few days that must be experienced unless I have a medical accident.

4. In the meantime, I will continue to enjoy each day with my family and friends and to circulate among them in my locality; to travel with them to nearby points, such as the mountain peaks that surround my home; to occupy myself with my favorite pursuits of reading, bird watching, walking, and debating issues with my closer friends—issues in which we are mutually interested—that include among many others my religion and my philosophy, which I think of as two separate personal attributes.

5. My religion is, I think, a universal one that finds good in many, if not all, of the major religions and contains feeling and emotions that started in my youth and have followed throughout my life, making me what I am. In this I have a faith, a security that I think I will not lose and that is my own personal experience modified by many years of searching.

6. My philosophy is my critical mind, ever standing to one side and watching me and my religious feelings, ready to question every point of faith and to enjoy speculations about what might be the truth, knowing that with a finite mind I cannot ever reach the infinite truth.

7. I would like to hope for a personal immortality, but I cannot imagine one that would not become stale and boring to me after a period of time. My religion and faith tell me that I may be given new knowledge so that I can understand after leaving the present world in which I live as an active being.

Finally, I have been strangely drawn to poetry and prose writings, that touch on the subject of thanatology and have discussed this with many friends at various times. One of them told me that this strange attraction was no more than looking at black and white, that the white could not be enjoyed without the black contrast, and that life could not be meaningful and rich and full without my knowing that a part of it is death. I am trying to bridge the gap between this normal lifetime attitude and the necessity for a compromise surrender, which I must now face, both as a matter of faith and of being.

On Human Behavior
and the Fear of Death

MAX M. STERN

FREUD'S PREDICTION MORE than 50 years ago that in a few dozen years progress in biology would blow away "the whole of our artificial structure of hypotheses" (1920:60) has come true. Recent discoveries of biology, especially those of molecular biology and neuropsychology, have rendered obsolete the fundamental thesis of the classical theory of psychoanalysis according to which the motivation for all organismic processes is the *need for discharge of instinctual energy*. From these findings arose the teleonomic theory formulated by the French biologists (Monod 1971; Jacob 1973; and others) and the Russian neuropsychologists (Luria et al. 1973).

The teleonomic theory is based on the Darwinian-Mendelian theory of selective survival. It postulates that survival is guaranteed by the operation of structures that emerged from evolution because of their success in overcoming trauma and death. In this theory, the development of the structure is guided by the teleonomic program encoded in the chromosomes of every cell. Their operation is regulated by the operation of the reticular activating system, a structure in the brain that coordinates the parts of the central nervous system.

The term *teleonomic* refers to a goal directedness determined, not by a vitalistic force (as the term *teleologic* does), but by the historical process of evolution. This does not mean that evolution works with a goal in mind. It means that in evolution, through selective survival, chance occurrences become necessities. According to Monod, all teleonomic structures, all the performances, all the activities that contribute to the success of the essential program are called teleonomic (1971:14).

The operations of all structures are induced by adequate stimuli. They contain information about the meaning of a situation and activate a pressure that we should call teleonomic pressure. The teleonomic pressure emerges like the teleonomic code from natural selection. Unlike the instinctual drives, it has no directing quality and does not dispense energy but uses energies that stem from the oxidation of metabolites activated by the stimulation.

Death

In the classical psychoanalytic theory, death is the effect of an instinct pressing for discharge, be it the death instinct or the aggressive instinct turned toward the self. The mere fact of death seems to contradict the teleonomic theory. Actually, the existence of death points to the dialectical aspect of the life process. On the one hand, structures evolving from evolution do guarantee survival of the individual, while on the other hand, they instigate his death in the interest of the survival of the species. This ambiguity is the effect of the introduction of sexual reproductivity. Unlimited sexual procreation would threaten extinction because of the limited quantities of provisions indispensable for the maintenance of life, such as oxygen and food.

While the individual cell is dissolved in reproduction by the fission of unicellular organisms, the parental cells survive in multicellular organisms with sexual reproduction. In the latter case, the individual's death becomes a necessary condition for the survival of the species. Not death from without, as a result of some accident, but death imposed from within—that is, by biotrauma. Jacob, the famous biologist and Nobel Prize winner, stated that there had to be an equilibrium between sexual effectiveness and the disappearance of the generation that had completed its role in reproduction. The adjustment of these two parameters was also the effect of natural selection, determining the maximum duration of life of individuals and species. Just as other functions, e.g., the mating period, so was the span of life *"prescribed by the [teleonomic] programme* which, from the moment the ovule is fertilized, fixes the genetic destiny of the individual"* (1973:310; italics added).

Thus, the life process reflects a dialectical ambiguity: processes promoting death, manifest in the role of ubiquitous traumata from within, are countered by processes warding off disorganization and death. This ambiguity explains the role that trauma and death have in the extraordinary development of the human mind.

Biotrauma and Mental Development

That every human infant goes through trauma from within is the effect of the immaturity of the human organism at birth. It is the necessity to ward off trauma that accounts for the spectacular development of the human mind.

The immaturity, most conspicuous at birth, ends only with the emerging of the mature organism in late adolescence. This immaturity underlies the diphasic nature of man's adaptation—that is, that the mode of adaptation in the infantile phase is different from that of the adult.

Infantile Dependency

In the infantile phase, survival is predicated on the fulfillment of symbiotic needs by parental objects. Symbiosis, from the Greek, meaning "living together," refers to an intimate association or close union of two dissimilar organisms. The term is ordinarily used in cases where the association is advantageous or even indispensable for survival to one or both parties. Symbiosis exists in all species, be it in the form of group formation, as in elephants, wolves, ants, bees, termites; or in the form of parasitism, as in bacteria, fungi, and so forth.

Mahler describes in detail how the symbiotic relationship of mother and child in the early infantile phase is complemented by its antithesis, the individuation separation. In the infantile phase, both symbiotic and individuational trends are running side by side. The individuation separation finally takes over in the transitional phase of adolescence and leads to the final individuation separation that characterizes adulthood. In the phase of infantile immaturity, survival is predicated on symbiotic dependence; in adulthood, it demands independence of judgment and action.

The Biotrauma in Infancy

Characteristic of the early infantile phase are biotraumata evolving from the immaturity of the infant's organism at birth. Their prototype is the postnatal biotrauma. These traumata have been described under various names: loss of object (Freud 1923), postnatal shock (Ribble 1944), separation trauma (Bowlby 1969), and maturation crisis (Benjamin 1961). The majority assume that at birth the immaturity of the central nervous system functions as a protective "passive stimulus barrier" and that when through neuronal and hormonal maturation this protective barrier is removed, postnatal biotraumatic phenomena develop.

The biotraumata or maturational crises appear, according to child observers, toward the third month (Benjamin 1961). They are the effects of frustration of needs of the immature and helpless child. They are recognizable in the increasing signs of unpleasure, such as irritability, crying, screaming, restlessness, and kicking. They induce maturation and the formation of the final active stimulation barrier.

Nature of Biotrauma

The concept of homeostasis provides the rationale for behavior in the maturational crises (Selye 1950). In the postnatal phase, because of the relative immaturity of the homeostatic equilibration apart from specific responses, deprivation induces nonspecific reactions, namely, the alarm reaction (Selye) and the primary defenses (Stern 1951). The general adaptation syndrome consists of a phase of disorganizing transitory paralysis of vital functions (shock) counteracted by compensatory counterreactions or biodefenses. The counterreaction consists either of an increase of motility, respiration, circulation, and central nervous activity (the baby is kicking, crying, and hallucinating), called agitation; or of a retardation of vital functions, presenting the picture of a physiological primary depression—that is, a regression to a lower level of functioning. What appears in the description of Spitz and Cobliner (1965), Benjamin (1961), and others is less the biotraumatic disorganization than the biodefenses against it—agitation (irritability, increase of motility) or primary depression.

Pavor Nocturnus

The prototype of the infantile biotrauma is the pavor nocturnus occurring in the sleep of every child. In classical psychoanalytic theory, sleep is mentally a return to the womb, and the dream is the guardian of sleep. In the dream, instinctual energies are discharged into hallucinatory wish fulfillment (which includes the wish for reparative mastery of nonintegrated previous traumata).

Freud explained pavor nocturnus as overstimulation due to nondischarge of libidinal forces during sleep. The teleonomic theory explains pavor nocturnus as the result of inhibition of defensive motility and lack of input of stimuli in sleep.

This latter explanation requires a short digression into the meaning of sleep and dream. Sleep actually is not a situation of utmost security, which a return to the mother's womb connotes; it is, rather, a state of danger close to dying. This was obvious to the old Greeks, who presented sleep and death as twin brothers. It comes to the fore in the child's prayer:

> Now I lay me down to sleep.
> I pray the Lord, my soul to keep.
> If I should die before I wake,
> I pray the Lord my soul to take.

The feeling of utmost sweetness that usually accompanies the hypnogogic hallucination when one is going to sleep serves to overcome the general aversion against going to sleep.

We stressed that in sleep, motility, the defense against trauma, is paralyzed and stimulation from the outside is cut off. Since this stimulation is indispensable for the function of the regulating reticular system on which life depends, the dream hallucinations replace the stimulation from the outside by stimulation from inside. Hallucinations involve the repetition of previous experiences or states of threatening disorganization for the purpose of reparative mastery. To the baby in whom homeostatic equilibration is still inadequate and who is still unable to distinguish dream hallucination from reality, the hallucinatory repetition of previous traumata provokes a state of anxiety evolving from a state of danger that the individual is unable to undo in sleep.

In sleep, therefore, undoing usually occurs through awakening, which ends the ominous hallucination. In the case of a repetition in sleep of previous severe deprivation, there occurs a defensive regression to primary depression, which means paralysis of the vital functions, including paralysis of the waking function.

The paralysis of motility and of the waking function is one of the main characteristics of pavor nocturnus. The sleeper attempts to wake up and cannot; he attempts to move, to cry, but cannot. He feels unable to breathe, as if he is vanishing; in short, he feels as if he is dying. This feeling is not a fantasy; what the individual experiences is the realistic process of dying.

Pavor Nocturnus and Fear of Dying

Since the experience of dying underlies pavor nocturnus, it is not astonishing that clinical observations show that the uncanny experience of pavor nocturnus is—in children and adults—at the root of the fear of death. Children and adults conceive of death as being alive and unable to move, to breathe, to cry.

The patients report: "Death is being dead and not dead." "It is being unable to breathe, to talk, but you can still feel." "You can't do anything, you are paralyzed." "You can't get up and move when you want to. . . . you feel like a piece of wood." "There is inability to breathe, to cry and to yell." It is significant that children personify death as a ghost or a black angel coming at night and killing, or as a burglar coming out of the closet (Stern 1953). These observations are confirmed by all researchers (Anthony 1940; Barnes 1964; Chadwick 1929; Furman 1964; Kastenbaum 1965; Nagy 1965).

The preoccupation with death starts early in life. Anna Freud (1960) thinks that the child at the age of two or three already has some idea of death and that at the age of three and a half or four is able to mourn. The child identifies with deceased objects, such as relatives, friends, or dead animals, and projects onto them his own feelings in the biotraumatic experience.

The infantile biotraumata have antithetical effects. They foster, on the one hand, mental functioning such as the anticipatory process—the core of thought and reality testing as well as separation individuation (Mahler and Furer 1968); on the other hand, they induce clinging to a symbiotistic mother–child dependency whose protective as well as threatening power is at the core of all human object relationships.

The impact of the child's immaturity comes to the fore in the various stages of mental development. Development occurs by jumps of neurophysiological and hormonal maturation. Every stage repeats on another level the immaturity of the first, the oral stage that produces the early biotraumata.

In the anal phase, the disappearance of the feces revives the experience of the vanishing of the self in the pavor nocturnus of the separation trauma. This explains the child's stubborn resistance to toilet training, for it means a threat to existence (pars pro toto), as evidenced by the well-known fear of falling into the toilet bowl and being flushed away.

In the oedipal constellation, with the immaturity of the sexual apparatus, the impossibility of full gratification of the premature sexual excitation repeats the constellation of the postnatal phase and results in pavor nocturnus attacks.

Freud likened fear of death to the fear of castration. He stressed, however, that the danger of castration could not be a decisive one for the female sex, that in women "the [early] danger situation of loss of objects seems to have remained the most effective" (Freud 1926:143).

It seems to me that in both sexes the fear of castration is a defensive displacement of fear of death—arising from infantile immaturity—on the genital organs (Stern 1968a). The rationale for this displacement is the immaturity of the genital apparatus, which repeats the disturbance caused by the postnatal immaturity.

Two experiences seem to underlie this displacement: first, the varying shape of the boy's penis, which often seems to disappear completely into the fold of the skin, and the view of the little girl's body, where genitals seemingly have disappeared completely; and second, the immaturity of the genital apparatus of the male and female, whose excitation stirs up unpleasure and crying. (I must stress that the child's response is due not to overstimulation, but to the failure of the structure to perform adequately.) This experience *re-*

vives the uncanny fading into nothingness experienced in the infantile pavor nocturnus. The slogan "Rather dead than castrated" is not confirmed by reality, which speaks for the opposite slogan, "Rather castrated than dead."

The trends characteristic for adolescence, alternating between individuation and clinging to symbiotic dependency, marked by hero worship or gang loyalty, emanate from fear of death characteristic for this period of still painful immaturity. It is accompanied by depression (*Weltschmerz*) and suicidal thought alternating with hypermanic exuberance.

The adaptational pattern developed in the infantile period persists to some extent in the adult. One lives life under the shadow of the experience of dying because of the ability to anticipate events. This accounts for some overall persistence of the adaptational pattern developed in the infantile period. It is this fixation to the infantile phase that underlies neurosis and psychosis species-specific to man.

Neurosis

Classical theory assumes that neurosis develops because of the inhibition of the discharge of instinctual drives. In teleonomic theory, neurosis is perceived as the effect of a clinging to infantile dependency, which means persistence of the infantile biotraumata. These evoke, on the one hand, a clinging to the life-saving effect of infantile symbiosis (including the phase-specific libidinal gratification) and, on the other, an ever-present need for reparative mastery of the traumata threatening from clinging to the past.

The neurotic symptoms emerge from this fixation. They are a combination of attempts at reparative repetition of infantile biotrauma and the fixation to biodefenses against it, which alleviate the anxieties resulting from the fixation.

Psychosis

Psychosis seems to differ only in degree from neurosis (Arieti 1959; Arlow and Brenner 1964; Fromm-Reichmann 1939; Stern 1953). It can be defined as the effect of excessively strong early biotraumatic experiences (which may originate in innate somatic dysfunction). They call into action archaic emergency primary defenses against trauma and death,—that is, primary process behavior, including hallucinated and/or acting out of infantile libidinal and aggressional wishes and serve as protection against death. (The fragmentation in psychosis seems to be a defensive compromise between the repetition of the fragmentation experienced in the infantile disorganization and the life-saving coenesthetic identification with body parts of the mother.) That the psychotic does not sufficiently distinguish hallucination from actual experiences—because of the life-saving (albeit transitory) effect of hallucination—explains his almost invincible inaccessibility to psychic treatment aimed at renouncing primary process behavior.

The Treatment

The driving power of the cure is not the pressure for discharge of repressed instinctual energies but the pressure for reparative mastery of infantile biotraumatic experience induced by fear of death. It is through the amalgamation of the fear of repetition of infantile bio-traumata with the fear of death that the past biotraumata become per-petutated (Stern 1968a,b).

The treatment should make the patient aware of his clinging to infantile dependency (which involves clinging to infantile anxiety) and of the illusion that dependency on parental figures might protect him against repetition of early biotraumata, as well as against future death. The battlefield on which this conflict is fought out is the transference to the doctor, from whom the patient expects protection from all dangers—unrealistic ones, as well as the realistic danger of death. Case histories can show that working through of the fixation to infantile dependency effects a maturation in terms of a belated individuation separation and an adaptation of behavior to reality.

Biosocial Analysis

This presentation describes the biophysiological background of the behavior of the human individual. It should be complemented by an exploration of the biosocial forces that shape individual behavior. It is the individual's identification with the immortal group that hitherto achieved some adaptation to the fact of death. Through the influence of tradition, the individual's achievements really exert some enduring impact on the function of the immortal group. As infinitestimal as this influence may be, it amounts to an extension of the effectiveness of the individual's personal existence far beyond the limits of his personal life span and thus to a modicum of immortality. Yet the individual has to pay the price for it. He should be able to sacrifice his physical existence in the service of the survival of the group. That is the meaning of Goethe's saying: "Man has to give up his existence in order to achieve existence."

References

Anthony, S. 1940. *The Child's Discovery of Death: A Study in Psychology.* New York: Harcourt, Brace.

Arieti, S. 1959. "Schizophrenia: The Manifest Symptomatology (The Psychodynamic and Formal Mechanisms)." In S. Arieti ed. *American Handbook of Psychiatry,* New York: Basic Books, pp. 455–84.

Arlow, J. and C. Brenner. 1964. *Psychoanalytic Concepts and the Structural Theory.* New York: International Universities Press.

Barnes, M. J. 1964. "Reactions to the Death of a Mother." *The Psychoanalytic Study of the Child* 19:334–57.

Benjamin, J. D. 1961. "The Innate and the Experiential in Child Development." In H. Brosin, ed. *Lectures on Experimental Psychiatry. Pittsburgh Bicentennial Conference, Western Psychiatric Institute and Clinic (March 5–7,* 1959), pp. 19–42. Pittsburgh: University of Pittsburgh Press.

Bowlby, J. 1969. *Attachment and Loss,* vol. 1. New York: Basic Books.

Chadwick, M. 1929. "Notes Upon the Fear of Death." *International Journal of Psycho-Analysis* 10:321–34.

Freud, A. 1960. "Discussion of Dr. John Bowlby's Paper." *The Psychoanalytic Study of the Child* 15:53–62. New York: International Universities Press.

Freud, S. 1920. "Beyond the Pleasure Principle." *Standard Edition* 18:87–174. London: Hogarth Press, 1959.

—— 1923. "The Ego and the Id." *Standard Edition* 19:3–65. London: Hogarth Press, 1961.

—— 1926. "Inhibitions, Symptoms and Anxiety." *Standard Edition* 20:87–156. London: Hogarth Press, 1959.

Fromm-Reichman, F. 1939. "Transference Problems in Schizophrenics." *Psychoanalytic Quarterly* 8:412–26.

Furman, R. A. 1964. "Death and the Young Child: Some Preliminary Considerations." And "Death of a Six-Year-Old's Mother During His Analysis." *The Psychoanalytic Study of the Child* 19:321–33, 377–97. New York: International Universities Press.

Jacob, F. 1973. *The Logic of Life: A History of Heredity*, translated by B. E. Spillman. New York: Pantheon.

Kastenbaum, R. 1965. "Time and Death in Adolescence." In H. Feifel, ed. *The Meaning of Death*, pp. 99–113. New York: McGraw Hill (paperback).

Luria, A. R. 1973. *The Working Brain*, translated by B. Haigh. New York: Basic Books.

Mahler, M. S. and M. Furer. 1968. *On Human Symbiosis and the Vicissitudes of Individuation. Volume 1. Infantile Psychosis*. New York: International Universities Press.

Monod, J. 1971. *Chance and Necessity*, translated by A. Wainhouse. New York: Knopf.

Nagy, M. H. 1965. "The Child's View of Death." In H. Feifel, ed. *The Meaning of Death*, pp. 79–98. New York: McGraw Hill (paperback).

Ribble, M. 1944. "Infantile Experience in Relation to Personal Development." In J. McV. Hunt, ed. *Personality and the Behavior Disorders*, pp. 621–51. New York: Ronald Press.

Selye, H. 1950. *Stress*. Montreal, Canada: ACTA, Inc.

Spitz, R. A. and W. G. Cobliner. 1965. *The First Year of Life*. New York: International Universities Press.

Stern, M. M. 1951. "Pavor Nocturnus." *International Journal of Psycho-Analysis* 32:302–9.

—— 1953. "Trauma and Symptom Formation." *International Journal of Psycho-Analysis* 34:202–18.

—— 1961. "Blank Hallucinations: Remarks about Trauma and Perceptual Disturbances." *International Journal of Psycho-Analysis* 42:205–15.

—— 1968a. "Fear of Death and Trauma." *International Journal of Psychoanalysis* 49:457–61.

—— 1968b. "Fear of Death and Neurosis." *Journal of American Psychoanalytic Association* 16:3–31.

—— 1976. "Beyond the Discharge Principle: A Teleonomic Theory of Psychoanalysis."

The Meaning of Aging

GLENN M. VERNON AND
PAULINE LOVELESS

WHAT DOES IT mean to be old? What does it mean to the elderly person to be old? What does being old mean to those with whom the elderly person interacts? What does being old mean to society in general? In an era of racial liberation and sexual liberation, an era in which we are moving toward the liberation of the aged, these are important questions. What does it mean to be both old and dying? Our society is in the process of deciding.

The majority of people living today will die in old age. More than two-thirds of all deaths occur in hospitals, nursing homes, and similar institutions. Approximately 80 percent of all who die are aged. More often than not, death results from a prolonged, chronic disease rather than from a quickly terminating, acute illness. The professionals associated with these institutions in which people die will be involved in the death of many of the aged. It would be naïve to assume that the meaning old age has for these people would not influence how they relate to and treat the older person who is dying.

We are concerned here with the meaning of old age expressed in the literature. We identify some traditional patterns and some changing patterns.

To understand death in old age, we need to understand the meaning of both old age and dying. Our primary concern here is the meaning of old age. Those who decide what dying in old age means will see whatever meaning of old age is realized or believed. This presentation suggests that those who relate to old-age dying should know which meaning of *old age* they are using and should be concerned with finding out whether the meaning being used is the most accurate one according to the best available knowledge and consequently whether it is functional or dysfunctional in their efforts to maximize their relationships with the dying aged.

This presentation is informed by the symbolic-interactionist orientation to behavior in general. Such an orientation is guided by the paradigm statement that the individual-level behavior is in response to meaning, is relative to the audience, and is relative to the situation. This paradigm statement is presented in shorthand form as ISAS, each of these letters representing the major components of human interaction—Individual, Symbols (Meaning), Audience, and Situation. Individual-level behavior is contrasted with internal behavior. We are concerned with what individuals do, not with what some internal entity does. We are concerned with the death of the individual, not the death of some internal part. The meaning to which behavior is in reponse is socially constructed and is thus never finalized. The meaning of *death* changes. The meaning of *age* changes. The meaning of *death* changes as the meaning of *age* changes. The timing of death is an element to which considerable attention has been given and to which important meaning is attributed. Dying has different meaning when the dying occurs in infancy, childhood, teenage, young adulthood, middle age, and old age. Neither the dying process per se nor the meaning of the dying remains constant.

Age stages, such as old age, are socially constructed. There is no old age as an empirically delineated phenomenon in the world independent of human beings. We establish the boundaries.

Historically, aging has been interpreted in various ways. Accounts of biblical antiquity tell us about men who lived well past 100 and generally represent the patriarchs as completely able bodied. The doctrines of Buddha and Confucius present old age in a very affirmative manner. The poets of ancient Rome and Greece, however, appeared to view youth as the "only real age." And Shakespeare and Sir Francis Bacon paint a dismal picture of what it is like to grow old.

On the other hand, the early inhabitants of the Aleutian Islands held a deep respect and reverence for their aged. However, by 1954 a change of attitude toward the older person had been noted in the Aleut village. In the Navajo society, the attitude toward the aged was one of respect because with age comes wisdom, an important possession. Although the aged have been viewed positively and treated accordingly in other societies, the American view of aging seems to have been taken predominantly from an English and French heritage. Aging from this perspective is seen primarily as an irreversible biological process that leads to negative mental and social consequences.

Aged individuals, as well as the behavior and accomplishments of the aged, can be evaluated in any number of different ways. Instead of a negative view of the biology of aging, it is appropriate to ask if aged people behave as they do because they are biologically aged or because they are rejected and defined negatively, being told directly or indirectly that that is the way they are expected to behave. Are such definitions then a self-fulfilling prophecy?

Evaluations that focus on economic productivity are quite different from evaluations that focus on loving ability, as well as on just being.

Biology per se has no inherent meaning. It has no behavior-directing aspects or components. People frequently turn to the professional to tell them what is happening or what the biological changes being experienced mean. The available literature suggests the types of answers frequently provided by the professionals involved and identifies broad changes in such meaning. The literature reveals that in the early research on aging, emphasis was typically placed on the biological and medical aspects. However, the biological theories of senescence show little or no cumulative historical development, being more of a catalogue than a process of developing scientific awareness.

This biological approach to the fundamental question of what aging is and how it affects the organism does little to explain human behavior. Knowledge about biological and medical factors alone does not turn out to be a very good predictor of human behavior. What individuals do about their internal behavior, including biological aging, is not directly related to the internal behavior per se but is mediated through a set of symbols that create the meaning of the internal behavior. This is equally true of the behavior of the physician and any other helping person. The biological condition is a cause but not *the* cause involved in the behavior. It is not the immediately antecedent causative factor involved. The immediately antecedent causative factor is the symbol or the meaning that the individual attributes to the biological "cause."

Interest in aging continues, however, and is reflected in the increased theoretical explanations of human aging in the past three decades. The late 1930s and early 1940s were apparently a turning point in the creation of theoretical concepts to explain the phenomenon of aging. Interest in aging was no longer exclusively biological, and various disciplines in the social science field turned their attention toward the phenomenon of aging, the process, and the behavior of older people.

Several writers (Pollack 1948, Linden and Courtney 1953, Tibbits 1960, Barron 1961, Philbert 1965, Kastenbaum 1965, Breen 1970) have suggested that the growth of gerontology and theoretical concepts explaining aging and the process of aging were given impetus by many factors. Some of these factors were as follows: (1) the determination that if physiological changes could not be reversed, then some way had to be found for the individual to adjust psychologically to the process; (2) the decline in the death rate—the increase in the number of older persons in a culture seems to bring into sharper focus psychological, economic, and social problems; (3) the shift from economic independence of the individual to reliance on the government and employer for economic security; (4) the change from gradual retirement to compulsory retirement; (5) the relegation of the older person to the status of a has-been, and increases in the incidence of chronic disease and disability; (6) society's negative feelings about the means of caring for the older person, such as almshouses and homes for the aged as institutional forms of rehabilitation; (7) older people organizing themselves into viable social groups in interaction and the recognition of older people as a source of political pressure; (8) increased social legislation on behalf of the older person; (9) a developing awareness by many professions, such as sociology, psychology, anthropology, social work, and medicine, that their interests converge on aging and that there is a need for theoretical frameworks to explain the phenomenon of aging; and (10) the availability of money that would permit research on the aging process, on the behavior of the older person, and on what has been called the third age in our culture. This configuration of societal factors has led to the creation of new theoretical concepts to explain the phenomena of aging, as well as to the modification of existence concepts.

Gerontology Literature

A survey of the literature in gerontology in Loveless (1975) identified 75 separate theoretical concepts of aging. These are categorized and tabulated in table 3.1.

These concepts are categorized according to the components of the ISAS, or interaction paradigm. The basic premise of the ISAS paradigm is that all four of the major components are interrelated. Behavior of the individual is in response to symbols and is relative to the audience and relative to the situation. However, for the categorization, two of the individual components of the ISAS paradigm were used singly to categorize six of the concepts.

Individual

Three of the perspectives gave primary emphasis to the individual, proposing the view that there are sets of personality processes, primarily intrapsychic, that show developmental changes throughout the life cycle. Other concepts formulated either a formal stage of last life crisis, such as "ego-integrity versus despair" or stages such as "ego-differentiation versus work role preoccupation," "body transcendence versus body preoccupation," and "ego-transcendence versus ego-preoccupation" or other developmental tasks that must be accomplished by the individual in the last stage of the life cycle. The creators of some of these concepts suggested that they replace models that regard aging as a biologically defined state of deficit.

Symbols (Knowledge-Culture)

Three of the aging concepts emphasized this component. One of these gave emphasis to concepts such as autonomy and dependency, persistence and precariousness, which were used as the exclusive basis for judging successful aging. If individuals' reactions to the social system were both autonomous and persistent, they were seen as aging successfully. Another perspective had as a central variable the older person's view of self. As older people are forced to make changes in their social positions in the later years, a crisis is precipitated in their ability to achieve a satisfactory identity in the new status. Another perspective placed in this category gave emphasis to coping needs, expressive needs, contributive needs, and influence needs. From this perspective older people are constantly engaged in a struggle to maintain the margin of energy and power they enjoyed in earlier years in order to continue to fulfill these needs.

Individual-Audience Emphasizing Social Systems

Two other components, individual-audience, of the ISAS paradigm were combined to provide a heading under which seven of the social science concepts of aging could be categorized, because these perspectives emphasized elements such as "the interface between the individual and the social system." Other theoretical perspectives emphasized prejudice and discrimination against the older person by the majority of young adults, prejudice and discrimination by employers against older people, and the enactment of social legislation against such discrimination and thereby showed the efficacy of using a particular theoretical perspective to explain human behavior and relationships.

Concepts that focused on the negative response of society toward the older person, which forces them to interact with one another across class and other social barriers, were placed in this category. Also other perspectives that gave emphasis to the relationship between the aged and the young, particularly with the families of the aged, seemed to "fit" in this category. The final theoretical concept categorized under this same heading emphasized isolated living without the stimulating input of meaningful repeated human interactions and the resultant psychologically degenerative processes, which hastened natural depletion in the older person. Two of the writers (Miller and Schooler 1972) viewed the crucial issue for social gerontology as the divergence between approaches emphasizing the social and those

TABLE 3.1

Biological Theories of Aging

Wear-and-tear or *Abnutzungstheorie*	A counterpart theory of aging
Rate of living theory	Cybernetic theory
Major involution	Somatic mutation theory
Exhaustion theory	Autoimmunity theory
Fixed store of energy	The collagen theory
Aging is not inevitable at all	Diffusion theory
The cross-linkage theory	Waste-product theory
Connective-tissues theory	Composite theory of aging
Stress theory of aging	"Multiple" theory of aging
Theory of mortality	Disturbed normal relations
Information on theory	Integrated theory of aging
Mathematical theories based on "Gompertz	Mean time to failure
function"	Accumulation of copying errors
Stochastic theory	Free-radical theory
Other explanations of the "Gompertz	
function"	

Individual (Psychological)

Personality theories	Cognitive theory of the aging personality
Developmental theories	

Individual-Audience, Emphasizing Social Systems

Disengagement theory	Subculture of aging
Quasi-minority group theory	Integration versus segregation theories
Propositions for a sociological theory of	Theory of sensory deprivation
aging and the family	Role theory

Individual-Audience, Emphasizing Symbolic Meaning

Life satisfaction theory	"Embryonic" theories of retirement
Utility theory of old age	Option-maintenance model
Development theory of successful aging	Systems-analysis approach
Theory of life course	Dimensions of cultural reality
Dissociation theory	Manipulation of social policies
Integration theory	New learning
Deviance theory	Direction instruction
Continuity theory	Accommodation and substitution
Activity theory	Crisis model
Life-cycle conception of aging	Crisis and crisis resolution
Multiple-deficit-repair theory	Normative-transition model
Theory of leisure	Evolutionary view
Retirement theories:	Social welfare theory
Equivalence of work and play	Stratification theory of aging
Retirement a function of rigidity in social	Comparative theory of aging
organization	Theory of aging in cross-cultural perspective
Social reconstruction theory	
Employment theory	
Manpower theory	

TABLE 3.1 (*Continued*)

Symbols (Knowledge-Culture)	
Theory of optimal aging	Margin theory of needs
Identity crisis theory	

Situation Component

Although aging and interaction with older people take place on some "stage" or in some environmental setting, no theory of aging focused primarily on the situation. The significance is the definition of the situation, which is a meaning component.

Individual-Symbols-Audience-Situation (ISAS)

Symbolic interaction theory

stressing the personal explanations of behavior, rather than what has hitherto been viewed as the crucial issue—the divergence between biological and psychosocial emphasis in social gerontology.

Individual-Audience Emphasizing Symbolic Meaning

Thirty-three of the concepts fell into this category. Emphasis was given to elements such as life satisfaction, which is positively related to activity involving others for some kinds of people and to disengagement for others, or the utility (quality of being careful) ceiling established by culture. When the utility program created by society runs out, energy dissipates. Consequently death is timed by the parent sociocultural program. As culture develops, the age of death changes.

Emphasis was also given to adaptation to aging as a series of problems to be solved. A person has to learn what the cultural expectations are in growing up. As with the younger person, failure to conform to these expectations results in a conflict situation between the individual and society. Another concept gives emphasis to the goals of development that are formed and transformed by society. This focus involves more than the means of living. One of several scripts may be written by an individual. One may have constructed a framework for life that needs the particular experiences of old age for psychological completion, or a psychological script that has no use for old age, or old age may have been completely deleted. Other emphases were on aging as a normal process, in which each period of life evolves into the next. Each phase offers new challenges and possesses its own core set of values as past experience, interaction with others, and cultural patterns continue to influence adjustment in each phase of one's life course.

The emphasis of other concepts was on the inevitability of devaluation, losses, and alienation in later years, suggesting that significant group support insulates people from the social insults of aging. Another perspective contends that an individual's adaptation to aging can proceed in several directions, depending on the individual's past life. Most older people, however, want to remain engaged with their social environment; the source of the failure lies in the social environment and not the age.

In yet another perspective, continuing the activities and attitudes of middle age as far and as long as possible is the major determinant of successful aging. Other concepts give emphasis to a life-cycle conception of aging, which contains a creative period, a moral and ethical reaffirmative period, and a period characterized by a need to correlate the present with the past through a conscious process of reasoning and intuition. Other concepts emphasize the behavioral deficiencies of the older person who can no longer produce in society or reinforce society with pleasant conversation and thus becomes extremely abrasive and subject to social neglect.

Some of the concepts used to explain another aspect of aging—retirement—were also placed here. An analysis of these concepts indicated that emphasis was variously placed on factors such as the number of options the older person has available in retirement; this influences self-esteem and society's responsibility to develop alternative courses of action. Also, emphasis was placed on the elements in the relationship between the individual and the culture, such as self-concepts, motivations and values, and social relationships. Adaptation, in another theoretical perspective regarding retirement, was seen as a function of the person and of the social setting, as they are perceived by the individual.

Another concept emphasized elements such as the fact that the aged always constitute a minority group within the total population, or that all societies value life and seek to prolong it even in old age. Other factors were also emphasized, such as the classification of people as "old" at an earlier age in a primitive society or the individualistic value system of Western society, which tends to reduce the security and status of older people.

Situation Component

Although aging and interaction with older people take place on some stage or in some social setting, no theory of aging focused primarily on the situation per se or on the definition of the situation.

Individual-Symbols-Audience-Situation (ISAS)

All individuals, including the aged individual, respond to symbols-meaning and relate to various audiences in various situations. Biologically, individually, socially, and situationally, nothing remains at rest; change is constant. Changes, evolution (life course), development are constant. Some behavior/beliefs are essentially eliminated (disengagement, retirement), some are added (such as increased leisure and recreation), and some are maintained at a fairly constant level (activity). Definitions (beliefs) of what one individual *needs* to function in a given situation are socially constructed. Needs are developed from the symbols (meaning-culture) to which individuals respond.

Aged individuals relate to different audiences or form different groupings. Group affiliations and attachments can and may be changed as the individual changes and as the opportunity structure for such change exists. To the extent that interaction between aged individuals becomes somewhat standardized, groups or quasi-groups may be formed and subcultures created. Such groups may be minority groups in terms of either power or numbers. Relating one way or another to family groups is usually important. The power structure of a society is influenced by such groupings. With reference to any group from a dyad to a whole society, we can distinguish various identifiable patterns, such as engagement and disengagement, dissociation and integration, accommodation and lack of accommodation (or deviancy), employment and retirement, and behavior-belief continuity and discontinuity. How one individual fits into or relates to any given group influences behavior and may produce satisfaction or crises. Any of the elements may vary from society to society (comparative) with the study of different societies, providing input on the relative influence of any given combination or configuration of elements.

Aged individuals, as well as those who relate to and study them, evaluate any or all of these factors and reach decisions about such things as life satisfaction, optimal aging, utility, manpower re-

quirements, and successful aging. Such evaluations involve nonref-
erented concepts and hence have no empirical absolute criteria—their
meaning is socially constructed. Lack of consensus usually exists.
Theorists, gerontologists, social workers, government and business
people, and other professionals, as well as individual people, frequently disagree on the meaning of such concepts. Such behavior
lends support to a basic premise of the sociology of knowledge that
anything is multidimensional and can be viewed in any number of
different ways.

In the early 1970s theorists viewing aging and the aged in a
different way marked another turning point in regard to theoretical
concepts relating to aging. At this time it was suggested that the use
of theoretical analysis of behavior would permit recommendations of
social policy pertaining to the health and welfare of the aging population (Miller and Schooler 1972). Another writer created a theoretical concept that emphasized the need for social structural alterations
to enhance the quality of life of older people (Bengston 1973). These
newly created theoretical concepts regarding the phenomenon of aging also have implications for the professional in the area of applied
gerontology. Previously created theoretical concepts that explain some
aspects of aging, such as activity theory, have been used by professionals in this field. The focus of these concepts appears however to
place the responsibility for "successful" aging on the older individual. Hence the professionals' attention would be on the behavior of
the older person. Acceptance and use of the concept of Miller and
Schooler (1972), as well as the perspective of Bengston (1973), by
the professional in applied gerontology also have implications for the
older segment of our population but focus the attention of the professional on the need for social structural alterations to enhance the quality of life for older people.

As we look ahead to the development of gerontology, the use
of the ISAS, or interaction paradigm, would offer a means of understanding a broader perspective in regard to human behavior in both
the social and applied sciences. Any one-dimensional attempt at explaining aging leaves out important factors, such as changes in behavior or appearance or even the physiological functioning of the
human organism. When we focus on only one component, behavior
appears to have a status rather than a dynamic emergent nature.

Those working with the aged dying have not merely to look for new materials but to reexamine and fit together the existing materials in a new way. There is a standing invitation among the scientifically inquisitive and those willing to pursue new directions. Theory creation and modification are limited only by the human capacity to imagine.

Dying in old age involves biological factors but is much broader in scope than that. A body dies, but a person also dies, and that person is typically related to others, so that relationships also die. Social death takes place. Meaning is also destroyed—symbolic deaths take place. There is, in fact, an interactive or reciprocal relationship between these factors. All these processes take place on some stage or in some larger setting that influences them. There is value in using a broad ISAS approach in deciding on the meaning of old age per se and of dying in old age.

References

Barron, M. L. 1961. *The Aging American: An Introduction to Social Gerontology and Geriatrics*. New York: Crowell.

Bengston, V. L. 1973. *The Social Psychology of Aging*. New York: Bobbs-Merrill.

Breen, L. Z. 1970. "The Discipline of Gerontology." In M. Hoffman, ed. *The Daily Needs and Interests of Older People*. Springfield, Ill.: Thomas.

Kastenbaum, R. 1965. "Theories of Human Aging: The Search for a Conceptual Framework." *Journal of Social Issues* (October) 21:13–36.

Linden, M. E., and A. Courtney. 1953. "The Human Life Cycle and Its Interruptions: A Psychologic Hypothesis. Studies in Gerontologic Human Relations." *American Journal of Psychiatry* (June) 109:909–15.

Loveless, P. 1975. "A Comparative Analysis of Theoretical Concepts in Gerontology." Ph.D. dissertation, University of Utah.

Miller, S. J., and K. K. Schooler. 1972. "Gerontological Theory and Empirical Research." In D. H. Kent, R. Kastenbaum, and S. Sherwood, eds., *Research Planning and Action for the Elderly*, New York: Human Science Press.

Philibert, M. A. J. 1965. "The Emergence of Social Gerontology." *Journal of Social Issues* (October) 21:4–12.

Pollack, O. 1948. *Social Adjustment in Old Age.* New York: Social Science Research Council.

Tibbitts, C., ed. 1960. "The Origin, Scope, and Fields of Social Gerontology." In Tibbitts, ed. *Handbook of Social Gerontology: Societal Aspects of Aging.* Chicago: University of Chicago Press.

Vernon, G. M. 1970. *Sociology of Death.* New York: Ronald Press.

—— 1978. *Symbolic Aspects of Interaction.* Washington, D.C.: University Press of America.

Aging as Ongoing Adaptation to Partial Loss

MARCELLA BAKUR WEINER

The work of mourning consists in summoning
up to the mind the many memories connected
with a lost object and bidding each of them
good-bye, as it were.

—Freud

*I*N SPEAKING OF existential man, Becker states that one needs to protect oneself against the world and that one can do this only as any other animal would: by narrowing down the world, shutting off experience, developing an obliviousness both to the terrors of the world and to one's own anxieties. Otherwise one would be crippled for action (Becker 1973).

The great lesson of Freudian psychology is that repression is normal self-protection and creative self-restriction—in a sense mankind's natural substitute for instinct. This natural human talent has been called "partialization." It has been suggested that life is impossible without it (Becker 1973). Thus, what we may call the well-adjusted person has just this capacity to partialize the world for comfortable action. In order, then, to function normally, one has to achieve from the beginning a serious constriction of the world and of oneself. In some way we may say that the essence of normality is the refusal of reality. Assuming no distinct dichotomy between neurosis and normalcy, we may yet postulate differences in degree—that is, we call neurotic any life-style that begins to constrict too much, that prevents free forward momentum, new choices, and the growth a person may want and need.

At stake possibly in all human repression is the fear of life and death. Safety in the face of the terror of creature existence becomes a problem for a person. One feels vulnerable but reacts too totally, too inflexibly. One is paralyzed, as though saying: "If I do anything at all . . . I will die." Symptoms are thus developed as attempts to live, attempts to unblock action and keep the world safe. The fear of both life and death is encapsulated in the symptom. Neurotic symptoms thus serve to reduce and narrow, perhaps to magically transform the world so that the person may be distracted from concerns of death, guilt, and meaninglessness. In this narrowing in neurosis, the person seeks to avoid death but does it by killing off much of self; killing off the action-world, one isolates oneself and becomes as though dead.

At the opposite end of this type of person we have the creative individual. This person has difficulty narrowing experience. Possessed of a vivid imagination, one takes in too much experience; as such, one feels through one's isolation, one's individuality. It is this person who has difficulty partializing experience; as such, one has difficulty living. Unable to select out, one is susceptible to the world as a total problem—with all that this implies. We might say that both the artist and the neurotic bite off more than they can chew, but the artist spews it back out again and chews it over in an objectified way, as an external, active work project. The neurotic, unable to marshal this creative response, chokes on introversions. Becker, attempting to conceptualize normality and health, states: "With the truth, one cannot live. To be able to live one needs illusions, not only outer illusions such as art, religion, philosophy, science and love, but inner illusions which first condition the outer." He later suggests: "This constantly effective process of self-deceiving, pretending and blundering, is no psychopathological mechanism" (189).

The aging individual has spent a lifetime living out both the realities and illusions intrinsic to life. More concerned with the end of life than the beginning, the person may be involved in a process of "partial responses." Unlike the depressed individual who appears depressed at the late stage of life, the healthier person perhaps doles out partialized mourning responses throughout life. This is in response to the exigencies of aging per se. Despite individual variations, aging people today share general and fairly stable components. These include a universal pattern showing a dissociation of cognitive stability from a relentless slowing down of psychomotor functioning (Jarvik, et al. 1972). Generalized aging trends include physiological changes and decrements in various degrees of the sensorium. These changes, though common to all, do vary individually and are specific to an individual's genetic endowment and physical health status.

The vicissitudes of aging lie in the psychosocial variables that encompass ego threats and traumas. They lie in the narrowing of the interpersonal field engendered by such phenomena as forced retirement (Neugarten 1968), reduced physical stamina, loss of loved ones, and societal rejection. It is this totality of narcissistic blows that the aging ego has to tolerate. Yet these traumas and ego assaults do not descend at once; they may be doled out, beginning in the middle years. The capacity to deal with them adaptively will have, of necessity, been laid down in the early years—years that may now be indistinct in memory yet crucial for the understanding of effective responding—in other words, coping.

With the loss of close ties, in adulthood, through death, and the consequent narrowing of borders for receiving narcissistic supplies, loneliness may be experienced with the fullest impact; along with this one may experience a sense of the inevitability and imminence of dissolution and death. It has been suggested that loss, rather than isolation, has the closer relationship to loneliness. It is, perhaps, this loss that underlies the assaults experienced by the aging person.

As a result of these assaults, three major intrapsychic components emerge in direct proportion to the integrity of an elder's ego: grief, helplessness, and fears of abandonment. It is precisely here, in the weakening of repressive defenses, that one can trace the reemergence of and regression to an early conflictual developmental level; not merely repeating the phase as children, in their regression, they carry with them the experiences of their years.

If aging is seen with the stress of lifelong loss that goes with it, the aging person's ability to handle these stresses can be seen as determined by lifelong adaptive abilities and coping styles. Thus adaptive coping styles linked to the use of cognitive strategies in compulsive-obsessional defenses may lead to behaviors illustrated, for example, by the ninety-year-old man who, during a group therapy session in a nursing home, told the group how he labeled his bureau drawer: "My drawer looks like a railroad terminal, for I have signs for where to find my socks, where my 'good shirts' are and where my 'everyday shirts' are. I read the labels and then take the track that will lead me to where I want to go."

Nonadaptive responses to the stress of aging may include shame over aggressive impulses, fear of aggressiveness, survivor guilt, fear of identification or merger with others, and prolonged mourning. Prolonged mourning is distinct from normal mourning, which is viewed as intrinsic to aging and to maturity and which demands an "essentially passive acceptance of that which is painful and inevitable" (Zetzel 1965). This has been conceptualized as the process of partial mourning. The manner in which these losses are faced depends on factors such as the nature of the loss, the present physiological capacities, the strength of ego reserves, and the person's adaptive capacities; yet these losses are compounded with added years.

Thus, the most common clinical syndrome seen in the older adult is depression. Yet it may be that normal mourning—the partial mourning just described—may have been a consistent part of the personality. It is not deemed pathological in early years, because it has been considered an extreme of a natural reaction or perhaps because it was integrated within the individual's normal repertoire of responses. For in our society we tend to dichotomize: pathology is what comes to the attention of medical/health personnel; normative functioning, what is outside its domain. We obsess with pathology and tend to see either all devils or all angels!

Partial mourning may be analogous to the Kleinian view of the infant's normally depressive position in the first six months of life. Klein postulates that the infant accepts the fact that the "good mother" (she who gratifies) and the "bad mother" (she who frustrates) may in truth be the same person. It is, for the infant, within the scope of this theory, the awakening to the fact that "Paradise is lost." This depression appears transient and the infant soon comes to terms with reality. Such transient depressions are common in adult developmental phases. To leave the parental home or to marry may entail some depression. Parenthood as a developmental phase, involving redistribution of libidinal cathexis to include another object, also involves transient object loss and therefore depression. Normal mourning or the affective response of depression consists of gradual withdrawal of cathexis from an object who no longer exists in reality. When this is completed, new object relations can be formed. Normal mourning comes to an end. This is in distinction to melancholic depression. Further, in normal mourning or grief, the object has been loved and lost. In extended depression or melancholia, love is overridden by aggression.

Developmental psychology concerns itself with the young child's formative years (Mahler 1972). The first year or more of life revolves around symbiosis—that harmony or closeness with the mother where the world is experienced as a loving, trusting, dependable one. Thus nurtured, the child can later on, in the next year of life, move toward the separation/individuation period, best noted in the rapprochement phase when the mother encourages the child to move out on its own but offers herself sensitively to the child when needed; she responds on cue, staying accessible but nonintrusive to the child's need to experience for oneself. She thus nurtures and renurtures what needs to be replenished.

We may see a parallel to this in the aging process. The older adult has lived many years in a complex environment. The person has learned to rely on self and has been reinforced for this in our striving, independence-oriented society. Yet sometime in the middle years, loss sets in. One begins to experience the natural concomitants of aging. Though selective, loss is universal. Whereas one individual feels the assault of bodily changes, another may experience the trauma of the loss of others. Each loss is, however, an assault, to be reintegrated into the psyche through the adaptive, coping mechanisms in use throughout one's life. Yet, unlike the child, the adult has no nurturing environment to turn to. One is seen as an adult who has learned to be independent and is scorned for dependent behaviors. Dependency or the reaching out for prosthetics with which to cushion the blows of the assault are seen as weaknesses. For this person there is no mother sitting nearby, waiting for the child to reach out in order to fill in what is still needed; for this person there is only self and the ability to use self as the giver of self to self. All objects have now been internalized into a matrix that exists in memory. The real world is coated with illusion; only the illusion acquired throughout the lifespan still exists within oneself. Though one may mourn, one has these images within oneself to turn to. Where these images do not exist in sufficient number or intensity, one has only emptiness and depression.

One of the dynamics of depression may be the hunger for immortality. Throughout life, we seek it and get it where we can— in the small family circle or in the single love object. Depression may sum up both the terror of life and death and the hunger for self-perpetuation. Thus, "dependency is the basic survival mechanism of the human organism. . . . When the adult gives up hope in his ability to cope and sees himself incapable of either fleeing or fighting, he is reduced to a state of depression. This very reduction with its parallel to the helplessness of infancy becomes a plea for a solution to the problem of survival via dependency" (Blanck and Blanck 1974) It has been suggested that the depressed person experiences guilt owing to the failure to live one's own life, to fulfill one's own potential, because of the twisting and turning to be "good" in the eyes of the other. This other, the object, thus calls the tune to one's eligibility for immortality, and so the other takes up one's unlived life. Relationships are thus always slavery, leaving residues of guilt. Depressed persons also get those around them to respond to them, pity them, value them, and take care of them. In a society that offers the aging person few nutrients, this symptom may provide for adaptive solutions.

Not always can early conflicts be used to understand the dilemmas of adult life. Adhered to rigidly, they may remind us of the procrustean bed. For example, menopausal depression in the adult woman has been said to trigger unresolved castration anxiety. Here the woman is again viewed as the poor, castrated creature reliving her natural disadvantage. Clinical experience has shown that often menopausal women in the psychiatric hospital were there because of the social forces impinging upon them. Their lives no longer useful, perhaps divorced with children out of the home, they have seen the expiration of their role as mothers/wives. Alone with nothing meaningful to do, devoid of a social role, trade, or skill outside their work in the family, they are rendered literally useless.

Seen another way, it may be that the woman's experience of a repetition of castration at menopause is a real one—not in the narrow focus that early Freud used, but rather in a broader sense, an existential one. Castration fear here may be viewed as an inroad whereby the anxiety inherent in all existence may break into one's world. Menopause here simply reawakens the horror of the body, the bankruptcy of the body as a viable project—the exact experience that brings on the early oedipal castration anxiety. The woman is reminded in a most forceful way that she is an animal thing; menopause an "animal birthday" that specifically marks a point in the physical career of degeneration. It is like nature imposing a definite physical milestone on the person, putting up a wall and saying, "You are not going any further into life now, you are going toward the end, to the absolute determinism of death." Because men do not have such animal birthdays, such specific markers of a physical kind, they do not usually experience another stark discrediting of the body. For the man, once has been enough, and he buries the problem with the symbolic powers of the cultural world view. But the woman is less fortunate; she is put in the position of having all at once to catch up psychologically with the physical facts of life. To paraphrase Goethe's aphorism, death does not keep knocking on her door only to be ignored (as men ignore their aging) but kicks it in to show himself full in the face. It is no accident that menopausal depression is peculiarly a phenomenon of those societies in which aging women are deprived of some continuing useful place, some vehicle through which to transcend the body and death.

Yet it may be that woman has the advantage in this obvious ability to mourn, in her menopausal state, some aspects of her body functioning. One may see this in the ideas of "self-mourning," developed by Ruitenbeek (1969), the mourning of one's own eventual death and thus the working of it out of one's unconscious. In this view one works out one's own death from within one's own system. A parallel to this may be seen in Freud's early concept of "mourning labor" (Perls 1969), which reaffirms the total bodily character of this process. It may also be said that cultural forces conspire to produce menopausal depression in a society that lies to the person about the stages of life, that refers to the later years only as "golden" ones, and most of all that has no provision in its world view for the mourn-

38   *Marcella Bakur Weiner*

ing of one's finiteness. Further, no vehicles exist through which that finiteness may be mourned in a stage-by-stage progression, not merely as a function of chronology per se but rather as a function of felt life's experiences.

Thus, it is suggested not only that mankind, from early life on, be allowed and encouraged to restrict their experiences, and not just as a means of self-preservation—or what Becker (1973) calls "partialization" of responses—but also that early mourning be accepted as a means of living life and living death-within-life. As such, the work of mourning is, indeed, the painful yet joyful process of bidding goodbye to the internalized images within each of us. The bid for immortality takes place when we, in turn, become an internalized good image in another being; the process is circular and, therefore, never-ending.

References and Bibliography

Becker, E. 1973. *The Denial of Death.* New York: The Free Press.
Blanck, G. and R. Blanck. 1974. *Ego Psychology: Theory and Practice.* New York: Columbia University Press.
Freud, S. 1974. "Some Observations on Depression, on Nosology, on Affects and on Mourning." *Journal of Geriatric Psychiatry,* 6–20.
Jarvik, L. F., C. Eisdorfer, and J. E. Blum. 1972. *Intellectual Functioning in Adults.* New York: Springer.
Klein, M. and J. Riviere. 1964. *Love, Hate and Reparation.* New York: W. W. Norton.
Mahler, M. 1972. "On the First Three Subphases of the Separation-Individuation Process." *Psychoanalytic Study of the Child* 26:403–24. New York: Quadrangle Books.
Neugarten, B. L. 1968. *Middle Age and Aging.* Chicago: University of Chicago Press.
Perls, F. S. 1969. *Hunger and Aggression: The Beginning of Gestalt Therapy.* New York: Random House.

Ruitenbeek, H. M. 1969. *Death: Interpretations*. New York: Delta Books.

Zetzel, E. R. 1965. "Dynamics of the Metapsychology of the Aging Process." In M. Berezin and S. H. Cath, eds. *Geriatric Psychiatry: Grief, Loss, and Emotional Disorder in the Aging Process*. New York: International Universities Press.

5

Theoretical and Clinical Aspects
of Geriatric Thanatology

IRWIN M. GREENBERG

SEVERAL YEARS AGO, I attended a committee meeting whose purpose was to review proposals for novel and original mental health programs based in the community. One of the programs involved a plan whereby the community agency submitting the proposal would contract for personnel to visit homebound elderly people to detect early signs of depression and prevent "unnecessary" hospitalization, presumably psychiatric. I asked whether the possibility had been considered that depression in an elderly person is a prodromal sign of a systemic illness such as cardiac disease or an infectious process, and if it had been so considered, what the agency proposed to do. The program planner had apparently considered depression, not as a non-specific signal of an underlying process, but only as a single psychiatric entity. The community representative and other members of the review group surmised that a visiting nurse could be called. Eventually, someone suggested that the patient in question might be referred for prompt medical and psychosocial evaluation.

The critical point of this vignette is that the possibility of physical illness in an elderly person had not been considered seriously by a sophisticated agency with considerable psychotherapy and counseling experience. A little reflection would make it clear, however, that this should not be unexpected, primarily because classical and neoclassical personality theories (e.g., Freud, Sullivan, etc.) that treat psychological health and disease do not usually attend to the aging process, and if they do, they do not deal with the possibility that systemic illness may play an etiological, or at least a modifying role, in the conditions we term psychiatric diseases, emotional disorders, or personality disorders. Consequently, relatively little background has been provided to the mental health field that would furnish a theory of human mental health and disease taking into consideration both the ubiquity of chronic illness and the importance of the aging process, as well as the interaction of these two phenomena. Moreover, the biology of aging and systemic illness as they affect the psychological processes of the aging person has been relatively ignored by biological psychiatrists. Fortunately, these deficits in theory are now being filled as the demands of clinical practice become evident.

In particular, a compilation of papers on geriatric psychiatry, published by the National Institute of Mental Health (Stevry and Blank 1977) should be mentioned. The volume contains helpful material on treatment, including an article by Goldfarb and Scheps (1954) on the psychotherapy of institutionalized aged persons with systemic illness. However, no theory is presented on the interaction of aging as a developmental phase and the role of chronic illness in psychodynamic development throughout life. There is also no systematic treatment of death anxiety in the aged.

In what follows, five topics are developed. The first is a brief review of classical and neoclassical psychoanalytic theories with respect to their viewpoints on aging. The second issue addressed deals with the concepts of those theories with respect to systemic illness, and in particular, the interaction of the psychodynamics of aging with those of systemic illness. The third subject is a review of death anxiety from the classical and neoclassical point of view. Fourth, philosophical and value systems assumptions underlying psychoanalytic theories are elaborated. Lastly, a general systems approach to the aging process is outlined, and dependency, illness, and death anxiety are discussed in this context.

The imprint of psychoanalytic theory on American thought can hardly be exaggerated. As part of the scientific evolution of the first half of the twentieth century, both intrapsychic and interpersonal theories have markedly affected childrearing, value systems formation, education, concepts of personality formation, views of mental illness, the practice of medicine, and legal issues. A review of the classical concepts of Freud (1938, Hall 1954) and Sullivan (1970, Mullahy 1968) reveals certain disparities of viewpoint and a good deal of agreement. The essential difference between the Freudian and the Sullivanian views centers about the importance of normative biological predetermined development. Freud saw the function of certain affective and cognitive phenomena as inevitable consequences of man's lot, e.g., the Oedipus complex, whereas Sullivan saw these same phenomena as consequences of interpersonal and familial events. As a corollary to the difference, Sullivan viewed cultural differences and influences as much more important than Freud did.

The similarities in the theories are much more striking, however. Both regard infancy and childhood as critical times for personality development and both affirm the importance of the nuclear family during those periods of development. Both theories posit the possibility of personality change through psychotherapy and postulate the existence of similar, although somewhat different, processes. The Freudian scheme proposes the use of transference in dissolving past conflicts and hence in freeing the ego to develop as it sees fit, unconstrained by unconscious conflict. The Sullivanian theory invokes the patient-therapist relation as an interpersonal experience that alters and corrects the patient's view of the world, particularly the interpersonal world. Neither Freud nor Sullivan described normative development in adulthood, and both neglected the later years of life as a developmental period. In addition, despite their both being physicians, neither discussed the causes or effects of systemic disease on intrapsychic or interpersonal functioning.

Of Freud's contemporaries and early students such as Adler, Jung, Abraham, and Reich, none dealt with the aging process, and only Adler (1946) treated systemic disease, though Adler invoked it only as an etiological factor in illnesses occurring during infancy or childhood. He speculated that systemic disease in the early years of life left the patient with an "organ inferiority" that affected his intrapsychic functioning and caused him to develop compensatory mechanisms to defend against the sense of inferiority. Adler did not carry this useful concept into its role in the psychodynamics of aging.

Karl Abraham wrote a brief and illuminating article in 1919 on the possible usefulness of psychoanalytic treatment of older persons, namely, people over the age of forty, or even fifty. In doing so, he contradicted Freud, who held that such older people were too rigid to be treated.

Later developments in psychoanalytic theory added depth in several areas. Neoclassical theorists such as Erich Fromm (1947) pointed out the great importance of culture and value systems in personality function and personality disorder. Flanders Dunbar and Franz Alexander pioneered in the major field of psychosomatic medicine (Kolb 1968), with a better understanding of the role of systemic illness in psychiatry, but frequently with an undercurrent of a search for a psychological, usually intrapsychic, "cause" for certain illnesses. Only Erik Erikson (1963), in a classical psychoanalytic work, studied the stages of development from childhood to aging in a systematic manner. Despite Erikson's breadth of understanding and scope of concept, he neglected to discuss systemic disease in the aging person. He cited previous competence in life, capability of adapting to changing roles, integrity, and resolution of earlier conflicts as psychosocial prerequisites necessary for coping with the normative psychodynamics of aging. He has a summarizing sentence on anxiety: "Healthy children (i.e., emotionally healthy children) will not fear life if their elders have integrity enough not to fear death."

Berezin (1963) used Erikson's idea of older age's being a "generative stage" and extended it into a "consultative" stage, characterized by being consulted, regardless of the usefulness of the advice offered. Berezin makes a helpful value system contribution, namely, that there is a role for the nonproductive elderly. He does not, however, put this into a theoretical formulation that includes consideration about less fortunate elderly persons, i.e., those who do not get consulted.

Thus, the predominant modes of psychoanalytic thinking, which have influenced our society so greatly, have given almost no recognition to the interaction of systemic disease with the psychodynamics of the aging process, and with it, have neglected the role of death anxiety in the elderly ill. Erikson mentions death anxiety only tangentially, stressing the need for "integrity" to cope with it. Almost all psychoanalytic thought prior to the last decade maintained the viewpoint that since people could not conceive of not existing, they could not be afraid of it. Therefore, no one could really be anxious about death; rather, the person is anxious only about what death is thought to represent. Presumably, if intrapsychic conflicts and interpersonal distortions could be resolved, there would be nothing about which to be anxious, including death. Twenty years ago, the study of death anxiety was not regarded as relevant or important. Only in the past decade has the study of the care of the dying person received attention. There is still a dearth of studies on the influence that a human being's knowledge of personal death has on intrapsychic and interpersonal functions throughout the life cycle.

Two related questions may then be raised: firstly, why should serious-minded and intellectually courageous scholars avoid confronting death anxiety, and secondly, why should they avoid studying the psychodynamics of aging? The answers herein suggested to both these questions are also related. They are embedded in the interaction between the philosophical traditions of the West and the sharp changes in life-styles and longevity wrought in postindustrial society.

The civilized West is essentially an Indo-European society that endeavored to resolve the psychological problems inherent in coping with death well before the spread of its dominant Christian beliefs. Greek thought expressed this attempt at solution most succinctly, although in a variety of forms. Prime examples may be found in the writings of Democritus and Plato, as well as in those of Pythagoras, Plotinus, Porphyry, and others (Russell 1945, Fremantle 1954). Essentially, the Greek solution, and hence the basic Western solution, to death anxiety consisted of the assertion separating corporeal from noncorporeal entities.

Democritus' original atomic theory defined the world as constituted of two distinct kinds of atoms, *somatic* and *psychic* atoms. These two atomic species have independent existences, and although the psychic atoms are capable of *interacting* with somatic atoms, they do not require the latter in order to exist. Plato defined his theory of ideals, in *The Republic* (Lindsay 1957), in a somewhat different manner, but essentially with the same assertion: life as we see it only reflects the shadow of a greater reality, a universal reality that exists independently of the material or somatic world. According to Plato, there are *real* universals that are ideal and require no corporeal expression. These universals are divine, immutable, and only poorly represented somatically to human beings. The idea, the ideal, and the universal are immortal. Although Plato did not specifically refer to these as being comparable to Democritus' psychic atoms, they clearly represent the same kind of entity. The difference may be likened to that between alphabetical and hieroglyphic writing: alphabetical writing is put together by basic elements of sound, (i.e., atoms), whereas hieroglyphic writing is based on each pictograph's representing a thing or a concept (i.e., ideals). The basic similarities between Democritus and Plato are those concerned with the separation of psychic from somatic entities and the immortality of the psychic entities.

The detailing of the psychic or ideal's interacting with the somatic occupied the thinkers, philosophers, and theologians of the West from the time of the Greeks until today. The refining of the concepts of morality, social responsibility, and sin onto the psychic-somatic dichotomy was essential to the development of social systems after the fall of Rome. In the Mediterranean view, each person determined the fate of his or her soul or psyche by virtue of morality and avoidance of sin. Immortality, at least of psychic atoms, was attainable by proper behavior and thought. The Gothic tradition was somewhat bleaker in outlook: at first Wyrd (Morris 1962), the god of Fate, decided who would be immortal. Later, with Calvin's (Smith 1972) and Luther's writings (Simon 1972) of the Northern European Reformation, it was revealed that the Deity, and not Fate, decided each person's lot. A person's behavior and thoughts were then construed to be manifestations of God's will. Immortality and the nature of that immortality were considered to be essentially preordained, but the separation of somatic and spiritual or psychic entities was never in question in the West.

The vicissitudes of this basic dichotomy continued into the nineteenth century. Hegel (Russell 1945), in many ways, epitomized the belief in a separate existence of a mind that interacts with nature, i.e., the somatic world, repeatedly to form new syntheses. Darwin's evolutionary theory was resisted on the grounds of denial of separate somatic and psychic entities. The "mind-body problem" continues to be debated today (Engelhardt 1977). Although Freud categorically denied the separate existence of psychic atoms, and although Sullivan never spoke as if he believed in their existence, both wrote about what is called "the mind" in the Western world.

It mattered little whether or not the formulators of today's theories were monistic or dualistic. It was of much more consequence that their audiences were raised in the dualist tradition. A conspiracy developed, formed by no one, but inherent in the belief system of our civilization, to allow belief in the separate existence of mind or psyche, apart from somatic existence, to continue. Psychoanalytic psychology, by its very emphasis on the activities of nonmeasurable functions, such as "intrapsychic economy" or "interpersonal distortion," fit into the vision characterized by the psychic atoms of Democritus, the ideals of Plato, and Hegel's mind externalizing itself through nature, *whether or not* the formulators of the theories intended it to be that way. As a consequence, death anxiety, which should not have existed for those who were moral, was once again ignored with the explanation previously described.

Purely philosophical considerations are not, however, sufficient to explain the lack of interest in the psychology of the aging process. The value systems of our society, although related to its philosophical foundations, must be examined separately. The basic tenets of Western values include two remarkable axioms. One asserts that all persons should become whatever their capabilities allow. This axiom frequently, but not always, has a hidden companion that states that all persons can become anything as long as they exert enough will and effort to do so. The second remarkable axiom is that of the equivalence of being and productivity: only the productive can become anything worthwhile. It follows from these axioms that since there exist several kinds of people who cannot be productive, they cannot, therefore, become anything worthwhile. Clearly, these groups of people are going to present rather difficult questions for the social structure to answer.

Since it is not the purpose of this discussion to contend with the problems presented by the descendants of previously enslaved or exploited peoples or other socially defined disadvantaged groups, the issue is presented only in passing. More central to this thesis are the problems raised by the aged and by the chronically or recurrently ill.

Neither of these two groups can ordinarily be productive as defined by our social customs, and if any member can be so productive, it is usually in a somewhat limited fashion. Only the rare individual in these groups is able to be fully productive in the commonly understood sense. It is next to impossible for the aged person who is also chronically ill to conform to the criterion of productivity. Consequently, there has been an important determinant in allowing personality theories to avoid the problems of aging, illness, and their interactions, which may be briefly stated as follows: "Why concern ourselves with the problems of third-class citizens?"

There is still another reason for the systematic avoidance of the issues raised by the aged and by the chronically or recurrently ill. As stated earlier, this reason is a complex one that postindustrial society has helped engender. The issues themselves may be stated simply, although the underlying processes are complex: (1) There are many more people living today who at one time would not have been able to survive the birth process and the postnatal period. Many of these people have mild to moderate birth defects that contribute toward chronic illness. (2) There are more people living today who would have once succumbed to a large variety of surgical, obstetrical, and medical conditions. Some of these people, notably those with metabolic diseases or chronic or recurrent infectious illnesses, are chronically ill. (3) More people live to be older. Many of these people are chronically ill.

Thus, it is not difficult to see that the formulations of classical and neoclassical psychoanalytic and personality theories, based on the nature of our society and its subpopulations during the first half of the twentieth century, could not include reasonable accounts of illness or aging. There were not enough members of either group to concern anyone, at least as viewed by the theorists mentioned previously. (Freud, however, specifically mentioned the needs of the poor, the only one to have done so.)

Lastly, concomitant with the development of increased numbers of aged people and chronically or recurrently ill persons, there has been a marked decline in the integrity of the structure and function of the extended family. The goals of individualism and achievement, along with the practical possibilities for social and geographic mobility, have promoted this disintegration. As a consequence, there are *fewer* familial resources with which to cope with the familial, social, economic, interpersonal, and intrapsychic problems of those who are aged, or ill, or both. The lack of a social structure thereby becomes greater in its influence.

The remainder of this discussion outlines a theoretical structure that might be useful in handling the problems described previously. The framework is based on the original formulation of von Bertalanffy's (1975) general systems theory and has been more extensively described elsewhere (Greenberg 1982). Briefly, this framework views the individual organism as a *system,* embedded in a number of superordinate systems and including a number of subordinate subsystems. The superordinate systems include the nuclear family, the extended family, the interpersonal field, social reference groups, and the society at large. The subsystems include the various organ systems, which are themselves formed of a hierarchy of subsystems at the organ, tissue, cellular, subcellular, and molecular levels. The organism, usually in a steady state, may be thrown out of such a state by dysfunctional alteration in any of the superordinate systems or subsystems. Mention was made, for example, of the chronically ill person's receiving less care, at least psychologically, if the extended family is disrupted. Molecular dysfunction, such as is found in metabolic disease, e.g., hypothyroidism or diabetes, may alter the other organism subsystems and hence the intrapsychic and interpersonal functions of the organism, i.e., the patient. In turn, nuclear familial system dysfunction may occur, as well as social reference group dysfunction, especially with respect to work performance.

Implicit in these remarks are two assumptions. One of these states that there are degrees of anatomic integrity, functional capacity, and quality of function in each component system or subsystem. The other assumption deals with the interaction of these systems, again in terms of anatomic integrity, functional capacity, and quality of function. A disruption of any of these may result in a breakdown of the organism's steady state, physiologically, psychologically, or both.

It is evident that a chronic or recurrent dysfunction, i.e., "illness," of any system creates a good chance of disturbing the organism's adjustment to its internal and external milieux. In the context of this development, organ system dysfunction is central. Children with conditions such as celiac disease, minimal brain dysfunction, or asthma are simply not organismically equivalent to children who are free of systemic illnesses. Unless their limitations are understood and their needs met by the sociofamilial environment, such children run risks of future psychological and possibly physiological difficulties.

Examples of similar illnesses may be found at any stage of development. Seizure disorder may first appear in latency, puberty, or even later. Gastrointestinal diseases such as ileitis, colitis, or ulcers may appear in late adolescence, early adulthood, or later. Arthritis, diabetes, and other metabolic disorders have variable ages of onset. The critical point is that chronic and recurrent illnesses form an integral part of the lives of many people. Theories of personality development that deal with healthy people and ignore the impact of illness on the sociofamilial environment, as well as on the personality, will do little to enhance understanding or the intrapsychic, interpersonal, familial, and social dynamics of many people.

Another aspect of the general systems framework, and one that is essential to contending with the aging process, is that of the relationship of time to other considerations. As important as the structure, function, and quality of function of the component systems and their interactions is the time development of all of these factors. The fact that a child cannot walk until there is myelination of the long tracts constitutes an example of one kind of time-related phenomenon, the longitudinal. Other kinds of time-related events are cyclic. Some are diurnal such as sleep while others are monthly such as the estrus cycle. Similarly, families are born, develop, and have internal cycles.

The aging process can, therefore, be viewed as part of the life cycle, and not necessarily as senescence or incompetence. It has its own physiology, intrapsychic phenomena, interpersonal relations, and sociofamilial events. It can, with a little thought, be divorced from the aura of "nonproductivity." It can even be studied from the point of view of different kinds of aging people, including their attitudes toward death. Erikson may be right, and a sense of integrity in an aging person may be of great help in facing eventual death. However, this also means that death as an inevitable event should have been considered throughout one's life course. Phrased another way, this implies that only by the recognition of death during the earlier phases of life can death be confronted in older age.

There are the further problems presented by those whose lives have not furnished the basis for integrity sufficient to the task of coping with death anxiety. In the relatively intact old person, such defects may be partly amenable to psychotherapeutic intervention. Such intervention may be with individuals, groups, or families. It may use verbal or activity techniques. It may involve insight, or support, or replacement of psychological deficits. What is most necessary is to recognize the intrapsychic development of an older person as a bona fide stage of psychological life, even if it does not culminate in "productivity."

The problems are more difficult in persons who are systemically ill, especially if the illness involves the central nervous system (CNS), and particularly the cerebral function. Such dysfunction may be primary in the CNS or secondary to other systemic disease. It may be cortical, subcortical, or both. The degree of impairment may be fluctuant or stable. The setting may be home or institutional. It is clear that the multiplicity of factors affecting the anatomic and physiologic integrity and quality of function of the component subsystems and superordinate systems must be analyzed in detail. Therapeutic intervention may utilize chemotherapy for a system dysfunction, e.g., cardiac decompensation. It may use aids to daily living to restore musculoskeletal capacity. A visiting nurse might make rounds during the time in which the patient is more alert and better able to discuss areas of concern. Professionals may help the family and/or nursing personnel recognize the patients' limitations and fluctuations. Intrapsychic matters similar to those discussed in physiologically healthy persons may sometimes be well tolerated by those who are ill, if the timing is correct and if there is also family involvement. In institutions, the reference group system and social structure functioning often depend on the nursing staff, so that teaching the staff to cope with death anxiety and the reality of dependency will often help interpersonal functioning and provide a psychotherapeutic environment.

Issues such as the belief systems of patient, family, and staff must always be examined. Who is from a guilt culture and who is from a shame culture? Who is a believer in fate or predestination and who believes in free will? Who believes that lost loved ones will be seen in Heaven and who does not?

Death anxiety, even in the aged and ill, can be discussed verbally or dealt with nonverbally if a meticulous system analysis is made for each person. The principal requirement is thought, but the indispensable prerequirement is courage. It is possible that thought might engender courage. It would appear that analysis of our own values and those of our culture may be necessary before we have either courage or thought.

References

Abraham, K. 1919. "The Applicability of Psychoanalytic Treatment to Patients at an Advanced Age." In K. Abraham. *Selected Papers on Psychoanalysis.* New York: Basic Books, 1953.

Adler, A. 1946. *Individual Psychology.* London: Routledge.

Berezin, M. A. 1963. "Some Intrapsychic Aspects of Aging." In N. E. Zinberg and I. Kaufman, eds., pp. 30–39. *Normal Psychology of the Aging Process.* New York: International Universities Press.

Engelhardt, H. T., Jr., ed. 1977. "Mind-Body Quandaries." *Journal of Medicine and Philosophy* 2:2.

Erikson, E. 1963. *Childhood and Society.* 2d ed. New York: Norton.

Fremantle, A. 1954. *Age of Belief.* New York: New American Library.

Fromm, E. 1947. *Man for Himself.* New York: Holt, Rinehart and Winston.

Freud, S. 1938. *A General Introduction to Psychoanalysis.* New York: Garden City Publishing Co.

Goldfarb, A. I. and J. Scheps. 1954. "Psychotherapy of the Aged." *Psychosomatic Medicine.* Reprinted in Stevry and Blank, *q.v.*

Greenberg, I. M., 1982. "General Systems Theory: Social and Biological Interations." Submitted for publication.

Hall, H. 1954. *A Primer of Freudian Psychology.* New York: New American Library.

Kolb, L. 1968. *Noyes' Modern Clinical Psychiatry,* 7th ed. Philadelphia: Saunders.

Lindsay, A. D., trans. 1957. *The Republic of Plato.* New York: Dutton.

Morris, W., trans. 1962. *Volsuga Saga: The Story of the Volsuga*. New York: Collier Books.

Mullahy, P. 1968. *Oedipus: Myth and Complex*. New York: Hermitage Press.

Russell, B. 1945. *A History of Western Philosophy*. New York: Simon and Schuster.

Simon, E. 1972. "Martin Luther." In *Makers of Modern Thought*. New York: American Heritage.

Smith, T. B. 1972. "John Calvin." In *Makers of Modern Thought*. New York: American Heritage.

Stevry, S. and M. L. Blank, eds. 1977. *Readings in Psychotherapy With Older People*. Rockville, Md.: U.S. Department of HEW, PHS Alcohol, Drug Abuse, Mental Health Administration.

Sullivan, H. J. 1970. *The Psychiatric Interview*. New York: Norton.

von Bertalanffy, L. 1975. *Perspectives on General System Theory*. New York: Braziller.

6

Negative Attitudes Among the Elderly Toward Living

BARRY J. GURLAND

*T*HIS PAPER FOCUSES on an attitude that may undergo rapid and impressive change in the course of dying—namely, the desire to die. In particular, this attitude is examined in elderly patients who have not yet entered the end stages of dying. Background information is provided to aid in understanding the process of dying in the elderly and to raise a question about the extent to which the expertise of thanatology may be brought to bear on improving the situation for elderly people before the health care professional offers the prognosis of the relatively imminent termination of life.

Data have been derived from a study, the United States/United Kingdom Cross-National Geriatric Community Study (Gurland et al. 1983), which was conducted by the Center for Geriatrics (Columbia University and New York State Office of Mental Health) in collaboration with the Institute of Psychiatry in London. Random samples of the elderly, all of whom were 65 years of age or older, were examined by multidisciplinary teams in the communities of New York and London. A systematic, semistructured interview, the comprehensive, assessment and referral evaluational (CARE), as administered by trained raters in the homes of the elderly. Each interview lasted between one and a half and three hours and covered a wide variety of psychiatric, medical, and social problems, and service use. The cross-national reliability of the ratings between the two teams was good. In New York, 445 completed interviews were obtained, and 396 in London, the response rate being above 70 percent in both cities. Cases were seen again after one year, and the same measurements were then repeated.

The main aims of the study were to compare, between the two cities, the prevalence of the health and social problems of the elderly, the treatment they received, and their outcome over one year. The results are based on secondary analysis, and though they are revealing, these data are being used to answer questions that were not anticipated when the study was planned.

TABLE 6.1. Percent of Elderly Sharing Negative Attitude

	In New York	*In London*
Feeling that life is not worth living	11	11
Having empty expectations for the future	17	20
Regarding the future as bleak and unbearable	4	7
Recent suicidal impulses	3	5
Recent wishes to be dead short of suicidal impulses	7	6
Worries about being alone in the future	14	15

Certain specifics can be derived from this interview as giving some insight into the attitudes of the elderly toward living and dying. These are the following: feelings that life is not worth living, having empty expectations for the future, regarding the future as bleak and unbearable, recent suicidal impulses, recent wishes to be dead short of suicidal impulses, and worries about being alone in the future.

The first social context in which we examined these attitudes was at the macro level of the two cities. It was found that almost exactly the same proportion of the elderly in the two cities shared negative attitudes on these matters. These proportions were as shown in table 6.1. We were surprised at these findings, for we had been impressed with differences in the sociomedical climates of the two cities and had expected to see some effect on the negative attitudes toward living among these elderly subjects.

It is generally believed that the practice of geriatric medicine and the status of home care services for the elderly are, on the average, more advanced in London than in New York. Furthermore, the population in London is more homogeneous than that in New York; London has a larger proportion of elderly, this population is more stable, and it is less preoccupied with the need to be productive. Superficially, therefore, one might regard these characteristics as providing a more favorable setting for the elderly. Yet there is little or no evidence to support such a contention in the data reported here. The extraordinary similarities and the frequency of these negative attitudes in the two cities led us to hypothesize that fairly powerful factors shared by the two samples of elderly subjects were determining their attitudes. A hunt for these factors then ensued.

The following possible determinants of negative attitudes to living were examined: sex, age, race, nativity, marital status, living arrangements, religious affiliation, strength of religious feeling, quality of the neighborhood and housing, finances, social contacts, engagement in activities, level of disability, and a range of psychiatric and medical conditions. Items and scales were constructed to measure each of these factors.

An orderly and powerful relationship was found between these negative attitudes and physical illness or its attendant disability. Age, on the other hand, was found to be inconsistently related to these negative attitudes. In the first place, the relationship varied with the sexes. Although negative attitudes did increase with age, the discrepancy between the youngest and oldest age groups was much greater for men than for women. Furthermore, for men there was a distinct dip in the frequency of negative attitudes at age 70 to 74, compared with younger and older age groups. The quality of the environment—of the neighborhood and housing—was not a powerful determinant of negative attitudes.

These negative attitudes to life were found to be related to a complex of negative feelings falling into the domain of the depressive syndrome. The correlation of the negative attitudes with a scale of depression, which contained the usual clinically relevant items, was very high. However, negative attitudes to living were also found to correlate highly with items such as life dissatisfaction, unhappiness, and loneliness, which are more characteristic of demoralization syndromes than of clinical depression. Therefore, these negative attitudes cannot be neatly assigned exclusively to either the clinical depressions or the demoralization syndromes; they share the characteristics of both. Thus, both medical and social models are required to understand and change these negative attitudes.

Many of the items dealing with physical illness and disability are self-reported and thus vulnerable to response bias on the part of the subject. It could be argued, therefore, that depressed people give a jaundiced view of life and of their physical state and thus provide a spurious relationship between negative attitudes and physical disability. However, an independent appraisal of the subject's disability, based on tests of performance ability and on the interviewer's observation of the subject, also supported the strong relationship between disability and a negative view of life.

The following situations tend to strengthen the relationship between physical disability and negative attitudes to life: lack of a confidante, living alone, being white rather than a member of a minority group, having low religious participation, and being divorced or separated. These are all circumstances in which social supports can be inferred to be relatively weak. Consistent with this interpretation is that those who had negative attitudes were much more likely than the others to claim that they might lie unnoticed and neglected for more than a day and a night if they were stricken helpless and unable to summon aid.

During the year that these subjects were followed, 31 members of this group died in New York and 18 in London. Except for physical disability, the most powerful predictors of actual death were not those that most powerfully predicted negative attitudes. Depression predicted negative attitudes but did not predict death, whereas dementia did the opposite. Heart disease and neurological disorder also predicted death but not negative attitudes. Advancing age was related to death in an orderly, sequential fashion but was not related to negative attitudes.

I would like to put these facts together in a way that appears to be relevant to thanatology. It seems to be that thanatologists have a double-edged management problem in the end stage of dying—namely, to gain acceptance of imminent and inevitable death while encouraging the valuation of the continuing life that remains, with all its limitations and discomforts. Imbalance in either direction between the acceptance of dying and the valuation of life can be undesirable. With respect to the elderly, the management problems are compounded by the difficulty of gaining acceptance for remaining life on the part of the attendant staff and the family, as well as on the part of the patient.

In 5 to 6 percent of our community subjects, the interviewers felt that the subjects' negative view of life was fully justified. Between 26 to 30 percent of the elderly subjects themselves had negative attitudes toward life, while about 10 percent wished either to be dead or to kill themselves. Nevertheless, in most cases the elderly subjects who had negative attitudes toward life were able to describe these attitudes as a sense of emptiness about life and not as an act or desire to be dead, suggesting that the purpose of intervention, to improve the quality of life for the physically disabled, might relieve these feelings. Furthermore, it should be remembered that more than two-thirds of the elderly did not have predominantly negative attitudes toward life.

These elderly subjects were almost all yet to enter the end stages of dying. Whatever attitudes might develop in that end stage can be better understood in the light of these data. Most particularly, there seems every reason to preserve energetically throughout the end stages of dying the valuation of life that the majority of elderly people profess. The negative attitudes held by a substantial minority of these elderly subjects seemed subject to exacerbation by two major influences: incapacitating physical illness and weakness of their social support system.

By the time such people enter the end stages of dying, they may have already established attitudes that will complicate the management of terminal events. The elderly often, if not usually, have suffered a long, chronic illness before entering the end stages of dying. Thus, there are two pressing reasons for the application of thanatological skills to the problems of the sick elderly patient and his family, prior to entry into the end stages of dying: first, to forestall and prevent complications in the end stages, and second, to apply the expertise gained in the end stages of dying to the relief of distress in earlier stages.

If more were needed to draw the thanatologist to this challenge of early intervention and continuity of treatment, a case might be made that the physical disability, often underlying the elderly person's negative view of living, is evidence of an early stage of dying. These subjects did not regard themselves as being at the end stages of dying, but physical disability was, in fact, a predictor of the deaths that occurred within the following year.

Other predictors of death—such as advanced age itself, dementia, or the symptoms of heart disease—were not associated with negative attitudes toward living as strongly as physical disability was. One suspects that physical disability is prepotent in predicting negative attitudes because of a complex of effects, including loss of independence on the part of physically disabled people, a constriction of their range of interests and activities, financial strains arising from payments for treatment and services, and the reflected feelings of strain and burden in spouse, children, and other family members. I should point out that in our findings we noted that there was a higher rate of depression among those who were supporting the disabled elderly than among the disabled elderly themselves. And this reflects, I think, on elderly patients who are being supported when they see what their situation is doing to family members. And finally, there is the emotional withdrawal of close friends and relatives during a long, chronic illness. The unraveling of the tangled relationships among these effects, and their amelioration, are a challenge that thanatology could well meet.

Reference

Gurland, B., J. Copeland, M. Kelleher, J. Kuriansky, L. Sharpe, and L. Dean. 1983. *The Mind and Mood of Aging: The Mental Health Problems of the Community Elderly in New York and London.* New York: Haworth Press.

7

Anticipatory Socialization
for Death

AARON LIPMAN

CONTEMPORARY SOCIETY IS permeated by feelings of loss, impermanence, and disintegration, brought about mainly as a consequence of the exponential rate of societal change. Movies, popular songs, television, and novels reflect a yearning for the past and the perceived semblance of stability represented by that past.

Futurists contend that the rapidity of the changes assaulting our society may be as problematic as the changes themselves and may help explain these feelings of loss and nostalgic turning toward the past. While these societal changes undoubtedly represent a gain of new behavior patterns, situations, and conditions, it is significant that they also represent a loss of the old established patterns. It has been suggested that one reason for so much current concern and discussion about death today is that in a society confronted with change and loss at every turn, death may be considered as the ultimate, irrevocable loss.

Some valuable insights regarding this process emerge when losses and gains are viewed in the context of sociological role theory. Thus, in one's passage through life, one plays a series of roles associated with one's changing statuses; the transitions from one role to the next have been described by sociologists as role entrances and role exits, and in many cases will be seen to be losses and gains. It is through the process of socialization that one learns how to fulfill the assigned or achieved roles. Anticipatory socialization refers to socialization for a role, prior to occupancy of that role; it is directed toward the learning of future roles, rather than those roles that one has at the time one is learning to fulfill them. Anticipatory socialization consists of both learning and rehearsing the values and behavior associated with a particular role or group as a preliminary step to assumption of that role or membership in that group. If we view the life cycle in terms of these role exits and entrances, or transitions, each can be seen to serve as anticipatory socialization mechanisms, helping the individual deal with losses and gains and leading ultimately to acceptance of death; in this context, death would represent the terminal role exit.

The transitional losses, where one way of living is finished and another has emerged, can take place on a continuum—losses may be gradual and minuscule—or they may be abrupt and catastrophic. The exact dynamics depend on both the objective events and the way in which the individual subjectively perceives and copes with those events. Retirement, which represents an exit from the occupational role and an entrance into whatever role or roles replace the work role for the individual, serves as a case in point. For some individuals, retirement represents a crisis; the loss of the occupational role causes trauma and pain. Gerontologists have theorized that for these people, many other life transitions or turning points were also viewed and reacted to as crisis situations. Conversely, there are those individuals for whom retirement represents a move along a continuum, an exit from the role of worker, and an entrance to the role or roles involved in being a retiree—usually an increase in social, familial, or political roles.

There is a great deal of heuristic value in an approach that identifies the losses associated with role exits and various transitions in a person's life and considers them as a series of minideaths. In the same way that we apply anticipatory socialization to the role of retiree and have been able to teach people to cope who might otherwise have reacted with a crisis mentality, it should be possible to use the concept of minidying in a positive and productive manner, understanding that the losses and change represented in minideaths involve some of the same entities of grief and mourning attendant upon actual death itself. The French saying, "Partir, c'est mourir un peu," is a recognition of the reality and poignancy of minidying. These losses or minidyings can be viewed as little rehearsals to the actual death that we all face eventually. The construct is not to be understood on a physical, absolute level, but rather a symbolic one; loss may be viewed as an analogue of death.

In the light of this approach, midlife crisis can be interpreted as an accumulation of losses and transitions that have reached proportions that the middle-aged person can no longer deny or ignore. Up to this time, the individual had been dealing with role transition increments. As he went through the life cycle he acquired a job, a wife, children, promotions, raises, and a general increase in money, power, and prestige. Even when role transitions represent gains, they often involve difficult adjustments; they are much more difficult when they involve decrements or losses. These turning points of loss may elicit feelings of helplessness, confusion, anger, pain, surprise, sacrifice, grief, and mourning—feelings similar to those associated with death.

When a national sample of individuals was asked to tell which period of the life cycle could be considered the worst, those that identified the ages 50 to 60 as being the worst years of a person's life mentioned poor health as the most frequent reason. The second most frequent response was "aging, feeling older, going downhill." The feeling pervading the explanation is an awareness of loss and depletion, a turning point from ascendancy to decline. Vocationally during these years, the individual is at what Super (1972) has called the "maintenance stage" of career development. Here the person who formerly had been concerned with advancement is now involved mainly in attempting to maintain the gains made already and defending the status quo against the inroads and encroachments of younger individuals, still in the "advancement stage," who are in competition. The person is at the penultimate stage in the vocational cycle; while all the stages up to this point represented advancement, the last step in Super's vocational development paradigm is called "decline stage" and involves such negative-sounding vocational developmental tasks as "deceleration" and "disengagement" before actual retirement. Economically, the retirement stage of the vocational cycle usually represents a reduction in income and a consequent reduction in style of living as well. In status terms it can be thought of as a demotion in the work force.

This midlife decade (not literally the years from 50 to 60 for everyone concerned, but rather a recognizable configuration composed of time of life, frame of mind, and shared experiences) marks the onset of a host of other transitional or turning point losses, which continue chronologically into the aging process. The physical losses are pervasive; there are age-related changes in virtually all bodily systems and functions. The skin loses its elasticity and becomes wrinkled, hair turns gray or falls out, there are decrements in the senses of hearing, vision, taste, and smell, and in general psychomotor functioning. There are losses of youth, of beauty, of vigor, of libido, and with these losses a concomitant change in total body image and image of self.

Some psychological changes are physiologically based, such as the losses involving brain cells throughout the process of physical aging and the losses in short-term memory. Still other psychological changes occur as accompaniments to losses in different physical areas, such as those already delineated; the person's self-concept undergoes profound changes in the adjustment to the minideath or role exit from youth and the transition or role entrance into the middle years and approaching old age.

Psychological changes also occur along with important social changes and losses. As mentioned previously, role changes accompany changes in status; a number of these status changes are extremely significant: in the family of orientation, for example, the individual's parents are aging and dying. With both parents dead, no one stands between the individual and the grave, symbolically; there may consequently be an increased sense of vulnerability and mortality. In the family of procreation, children are maturing into adults, with the parental role receding or clouded in ambiguity and redundancy. Nurturing roles change to occupational or recreational ones. Marital statuses change, with losses and changes occurring through both death and divorce. There is attrition of old friends; changes occur through dispersion to different neighborhoods, to the homes of children, to retirement communities, and through death. Changes also take place in societal value systems; norms that had helped define appropriate behavior for different roles have suddenly shifted with a consequent shattering of reciprocal noncontractual exchange obligations.

It is the thesis of this paper that providing individuals with insights and coping mechanisms with which to handle their significant role transitional losses or turning points may give them the means to deal with the ultimate loss represented by their own death. Mini-dying in this sense can serve an extremely important function, as a series of small rehearsals for death itself. Conversely, by learning to confront and understand one's own death, it is possible that one will be able to confront and manage each of the changes in one's life more effectively. Therapists should be concerned with the integration of these two processes in their attempts to make awareness of death function as an educational tool for a fuller life.

Reference

Super, D. 1972. "Vocational Development Theory: Persons, Positions, and Process." In J. M. Whitely and A. Resnikoff, eds., *Perspectives on Vocational Development*, Washington, D.C.: APGA.

8

Can Suicide
on Grounds of Old Age
Be Ethically Justified?

H. R. MOODY

*T*HE ISSUE OF suicide and old age today assumes an importance that is historically unprecedented, for two major reasons. First, technological advances in medicine have increased life expectancy to the point where an unprecedented proportion of the population lives into old age, and new medical technology offers prolongation of life for elderly patients suffering from chronic diseases and disabilities. (For a good discussion of some of the social, economic, and philosophical questions here, see Neugarten and Havighurst 1977.) Second, the rapid rate of cultural change has brought a state of affairs in which many older people have, in effect, outlived their previous roles, values, and sources of subjective meaning—in short, reasons that make life worth living. We know from statistics that the rate of suicide, in general, increases with each decade of life to reach a high point in old age. From these empirical data we know something of the magnitude of the phenomenon, but we do not know what to make of it. My purpose here is to provide some philosophical clarification of the issues at stake in suicide and old age and to suggest some answers to the ethical dilemmas that are raised.

The Basic Question

Is suicide on grounds of old age ethically justified? This is the question I propose to consider, but before proceeding we must be clear about what question is being asked. First, I am concerned here with *suicide* in the strong sense of the term: with intentional acts of self-killing, not with "allowing to die," with negligent actions resulting in death, or with other acts indirectly related to the ending of life. Second, I am concerned with the choice of suicide *on grounds of* old age, not simply during the period of old age. Specifically, I am not concerned with other grounds for suicide: for example, with arguments over euthanasia, either active or passive, in cases of painful terminal illness. (For a closely reasoned philosophical analysis, see Foot 1977; on the ethical problems of suicide in general, see Novak 1975 and Landsberg 1953.) Third, I am concerned with the question of whether the choice of suicide on account of old age can be *ethically* justified. That is, what reason or justification can we offer for the claim that suicide in old age is a good or a bad thing, an action to be encouraged or discouraged? This is clearly a question of philosophical ethics and not a matter of law or of the so-called "right to die" (Jonas 1978:4), the legal right to commit suicide (Tonne 1974). I do not argue that suicide, among the elderly or any other group, should be subject to sanctions of the criminal law. But if we accept suicide as a legal right, it does not follow that it is an ethically justified course of action. *Whether* suicide on grounds of old age can be ethically justified is precisely the question we need to examine.

The Rationality of Suicide

I assume at the outset that the choice of suicide can itself be a "rational" option, in the sense that it is a serious life choice, the outcome of a process of intelligent deliberation where the agent has an option *not* to commit suicide. That is, I assume that suicide, at least in some cases, is a free action in the simple sense that the agent "could have done otherwise." Thus, when I call suicide a "rational" choice, I do so in the same sense that we could describe a person planning a bank robbery as engaged in a "rational" choice. The person may be mistaken, may be acting unethically; to call the action "rational" or "free" is simply to say that the agent could have done otherwise. Unless these conditions of freedom and rationality are present, we cannot seriously address the question of whether suicide on grounds of old age is ethically justified.

Three common points of view dominate discussion of suicide, and I must dispose of these before proceeding further. These are the sanctity-of-life argument, the libertarian argument, and the view that suicide is a form of mental illness. Each of these views, in different ways, weakens any genuine effort to assess whether suicide on grounds of old age is ethically justified.

Sanctity-of-Life Argument

The sanctity-of-life argument maintains that suicide is *never* permitted, because the choice of life or death is not a decision that belongs to human beings to make. Human life, and perhaps all life, is held sacred, and there are no good grounds for killing, either oneself or others. The sanctity-of-life argument against suicide is based on the same claim as the argument of this kind against capital punishment. Believers in sanctity-of-life as an absolute value, for example, would not be persuaded by utilitarian arguments that capital punishment may serve as a deterrent to crime. "Sanctity-of-life" is a deontological principle beyond any possible refutation by empirical consequences.

The sanctity-of-life view is supported not only by religious doctrines, such as Aquinas' third argument against suicide, but also by more vague religious sentiments, such as the "reverence-for-life" principle associated with figures like Schweitzer, Gandhi, or Tolstoy. Sanctity-of-life should by no means be dismissed as simple-minded dogmatism or religious superstition; as a prohibition of suicide, it expresses a moral idealism concerning the destiny of life in the universe.

I do not intend to argue for or against the sanctity-of-life view, but rather to set it aside from consideration. If its absolutism is accepted, then *no* decision for suicide is ever justified, on account of old age or on any other grounds. The sanctity-of-life point of view is really a species of moral intuitionism, appealing to a standard of absolute value—the sacredness of life—that must simply be accepted or rejected by pure intuition. In this sense, the argument forecloses serious consideration of suicide as a life choice, and for this reason it cannot enter into discussion here.

Libertarian Argument

The best statement of the libertarian argument is to be found in David Hume's essay "On Suicide," published in 1777, a year after his death. (For a definitive philosophical treatment, see Beauchamp 1976; for the historical background, see Sprott 1961). Like contemporary humanist writing on the subject (*The Humanist,* 1974; for a philosophically informed treatment, see Hook 1927), Hume's intention is to show that suicide is not a crime, that everyone ought to have the right to commit suicide. Hume argues that for suicide to be a crime, it must be an offense against God, society, or ourselves. It is not an offense against God, because our God-given reason offers us suicide as a release from misery. As regards the place of man's life in the cosmic scheme of things, Hume asserts that "the life of a man is of no greater importance to the universe than that of an oyster." Is suicide then an offense against society? Hume rejects this claim, too, arguing instead that "A man who retires from life does no harm to society; he only ceases to do good; which, if it is an injury, is of the lowest kind." Hume's argument seems even stronger in the case of suicide on grounds of old age when one's duties to others are minimal and one may even be a burden to society.

Finally, as to the claim that suicide is an offense against oneself, Hume simply points out that suicide may be strongly in one's self-interest. In any case, the decision about whether suicide is really in one's self-interest is strictly up to the individual, who is his own best judge of his interests. It is this last argument that we shall return to shortly, with the particular aim of clarifying the meaning of "self-interest."

The libertarian argument on behalf of suicide today has become widely accepted. But the argument does little to clarify whether suicide on grounds of old age is ethically justified. We may set the libertarian argument aside simply by accepting its major conclusion: yes, suicide ought *not* to be considered a crime—people have a "right" to commit suicide. But is the exercise of this right *ethically* justified on grounds of old age? The answer to this question will depend on the *reasons* given for the decision. Unfortunately, the libertarian argument in practice often passes over into sheer relativism or nihilism: that is, the belief that it does not make any difference what reasons a person has for the decision as long as it is one's own free and private action. This crude version of the libertarian argument we must set aside, since it prevents us from taking suicide seriously and from examining the ethical justification for the decision.

Suicide as Mental Illness

Finally, we must dispose of the view that acts of suicide are always forms of mental illness. This presumption is today quite commonplace. In fact, it is the bulwark of the ideology behind the mental health industry concerned with suicide prevention. (The literature of "suicidology" is vast: see Shneidman and Farberow 1975.) But a problem arises here because of a contradiction between two of our cherished beliefs: first, that society has no business interfering with free, private decisions and, second, that killing oneself is a bad thing and should be prevented. We find it possible to reconcile these two propositions by concluding that anyone who decides to kill oneself is not really free: that is, by *deciding* that an act of suicide is, prima facie, a sign of mental illness.

As a rule, the claim that suicide shows mental illness does not even require proof; it is taken for granted. In this circular logic, suicide is a sure sign of mental illness, because only people who are crazy would try to kill themselves. To contemplate suicide is a sign of a disturbed mind to begin with. From this assumption follows the rationale for programs of suicide prevention. Yes, people have a perfect right to kill themselves, but if they try to do so, they prove that they are not really free and rational agents, and so they need treatment for their emotional disorder. If they are treated and still decide to kill themselves, that simply shows the treatment was not successful.

It is, of course, impossible to argue against this claim, because the claim itself is a form of psychological reductionism that converts every rational question into a symptom. A reductionism of this sort seems to be implicit in Freud's remark that the moment a man begins to question the value of living he is already sick. But there is no reason why we need to accept what Thomas Szasz called "the myth of mental illness" with respect to acts of suicide. Certainly, *some* acts of suicide are motivated by desperate states of mind, but other acts of suicide seem to express a rational choice consistent with the agent's long-held values. The presumption that acts of suicide are invariably forms of mental illness is an arbitrary imposition of psychiatric imperialism that effectively prevents us from taking suicide seriously as a rational life choice.

Suicide in Old Age: A Reasonable Alternative

The ideology of suicide prevention, whatever its psychological underpinnings, essentially expresses a commonsense belief that life is a good thing and that it is better to live than to die. The commonsense view may be widespread, but it hardly constitutes a serious argument against suicide, and in the case of suicide on grounds of old age, it does not work at all.

In the case of attempted suicides who are young or middle aged, it is easy to produce arguments in favor of suicide prevention: (1) The person attempting suicide very likely has external obligations—if not financial dependents, then at least people who would be affected emotionally by his death (spouse, parents, friends). (2) The state of mind leading to suicide may be only temporary; people often change their minds, provided only that they are alive in the future to do so. (3) Even if circumstances are bad now, no one can predict the future; things might be different in the future. (4) Suicide in youth or middle age is a violent cutting short of the natural life cycle, and this is to deprive oneself of a full life.

Only the first argument here is based on the moral force of duties to others; the last three arguments are based on a conception of duties to oneself. The first argument has a long history going back to Aristotle and Aquinas, who both argued against suicide on grounds that suicide deprives society of a human resource, by analogy to a soldier deserting his post. Even if this argument fails in certain cases—for persons who have minimal utilitarian value to society—still, it is likely that interpersonal obligations remain persuasive, since other people may be emotionally affected by the suicide. Thus, in terms of this first argument, our duty toward others may at times be a sufficient reason for not killing ourselves.

The last three arguments are more interesting, since they all revolve around some conception of "duty to oneself." At the very least, this kind of duty amounts to prudential self-interest. In the first place, we may be mistaken about whether some course of action is in fact in our interest, given that we know what that interest is. But, more fundamentally, there is a question of how to know what "self-interest" actually means, if "self-interest" counts as something more than "what I want" at a specific moment in time. In the case of rational suicide, it becomes extremely important to know whether the agent has correctly judged his self-interest. The last three arguments all amount to a claim that the person attempting suicide has misconstrued his own best interests.

These arguments against suicide proceed by emphasizing the role of future self-interest over the whole lifespan. The second argument, for example, maintains, not that suicide is a form of mental illness, but only that the choice of suicide expresses a temporary mental state on which it is unwise to act, since the act precludes future choices. The third argument, in turn, does not deny that current circumstances might very well warrant killing onself; it does remind us that the future is unpredictable. With long enough future life expectancy, things may turn out to be different from what we expect. The fourth argument appeals to the notion of a "natural" lifespan, to which each person is entitled. Premature death, even by suicide, means to deprive oneself of this full lifespan.

Regardless of whether these arguments for suicide prevention are successful for other age groups, in the case of old age none of the arguments retains its force.

1. *Deliberate choice.* The aged person who chooses suicide after years of reflection and deliberation (not a temporary disposition) expresses fundamental values, not a momentary mental state.

2. *Negative future outlook.* While the future may be unpredictable in youth, old people face a limited life expectancy, with the likelihood of diminished quality of life and irreparable losses of meaning and happiness.

3. *Disengagement.* Old age is typically a period of disengage-

ment, or withdrawal from external obligations. With retirement, with children moving away, with the death of friends and relatives, fewer and fewer interpersonal obligations remain. In many cases, there is no one left to be negatively affected by one's death.

4. *Natural death.* Upon reaching old age, people have lived out their "natural" lifespan of three score years and ten. When an aged person dies, we usually do not feel that their death is "premature" or "unfair." Indeed, the very prototype of "natural death" is death in old age, which does not cease to be natural death even if it is brought about by suicide.

We can summarize this discussion in the following question. What objection can there possibly be to an old person, who has lived a full lifespan, whose external obligations are fulfilled, who faces the prospect of infirmity and decline, and who rationally and deliberately chooses suicide as the form of death? The usual arguments in suicide prevention do not work here. Both duty to others and duty to oneself fail to offer convincing reasons to live when a person, on grounds of old age, chooses to end his life. Having shown that these objections to suicide fail, let me now consider more carefully the principal arguments offered on behalf of suicide on grounds of old age.

The Balance-Sheet Argument

The first argument to consider is what I describe as the "balance-sheet" argument for suicide on grounds of old age. We can introduce this argument by means of a case study. The cases I examine are the suicides of Karl Marx's daughter and of her husband, Dr. Paul Lafargue.

Suicide of Karl Marx's daughter & her husband Dr. Paul Lafargue. Their joint suicide took place in 1911. The gardener discovered their bodies in a room off the garden of their home in Paris. "He was lying fully dressed on a bed; she was in an easy chair in an adjoining room. Before committing suicide Dr. Lafargue had written out a reference for his domestic help, signed his will, and even drafted the text of a telegram to be sent to his nephew (announcing their deaths)."

In his suicide note to friends Lafargue said:

"Sound of mind and body, I am killing myself before pitiless old age,

which gradually deprives me of the pleasures and joys of existence
and saps my physical and intellectual forces, will paralyze my energy,
break my will power, and turn me into a burden to myself and others.
Long ago I have promised myself not to live beyond the age of seventy. I have fixed the moment for my departure from life and I have
prepared the method of executing my project: a hypodermic injection
of hydrocyanic acid'' [cited in Choron 1972:100].

In my analysis of this text, I set aside for the moment the
reference to fear of becoming a ''burden to others''—which involves
us in utilitarian considerations—and concentrate instead on the main
thrust of Lafargue's note, which really justifies their personal life
choice. Clearly, the Lafargues were unwilling to wait to experience
the decline of old age and, instead, chose preemptive suicide at the
point when the future began to look grim. Sizing up their life prospects, the Lafargues came to the rational conclusion that the balance
of losses outweighed the gains of living longer, and therefore suicide
was justified. This classic paradigm of balance-sheet suicide cannot
in any sense be described as caused by mental illness or psychological depression. The choice of suicide was, in fact, made many years
before: in his note, Dr. LaFargue wrote that long ago he had promised himself not to live beyond age seventy. Over a period of years
both he and his wife had many opportunities to discuss their choice,
and in this respect we cannot view it as anything other than a rational
decision. Jacques Choron cites a similar example of the French doctor Thierry de Martell, who had often told his associates that he
planned to kill himself at age 65, and he proceeded to carry out his
plan. The case of Marx's daughter, then, is not an aberration, though
it is a striking example of cold-blooded rationality and a bleak assessment of old age.

But even if such a decision is rational, we are left with the
further question: is it ethically justified? This is the question considered by Kant, who takes up the problem of suicide in several places,
including his treatise *The Metaphysical Foundations of Morals*. Here
is Kant's example:

A man, while reduced to despair by a series of misfortunes and feeling
wearied of life, is still so far in possession of his reason that he can
ask himself whether it would not be contrary to his duty to himself to
take his own life. Now he inquires whether the maxim of his action

could become a general law of nature. His maxim is: out of self-love
I consider it a principle to shorten my life when continuing it is likely
to bring more misfortune than satisfaction (1969).

Note that Kant here excludes any extraneous causes such as mental
illness or senility by stipulating that the person is in possession of his
reason. The motive or maxim for the decision is couched in the he-
donistic terms of a balance-sheet suicide: does the balance of pleasure
over pain offer a favorable outlook for the future?

Kant cites the example of the balance-sheet suicide as one of
several instances where a moral problem forces us to clarify the rational foundation of our ethical ideals. Where is such a foundation to
be discovered? After appraising and rejecting a series of alternative
conceptions of the moral law put forward by philosophers throughout
history, Kant arrives at his own formulation of the supreme principle
of moral judgment, his well-known categorical imperative. Kant's
conception of the categorical imperative echoes the moral teachings
of the Golden Rule but reformulates the principle into a complex
philosophical structure. In *The Metaphysical Foundations of Morals,*
as well as in *The Critique of Practical Reason,* Kant argues that we
must evaluate the moral justification for balance-sheet suicide by
means of the categorical imperative.

In brief, Kant argues strongly against the justification of balance-sheet suicide, and he does so through several different versions
of the categorical imperative. His first version of the categorical imperative runs as follows:

Act only on a maxim by which you can will that it, at the same time,
should become a general law.

We can express this version of the categorical imperative in simple-
minded terms by the ethical question, "What would happen if every-
body acted as you are about to do?" How does this version of the
categorical imperative lead us to evaluate the balance-sheet suicide?
Would the Lafargues, or other preemptive suicides in old age, be
willing to see their example adopted as a universal practice or general
law? Putting the question this way, we immediately see that Kant's
argument is unsuccessful. Perhaps the Lafargues would be eager to
see their example adopted, even made universal throughout society.
There is no apparent contradiction involved in willing such a social

order. We cannot argue that such suicides in old age are "setting a bad example" unless we already *assume* that it would in fact be bad for the action to be adopted at large in similar circumstances. Simply to say that suicides like the Lafargues' case are a "bad example" to others begs the question by circular reasoning.

Kant wants to argue against the balance-sheet suicide on the grounds that, if the maxim of the action were to be universalized, it would lead to a contradiction and therefore be shown to be without rational foundation. This kind of argument against the balance-sheet suicide may work when applied to the "system of nature" (that is, human nature) as a whole, for the clear reason that if the practice of balance-sheet suicide became widely adopted—as in similar cases of widespread adoption of lying, giving false promises, etc.—it would certainly contradict the maintenance of any stable order of human society. Conceived in these terms, suicide is sometimes condemned as a sort of "cowardice" akin to deserting one's post in times of military duty. Certainly, judged by this test of Kantian "universalizability" within a systematic harmony of human purposes, the balance-sheet suicide is not ethically justified and can be condemned. But when there are no duties toward others, as Hume argues, and especially when the range of universalization is restricted to old age, why then can we find any objection to balance-sheet suicide on grounds of old age? There seems to be no valid objection, at least when measured in terms of the universalizability criterion of Kant's first version of the categorical imperative. Indeed Paton (1948:154) argues that Kant gives the answer he does only because he assumes to begin with that suicide is morally wrong, and, with respect to Kant's reasoning, Paton adds that "This is the weakest of Kant's arguments."

But Kant's use of the categorical imperative to argue against balance-sheet suicide takes other forms. A second version of the categorical imperative runs as follows:

> Act as if the maxim of your action were to become by your will a general law of nature.

The balance-sheet suicide, with its rational determination of the balance of pleasure and pain, is clearly motivated by a certain conception of self-interest or self-love. Does then the principle of self-love implicit in balance-sheet suicide satisfy the condition of the second version of the categorical imperative? Kant argues in *The Metaphysical Foundations of Morals* that it does not:

> we see at once that a system of nature, whose law would be to destroy life by the very feeling designed to compel the maintenance of life, would contradict itself, and therefore could not exist as a system of nature; hence that maxim cannot possibly be a general law of nature and consequently it would be wholly inconsistent with the supreme principle of all duty.

The ethical problem of suicide—in the present case, the justification of suicide on grounds of old age—is now treated in a very different fashion. The ground has shifted from the harmony of human purposes to some conception of the harmony of nature. There is an echo here of Aquinas' prohibition of suicide in terms of a principle of self-love understood as "natural law," but for Kant the formulation of natural law has been replaced by a concept of duty, in this case a duty to oneself (or to the rational principle within oneself) rather than duty to others. (For a detailed treatment of the problem of suicide in Aquinas and Kant, see Novak 1975.)

We can understand the force of Kant's second version of the categorical imperative only by grasping the meaning of his concept of natural teleology. Kant's claim is that the maxim of balance-sheet suicide betrays a contradiction between the ends of action and the teleological purposes of nature. This doctrine of natural teleology is implicity contained in Kant's notion of what a "system of nature" ultimately must be. Kant here presupposes that the feeling of self-love exists in man for the teleological purpose of maintaining that life which constitutes the system of nature as a whole. To destroy life by reason of this same principle (self-love) that exists only in order to preserve it would lead to a contradiction. Therefore, suicide on grounds of old age, when undertaken with this maxim in mind, is inevitably wrong.

But does suicide in old age contradict the teleological purpose of self-love in the maintenance of life? If the feeling of self-love has this teleological function of maintaining life, still it cannot have the teleological function of maintaining life indefinitely, since the human life course does after all reach its natural termination in death. If finitude is bound up with the "natural" human condition, then any teleological conception of human nature must take this finitude into account. We have already seen that there is no contradiction entailed by willing suicide in old age as a course to be adopted by everyone at large. Is there then a contradiction that a teleological principle of nature—self-love—which ordinarily leads to preservation of life should in some circumstances lead to death? Why can the same principle not have different effects in different circumstances?

By introducing the concept of a teleological function within the order of nature, Kant has left open the possibility that the teleological purpose involved—"self-preservation"—may vary in its meaning according to the teleology of nature itself. For human nature, this teleology unmistakably includes the fact that the human life course goes through "seasons" or an unfolding of powers and potentialities according to successive stages of life. (The metaphor is ancient and recurs in modern investigations of lifespan development; see Levinson 1977.) On this point, however, we touch a fundamental weakness in Kant's thinking about human nature and therefore a limitation in his system of ethics. By virtue of his fundamental principle of man as a free, rational person, Kant conceives human beings as "noumenal persons": that is, timeless, purely rational agents who are thus abstracted from all empirical details of their actual historicity. In his critical *Commentary on Kant's Groundwork of the Metaphysic of Morals,* Robert Paul Wolff (1973:226–27) points out this limitation in Kant's thought and emphasizes that, for Kant, "the accidents of birth and death, the phenomena of growth and parenthood, the facts of the social origin of personality itself, in short, what Erik Erikson calls the life cycle, are treated as mere intrusions or embarrassments" (for a philosophical elaboration of ethics on a "life cycle" model, see Norton 1976).

Kant's philosophy of human nature, by projecting man as a timeless, rational agent, passes over the meaning of finitude and death as "natural" elements of the human life cycle. Once we include these elements, the moral problem of the justification of suicide on grounds of old age takes on a different significance. Death is not a mere contingency, but, as modern research in biogerontology increasingly makes clear, death is rooted in life and in the broadest possible "system of nature" that constitutes the evolution of living organisms on earth. From this perspective, it makes sense to say that the final stage of life, old age, points toward its teleological fulfillment in death. Natural death in old age is not only an effect or outcome but also, in Kant's terms, the teleological purpose of the last stage of life. For this reason it is difficult to see why suicide in old age should not be an entirely reasonable choice, a choice consistent with the supreme principle of morality, the categorical imperative.

We can restate Kant's arguments to this point as follows. His first version of the categorical imperative—the test of universalizability or general law—*may* argue against general adoption of balance-sheet suicide throughout society at large but in no way argues against it on grounds of old age alone. The second version of the categorical imperative—the test of conformity with a teleological law of nature—also fails to prohibit suicide on grounds of old age because the principle of self-love must be interpreted through the system of nature or the structure of the human life cycle. Since the last stage of the life cycle results in natural death as its outcome, suicide because of old age is not wrong.

We come now to Kant's third formulation of the categorical imperative as a critique of the balance-sheet argument for suicide on grounds of old age. It is in this formulation alone, I believe, that we can find a valid critique of the balance-sheet argument. In this formulation Kant transcends considerations of society and nature, human purposes and natural teleology, in order to arrive at a ground of moral action that is itself a principle of absolute value. This principle is nothing short of the rational nature of the human being existing as an absolute, or unconditional, end in itself. Kant expresses this version of the categorical imperative as follows:

> So act as to treat humanity, whether in your own person or in that of any other, always at the same time as an end, and never merely as a means.

Consistent with this supreme principle of morality, Kant rejects the balance sheet argument for suicide:

> the man who contemplates suicide will ask "Can my action be compatible with the Idea of humanity as an end in itself?" If he does away with himself in order to escape from a painful situation, he is making use of a person merely as a means to maintain a tolerable state of

affairs till the end of his life. But man is not a thing—not something to be used merely as a means: he must always in all his actions be regarded as an end in himself. Hence I cannot dispose of man in my person by maiming, spoiling, or killing.

The balance-sheet argument makes the balance of pleasure and pain the final criterion for whether human life is worth living. This remains true, incidentally, whether we calculate on selfish grounds— my private balance sheet—or on so-called altruistic grounds—the fear of being a burden to others. If we accept the altruistic version of the balance-sheet argument, then the logic of utilitarian ethics leads inevitably to the point where the welfare of society makes suicide in old age not merely permissible but obligatory in order to bring about the greatest happiness for the greatest number. (Hook 1927 makes this clear; for another view on the "duty" of death in utilitarianism, see Reed 1977.)

It is this line of thought—whether hedonism or utilitarianism—that Kant rejects entirely by his concept of man as an end in himself. Paton (1948) puts it as follows:

> If—apart from all questions of duty to others—there can be a right to commit suicide, this can be justified only on the ground that there is no longer any possibility of living a moral life and manifesting moral worth.

Suicide undertaken to avoid the decline and infirmity of old age puts limits on the dignity of the human being in the name of empirically contingent factors of happiness. But if man, as a moral personality, is an end in himself, he retains this intrinsic and infinite worth even in old age. In Kant's words:

> Man cannot renounce his personality so long as he is a subject of duty, hence so long as he lives; and that he should have the moral title to withdraw from all obligation, i.e., freely to act as if he needed no moral title for this action, is a contradiction. To destroy the subject of morality in one's own person is to root out the existence of morality itself from the world, so far as this is in one's power; and yet morality is an end in itself.

The Kantian reply to the balance-sheet argument, at least in the third version of the categorical imperative, is a reminder that the moral worth of the individual is not conditioned by any limits imaginable, even the limits of our own desires or happiness. The human being, even in old age, does not cease to be a member of the "kingdom of ends." The rational community of beings who, each in their own persons, constitute this kingdom of ends includes ends in themselves. The true dehumanization of old age lies, not in the loss of powers, but in the insidious tendency to see old people as somehow less than human and life in old age as not worth living.

The Quality-of-Life Argument

I turn now to a second major argument favoring suicide on grounds of old age, the quality-of-life argument. As with the balance-sheet argument, I offer a case study to dramatize the issues involved.

The Van Dusen Case

In 1975, Dr. and Mrs. Henry P. Van Dusen, aged 77 and 80 respectively, attempted suicide by taking an overdose of sleeping pills. Mrs. Van Dusen died immediately. Dr. Van Dusen survived but died two weeks later of a heart ailment.

The Van Dusens were well-known figures in American religion. Before his retirement, Dr. Van Dusen had been President of Union Theological Seminary and a prominent ecumenical leader. The couple's decision to commit suicide was evidently the result of a long and thoughtful reflection. Both Van Dusens were members of the Euthanasia Society and, according to the *New York Times* report, "had entered into the [suicide] pact rather than face the prospect of debilitating old age." In the suicide note left by them they explicitly vowed that they would not "die in a nursing home." Both Van Dusens suffered from chronic health problems: she from arthritis, he from the effects of a stroke that interfered with normal speech. The *Times* report noted that "For the vigorous articulate Presbyterian scholar and his active wife, the setbacks were serious impediments to living the kind of useful, productive lives to which they had become accustomed."

The Van Dusen case illustrates all the relevant features important for the claim that suicide on grounds of old age is ethically justified: (1) The Van Dusens killed themselves as a result of long rational deliberation: their choice was consistent with ethical values they had espoused over their lifetime (e.g., euthanasia). (2) Although subject to disability and chronic illnesses common in old age, the Van Dusens were not suffering from a painful terminal disease at the time of death (this is important, since most justifications of "beneficent euthanasia" tend to assume either that the person is in great pain or has become, as is said, a "vegetable;" neither case obtains here). (3) The Van Dusens, both elderly, chose to kill themselves because of distaste for the infirmity of old age (e.g., reluctance to die in a nursing home), and not on some other grounds. Here, if anywhere, we find a paradigm case of the decision to commit suicide on grounds of old age, as we saw too in the Lafargue case.

The Van Dusen case is a vivid one and was much publicized at the time, but the reasoning behind their decision has an ancient and venerable history. For example, in Plato's dialogue the *Crito,* the imprisoned Socrates turns down an offer of escape from prison, preferring instead to suffer death in honorable obedience to the laws of Athens. When his friend Crito asks him, "Don't you have a duty to save your life if you can?" Socrates replies, "The point, my dear Crito, is not simply to live, but to live well." Socrates' answer expresses the ethical principle involved in the Van Dusen case and in others like it. Aristotle, in this same tradition, maintained that it was not life itself that is worth living but only the good life. This ethical principle amounts to the claim that quality of life, not quantity of life, is the ultimate ground of value, and expressed in this way, the principle became a cornerstone for the ancient philosophical school of Stoicism. It is therefore no accident that the Stoics, more than any other philosophical school of antiquity, became associated with the view that suicide can be a justifiable course of action (Rist 1969). In their justification of suicide, the Stoics explicitly invoked this principle of quality of life. In the discussion that follows, then, I reconstruct what I take to be the Stoic quality-of-life argument in favor of suicide on grounds of old age, recognizing at the same time, however, that there is no single Stoic theory of suicide.

The Stoics held that the ultimate criterion for human ethical action was to be found in living in accordance with nature. Man's reason, freed from the turbulence of false desires and social convention, would lead him to an inner tranquility and state of virtue, which the Stoics identified as the achievement of the sage or wise man. For the wise man, ordinary objects of fear, including death, would hold no terror. Indeed, death itself should be a matter of indifference, they maintained. Only the inner condition of virtue and tranquility of spirit—defined as the ultimate stage in "quality of life"—should properly be the object of our aspiration. According to this view, suicide could, under certain circumstances, be an entirely justifiable course of action. In an image used by Epictetus and Marcus Aurelius, the wise man might commit suicide the same way one gets up to leave a smoke-filled room. One abandons life if the conditions of virtue or quality of life are no longer attainable.

The strongest defense of suicide is found in the writings of the Roman Stoic philosopher Seneca:

> mere living is not a good, but living well. Accordingly, the wise man will live as long as he ought, not as long as he can. He will mark in what place, with whom, and how he is to conduct his existence, and what he is about to do. He always reflects concerning the quality, not the quantity, of his life. As soon as there are many events in his life that give him trouble and disturb his peace of mind, he sets himself free.

The ultimate freedom of the wise man is the act of suicide. In Seneca's words:

> And this privilege is his, not only when the crisis is upon him, but as soon as Fortune seems to be playing him false; then he looks about carefully and sees whether he ought, or ought not, to end his life on that account. He holds that it makes no difference to him whether his taking-off be natural or self-inflicted, whether it comes later or earlier. He does not regard it with fear, as if it were a great loss; for no man can lose very much when but a driblet remains. It is not a question of dying earlier or later, but of dying well or ill. And dying well means escape from the danger of living ill.

This passage conveys well the general tone of Seneca's views on suicide, views repeated and amplified through his writings.

Interestingly, a close study of Seneca's work shows that he does not look on old age in purely negative terms, as a stage to be avoided. Like Greco-Roman society as a whole, he betrays an ambivalent attitude toward aging. At times, he writes explicitly that old age is the period of life when, after retirement from external duties, man can occupy himself with learning wisdom. Still, the drift of his thinking, and of Stoic principles, is clear: when the infirmity of old age unduly interferes with the quality of life, one is justified in committing suicide. The Van Dusens, for example, led an active life in retirement up to a certain point. But, finally, with health setbacks, they were, in the words of the *Times* report, unable to lead "the kind of useful, productive lives to which they had become accustomed." Their choice was based, not on quantity, but on quality of life. A newspaper article appearing at the time quoted one of the Van Dusen's colleagues as saying that their decision was perhaps more Stoic than Christian in its inspiration.

Objections to the Quality-of-life Argument

Yet the Stoic quality-of-life argument is open to certain objections. The most fatal objection is that suicide on grounds of old age contradicts the genuine first principles of Stoic ethics, in particular the assumption that virtue alone is the only good and that virtue is happiness. Taken seriously, this principle requires us to say that "quality of life" is never determined absolutely by external gains or losses but depends on the radical freedom of the mind to take up new attitudes toward life circumstances. The Stoics insisted that only the "things within our power" are our proper concern. Whatever fate may inflict by way of loss of fortune, bodily ills, or other contingent elements of life, the citadel of self-consciousness, and therefore the intrinsic freedom of the mind, remains untouched. For the Stoics, unlike, say, Aristotle, the good life is entirely a matter of *inner* attitude and awareness, not of external circumstances at all. As long as man's reason maintains this ultimate power, the infirmities of old age cannot diminish this authentic touchstone for the quality of life.

What about the argument that the wise man should act before decline sets in, as when the Van Dusens acted to choose suicide rather than face the prospect of debilitating old age? In this case, could not suicide be chosen as a form of "death with dignity" in contrast to the humiliating or dehumanizing fate symbolized by "dying in a nursing home," to use the Van Dusen's own image? As Ramsey has argued, we must view the arguments for "death with dignity" with great care and skepticism (1974). What goes under the name "death with dignity" today was what the Stoics called honor or nobility.

We know that death by suicide was common among the Romans as a means of avoiding dishonor. Brutus, Mark Antony, and Cleopatra, not to mention the philosopher Seneca himself, are only a few from the long succession of suicides for honor that were frequent among the Romans of antiquity. In principle, this suicide to preserve dignity or avoid dishonor has much in common with cultural practices such as *suttee,* the Hindu self-immolation of widows, or the Japanese *hara-kiri*. We should look upon all these claims of "dignity," "honor," or "ego-integrity" with a certain amount of critical doubt. Unless we are thoroughgoing cultural relativists, we need not approve of the practice of *suttee* or of the ancient Roman practice of suicide on grounds of dignity. When claims of self-killing are supported on behalf of a transcendent ethical ideal—as in cases of martyrdom or self-sacrifice—they may have an ethical justification. But when self-killing is supported solely by some conception of the ideal self, as in Stoic reasoning favoring suicide, then the claims of dignity or honor presuppose a certain purity or consistency of self-image that refuses any vulnerability. Rather than give up the ideal self, death is preferable. This excessive nobility of soul has a heroic grandeur, no doubt, but grandeur is very different from an ethical respect for human personality. Considerations of honor or dignity entailing suicide on grounds of old age seem to stand in contradiction to the very principles of universal human freedom enunciated by Stoic philosophy at its best.

Finally, we must consider the argument of "natural death" as a reason for suicide in old age. Daniel Callahan (1977) finds the paradigm case of natural death in the example of the death of an elderly person who has lived a rich and full life. Callahan's arguments were developed, in part, to provide an ethical rationale for public policy decisions putting limits on the aspirations of medical research and technological intervention to keep people alive artificially. (See Garland 1976 and Lebacqz 1977; for background, see Veatch 1976.) But the concept of natural death—that is, an appropriate death, a death that is "acceptable"—has an obvious ancestry going back to the Stoic principle of quality of life and to the broader

Stoic ideal of natural law as the basis for deduction of ethical judgments.

If we accept this notion of natural death, certain conclusions follow. For example, Callahan argues that the concept of natural death would lead us to allocate scarce health resources to enable as many people as possible to live out a normal human lifespan but not to extend the upper limit of that lifespan for its own sake. The entitlement to a "natural" lifespan takes precedence over extending life at the other end: thus, quality takes precedence over quantity. Although Callahan does not develop the argument in this direction, his formulation of the principle of natural death would also provide an ethical justification for suicide on grounds of old age. It may seem paradoxical to speak of suicide as a form of "natural death," but the semantics of ordinary language need not be an insuperable objection.

Yet the concept of natural death should not be accepted uncritically. Indeed, on closer examination the ideal of natural death may well turn out to be philosophically incoherent, a grab bag of concepts without a clear meaning (High 1978). On the surface at least, the concept of natural death has obvious appeal and seems to illustrate well the Stoic ideal of living in accordance with nature. But the Stoic ethics of dying may have its own contradictions. For example, the genuine Stoic concern was with dying *well,* yet dying "well" may or may not mean dying by the use of natural means alone. A "good death" may in fact require careful management and artificial intervention through medical practice.

But there is a further difficulty, and one that touches directly on the problem of aging. How old does one have to be before natural death is an appropriate course that in turn might justify suicide on grounds of old age? Callahan speaks of natural death occurring at a point late in life when one's major projects and responsibilities have been carried out, but a moment's thought reveals that in old age people are free to take up new projects and set new goals for themselves. Justice Oliver Wendell Holmes, who began the study of Greek in his nineties, is a homely example, but it reminds us that old age need not mean that life is "finished" or ready for premature closure.

Death in old age may be "natural" in the sense of being a predictable limit for our normal life projects and goals, but old age itself is also part of man's natural life cycle, and on Stoic grounds, it should be accepted as such. Even the alleged decline and infirmity of old age, as Seneca himself observes, may be the basis of wisdom in the last stage of the life cycle. Certainly the record of autobiographies produced by aged persons throughout history documents this possibility of new psychological growth in old age. These potentialities too are included in man's "natural" life cycle, which at this juncture in history we have only begun to explore. Whatever natural death may mean, it cannot mean avoiding the experience of old age, which, though not inevitable, is as much a part of man's natural life cycle as birth and death.

In summary, the quality-of-life argument for suicide on account of old age does not strictly follow from Stoic premises. On closer examination, in fact, it contradicts essential Stoic principles. "Quality of life" is not simply a datum of consciousness, given once and for all, but is conditioned by our attitudes and by the intrinsic freedom of the mind. For the Stoics, quality ultimately means virtue, and in Kant's terms, life is worth living as long as there is the possibility of living a moral life and manifesting moral worth. The ideals of honor and dignity, like the quality of life, ought not to be uncritically accepted. Scrutinized more closely, these ideals involve covert assumptions of cultural decorum and a fixed image of the self. Finally, natural death, despite its appeal, turns out to be unusable as a criterion for deciding whether suicide is ethically justifiable on grounds of old age. As a concept, natural death is unclear, and in any event, it does not tell us when or how death ought to come about. Old age, along with death, is a natural part of the life cycle.

Having sketched briefly the Stoic argument on quality of life, I think it may be helpful to see this argument, today so popular, against a broader cultural background. The ancient Stoics despised happiness and death alike in the name of a nobility of spirit that could triumph over all things in its radical freedom and inwardness. But what this spirit of antiquity did not understand was the possibility that its much-prized nobility—or glory, or honor, or dignity—could itself be open to doubt. For this reason, the moral heroism of Marcus Aurelius' *Meditations* becomes, in the end, both arrogant and suffocating: a cul-de-sac of worldly humanism that avoids boredom in the name of unceasing moral perfectionism. The aristocratic and sublime mood of Stoic ethics has its resemblance to the existential ethic expressed by Camus in *The Myth of Sisyphus,* where he makes the famous statement that suicide is the only serious philosophical problem.

Both the balance-sheet argument and the quality-of-life argument for suicide because of old age must be questioned through their fundamental premises. Both the concept of "happiness" and "quality" presume a fixed or determinate picture of the self: only a certain sort of self, or a certain sort of life circumstance, counts to make life worth living. Below some arbitrary level of happiness, or quality, life in old age does not measure up and so must be terminated.

Both the balance-sheet argument and the quality-of-life argument agree in rejecting sheer quantity or length of life as an ultimate value. Instead, they presuppose a different sort of "duty to oneself," or self-interest, which, under certain circumstances, makes suicide permissible on grounds of old age. Virtually everyone seems to agree that the extension of life for its own sake makes no sense. The technological imperative must be limited in the name of some ethical ideal, and recent advances in biomedical technology make it an urgent matter to discern what that ideal might be. As larger proportions of the population reach old age and as life prolongation technology becomes more sophisticated, these questions will only become more pressing. Obviously, disagreement will quickly arise when we try to specify what rational limits there ought to be to life extension. What we need to recognize is that these dilemmas arise for chronic illness, as well as for the more dramatic instances of acute treatment that capture the headlines. The major group in the population that will feel these dilemmas will be the elderly: the paradigm for the future is not Karen Ann Quinlan but the aged person suffering from heart disease, or emphysema, or chronic kidney failure.

What we now call the human condition includes the fact that, for those who survive into old age, chronic illness is a very high probability and death, as always, the great certainty. In contrast with earlier stages of the life cycle, old age usually means a decline in productivity, energy, health status, and other circumstances generally associated with happiness and quality of life. But the fact that old age may mean diminished happiness is not a new discovery. It is as old as the ancient Greeks, who, like twentieth-century Americans, worshipped youth and feared old age and death. The glory of dying young, from the Homeric point of view, was to die at the peak of one's powers and thus avoid the decline of old age. And so, from the standpoint of both happiness and dignity it was best to avoid old age altogether. Contemporary gerontologists might prefer to dismiss this attitude as ungenerous ageism, but I suspect that something deeper is involved here.

All of us would like to believe that old age can be made bearable, that social programs can improve the life of the elderly and can make our own old age more acceptable. We unconsciously want to believe that old age, like poverty, unemployment, and pollution, can be remedied if only we try hard enough. At the same time, we recognize too that old age involves unredeemable losses and irrevocable tragedy. This mixed mood—the insistence on social meliorism along with a recognition of intrinsic tragedy—is at work all through Simone de Beauvoir's book *The Coming of Age*. Perhaps this unresolved ambivalence is what gives that work its power. Yet against the background of this ambivalence, which we all share, the phenomenon of rational suicide on account of old age must appear as a disturbing and threatening event, for suicide always threatens the values of those of us who go on living. This, after all, is why society condemns suicide.

Arguments favoring suicide in old age come down to the proposition that life in old age is no longer worth living. What happens, all too often if not inevitably, in old age is that the sources of subjective meaning—the reasons that made life worth living—one by one disappear. Through retirement from work roles, through the death of friends and loved ones, through the completion of projects or the final failure of their realization; one by one the dreams and human purposes that made life worth living vanish. Without any larger religious or philosophic belief system, the individual in old age may be confronted by a void. This humanly felt void is set against a wider, cosmic void evoking the suspicion that "life is meaningless." Can we depend on convincing people that this is not so, that life does have a cosmic meaning?

If the answer is doubtful, another alternative presents itself. Perhaps it is possible, on a purely humanistic plane, to generate new goals, new purposes that make life worth living in old age. Of course, we may ask ourselves, why *should* we construct such purposes and goals, when time is short? Yet, in the long run, time is short for all of us, so why should any of us construct purposes and goals for which we struggle? These questions take us back to the biggest philosophical questions of all, but for the elderly person, the person in the last stage of the life cycle, the questions are concrete and unavoidable. It may well be that an older person cannot acquire the courage and perseverance to struggle for new goals—say, learning to walk again after a stroke—unless we are prepared to recognize some ultimate ground that could justify the specific subjective goals that the older person might set for himself. I have no ready answer to these questions except to insist that the intrinsic human possibility of setting new goals remains always, even in extreme old age, even until the last breath of life.

Conclusion

We live in a time when there are rising calls for the "right to die" and the need for "death with dignity." Today, ever larger numbers of persons are living to an advanced age where they are no longer economically productive and where they may become incapable of leading full and active lives. Under these circumstances, it becomes easy to describe the lives of the disabled elderly—those who are not terminally ill—as "meaningless." In this climate of opinion it is not difficult to foresee an extension of the growing tolerance for euthanasia to include a tolerance for suicide by those elderly whose lives have now been labeled "meaningless," by themselves or by others. A recent book on the subject of euthanasia concludes:

> It seems certain that it is only a matter of time until laws will be passed that will permit the administration of painless death when the only alternative is an agonizing or meaningless existence [Russell 1975:283].

We are embarked here on a very slippery slope, indeed. In the case of suicide on grounds of age, the tendency is dangerous *not* because of any remote possibility of Nazi-like laws for obligatory euthanasia for the elderly (see "Euthanasia at 80?" *Newsweek,* May 12, 1969). Opponents of euthanasia who raise the Nazi spectre overlook the legal safeguards that make its adoption unlikely. No, the danger is not legally enforced euthanasia for the elderly but rather the spread of a climate of opinion that treats suicide among the elderly as a matter of libertarian indifference or as a welcome refuge from their problems. It is not difficult to imagine that in such a climate of opinion the unproductive, chronically ill elderly would come to look on suicide as a ready alternative; they might even see avoidance of suicide as a matter of shame or cowardice—selfishly being a "burden on society." What was once a matter of disgrace would then become morally obligatory, even where not enforced by legal or institutional sanctions. When this happens, as Veatch observes, "natural death" will become, not merely a right but a duty.

If this possibility for such a radical reversal in moral attitudes seems remote, consider the way attitudes toward virginity and pre-marital sex have changed within a single generation. But we are not condemned to pure speculation in thinking about this subject, since historical precedents exist. The genuine historical precedent is found not, in the Nazi case, but among the ancient Romans, where suicide became common and acceptable, with philosophical support from the Stoic thinkers. The same Stoic arguments in terms of the "quality of life" of the elderly are increasingly being heard today. If life is "meaningless," then the logic of "administering" a painless death seems inevitable. But do we really want a society in which our best answer to the "meaningless" existence of old age is an encourage-ment for old people to kill themselves? Does this attitude itself not betray a contempt for dependency, a feeling that the lives of old people are somehow less than human, and, finally, a secret despair over the last stage of the life cycle?

On this point, I can do no better here than conclude with words from Erik Erikson that make clear just why the stakes seem to me so large in the question of suicide in old age. When we come to the last stage of the life cycle, writes Erikson (1964:132–33),

> . . . we become aware of the fact that our civilization really does not harbor a concept of the whole of life . . . As our world-image is a one-way street to never ending progress interrupted only by small and big catastrophes, our lives are to be one-way streets to success—and sudden oblivion. Yet, if we speak of a cycle of life we really mean two cycles in one: the cycle of one generation concluding itself in the

next, and the cycle of an individual life coming to a conclusion. . . .
Any span of the cycle lived without vigorous meaning, at the beginning, in the middle, or at the end, endangers the sense of life and the
meaning of death in all whose life stages are intertwined.

To live the span of old age in the fullness of vigorous meaning requires, in Erikson's terms, the psychological virtue of *ego integrity:* a strength and wholeness capable of withstanding the logic of
suicide and its promise of a one-way street to sudden oblivion. But
what we must understand is that the suicidal image of old age as
despair is built into our current cultural crisis; it is a philosophical
and ethical dilemma as much as anything else.

Eighty years ago William James wrote his book with the famous title, *"Is Life Worth Living?"* James certainly was a man well
acquainted with despair, but as a physician and psychologist, he saw
quite clearly that the despair of suicide could be overcome only by
answers that philosophical and religious thought would have to provide. Gerontology and thanatology alike need to look further in this
direction to find new sources of meaning in the last stage of the life
cycle. If our culture is to find an answer to this, perhaps ultimate
question of life, then those who study the phenomena of aging and
death will need to address the question that all of us must one day
face.

References

Alvarez, A. 1970. *The Savage God: A Study of Suicide.* New York: Random House.
Beauchamp, T. L. 1976. "An Analysis of Hume's Essay 'On Suicide,' " *Review of Metaphysics* (Spring) 30:73–95.
Callahan, D. 1977. "On Defining a 'Natural Death." *The Hastings Center Report* (June) vol. 7.
Choron, J. 1964. *Death and Modern Man.* New York: Collier.
—— 1972. *Suicide.* New York: Scribner.

Cioran, E. M. 1974. *The New Gods.* New York: Quadrangle.

De Beauvoir, S. 1972. *The Coming of Age.* New York: Putnam.

De Vleeschauwer, H. J. 1966. "La Doctrine du Suicide dans l'Ethique de Kant." *Kant Studien* 57:251–65.

Downing, A. B., ed. 1970. *Euthanasia and the Right to Death.* London: Low and Brydone.

Engelhardt, H. T. Jr. 1975. "The Counsels of Finitude." *The Hastings Center Report* (April), vol. 5.

Erikson, E. 1964. "Human Strength and the Cycle of Generations." In *Insight and Responsibility.* New York: Norton.

Farberow, N. L. 1975. *Suicide in Different Cultures.* Baltimore: University Park Press.

Foot, P. 1977. "Euthanasia." *Philosophy and Public Affairs* 6:85–112.

Gallon, R. 1970. "Suicide and Voluntary Euthanasia." In Downing (1970).

Garland, M. 1976. "Politics, Legislation, and Natural Death." *The Hastings Center Report* (October), vol. 6.

Harrington, A. 1969. *The Immortalist.* New York: Random House.

High, D. 1978. "Is 'Natural Death' an Illusion?" *The Hastings Center Report* (August), vol. 8.

Hirzel, R. 1908. "Der Selbstmord." *Archiv fur Religionswissenschaft.*

Hook, S. 1927. "The Ethics of Suicide." *International Journal of Ethics,* 37. Reprinted in Kohl (1975).

Humanist, The. 1974. "A Plea for Beneficent Euthanasia." (July–August).

James, W. 1896. *Is Life Worth Living?* Philadelphia: Peter Smith.

Jonas, H. 1978. "The Right to Die." *The Hastings Center Report* (August), vol. 8.

Kant, I. 1949. *The Metaphysical Foundations of Morals.* (T. K. Abbot, trans.), New York: Bobbs-Merrill.

—— 1971. *The Doctrine of Virtue.* Philadelphia: University of Pennsylvania Press.

——. 1972. *Critique of Pure Reason.* New York: Dutton.

Kass, L. 1974. "Averting One's Eyes or Facing the Music? On Dignity in Death." *The Hastings Center Report* (May), vol. 2.

Kluge, E. H. 1975. *The Practice of Death.* New Haven: Yale University Press.

Kohl, M., ed. 1975. *Beneficent Euthanasia.* Buffalo: Prometheus Books.

Landsberg, P. L. 1953. *The Experience of Death: The Moral Problem of Suicide.* New York: Philosophical Library.

Lebacqz, K. 1977. "Commentary of Natural Death." *The Hastings Center Report* (April), vol. 2.

Levinson, D. 1977. *The Seasons of a Man's Life.* New York: Knopf.

Neugarten, B. L. and R. J. Havighurst. 1977. *Extending the Human Life Span.* Washington, D.C.: U.S. Government Printing Office.

Norton, D. 1976. *Personal Destinies: A Philosophy of Ethical Individualism.* Princeton: Princeton University Press.

Novak, D. 1975. *Suicide and Morality.* New York: Scholars Studies Press.

Paton, H. J. 1948. *The Categorical Imperative.* Chicago: University of Chicago Press.

Ramsey, P. 1974. "The Indignity of 'Death with Dignity.' " *The Hastings Center Report* (May), vol. 2.

Reed, T. M. 1977. "The Paneuthanasia Argument." *Personalist* 58:84–87.

Rist, J. M. 1969. *Stoic Philosophy*. London: Cambridge University Press.

Russell, O. 1975. *Freedom to Die: Moral and Legal Aspects of Euthanasia*. New York: Human Sciences Press.

Seneca, L. A. *Epistulae Morales*.

—— Letter LXXVI. "On Learning Wisdom in Old Age."

Shneidman, E. S. and N. L. Farberow. 1975. *Clues to Suicide*. New York: McGraw-Hill.

Shneidman, E. S., ed. 1969. *On the Nature of Suicide*. San Francisco: Jossey-Bass.

Siegmund, G. 1961. *Sein oder Nichtsein: Die Frage des Selbstmordes*. Trier, West Germany: Paulinus Verlag.

Spanneut, M. 1973. *Permanence du Stoicisme: De Zenon a Malraux*. Gembloux: Editions J. Duculot.

Sprott, S. E. 1961. *The English Debate on Suicide*. La Salle, Canada: Open Court.

Tonne, H. A. 1974. "The Right to Suicide." *The Humanist* (July–August) 34:33–41.

Veatch, R. M. 1976. *Death, Dying, and the Biological Revolution*. New Haven: Yale University Press.

Von Andics, M. 1947. *Suicide and the Meaning of Life*. London: Hodge.

Wolff, R. P., ed. 1969. *Foundations of the Metaphysics of Morals with Critical Essays*. New York: Bobbs-Merrill.

—— 1973. *Commentary on Kant's Groundwork of the Metaphysics of Morals*, pp. 226–27. New York: Harper and Row.

Part
Two

Caregiving for the Physical and Emotional Well-Being of the Elderly

9

Nature, Convention, and the Medical Approach to the Dying Aged

BERNARD E. ROLLIN

FOR AS LONG as people have thought about man and nature they have tended to filter their images of the universe through dualistic lenses (Dewey 1960). In antiquity, the Greeks, the Persians, the Chinese all approached the world with expectations that it would conform to the dualistic conceptual schemes that they felt laid bare the skeletal structure of reality. This tendency toward bifurcative categorization, though in many ways beneficial, has also often served as a barrier to a clear understanding of nature. Thus, for example, the Aristotelian ontological/astronomical division of the universe into celestial and terrestrial was a serious impediment to the development of both astronomy and physics and to acceptance of the idea that one set of laws could be used to describe both mundane and supramundane phenomena.

One of the most pervasive dualisms in western thought has been the cleavage between *nomos* and *physis,* or convention and nature. Perhaps because of its ubiquitousness—it appears in the thought of virtually every major western philosopher (Rollin 1976a)—this dualism has become an unnoticed part of the categoreal apparatus with which we in all fields of study approach the world. Things have come to be seen as either fixed, universal, necessary, inevitable (i.e., natural) or as changeable, tentative, arbitrary, and culturally variable (i.e., conventional). Although a close conceptual examination of this dualism reveals its untenability and makes manifest that no clear-cut line can in fact be drawn between nature and convention (Rollin 1976b), the impact of our implicit acceptance of this schism cannot be overestimated. Even among those who have never consciously articulated this division, the sciences are seen as uncovering that which is natural. Hence, perhaps the historically late and certainly tentative development of attempts at social science—how, runs a hidden assumption, can there be a science of the conventional and variable? Biological science today is probably seen as the science most obviously concerned with what is natural. Whereas physics has for some time recognized a conventional dimension to its activities, stemming in part from the high level of abstraction and mathematization and abstract modeling endemic to recent physical theorizing (high-energy physics, quantum theory, gravitation), biology is still seen as directly and inexorably articulating the natural—perhaps in part because of the relative lack of abstract theorizing in biology. Biologists, more so than theoretical physicists, tend to view themselves as direct explainers of nature rather than as creators of abstract models.

One result of this has been a tendency among biomedical researchers and medical practitioners to "biologize" the human being, to equate a person with a body, and to assume that biological description exhausts the proper scientific approach to biomedicine. (This tendency has been further stimulated by the remarkable recent advances in molecular biology.) A human being is a natural biological mechanism; illness involves some problem with the mechanism and is thus by nature a purely biological question. In a recent paper (Rollin 1979) I have tried to mitigate this tendency and to show that this view of illness is another instance of an illegitimate application of a nature-convention bifurcation and that in fact the concept of illness and thus the practice of medicine contain valuational and conventional dimensions inextricably bound up with the purely biological, so that illness is as much conventional as natural.

It appears that seeing current biological science as laying bare what is natural has had direct implications for our contemporary view of death. Death is seen as being again by nature a biological event and problem, one to be studied biologically and one to be managed or approached biomedically. As medicine grows more scientific and sophisticated, more knowledge of the causes of death is gained, and familiarity with more ways of averting it is acquired. Thus, the "natural" significatory link between dying and medicine is strengthened. As the person becomes understood more and more as a biological mechanism, cessation of personhood becomes equated with biological running-down of the body. Any conventional or valuational elements of death and dying are ignored, for biomedicine must deal with what is universal, natural, and empirical, not with what is culturally variable or not subject to empirical test. It is believed that any problem of meaning associated with death must also be submerged or at least dismissed as irrelevant, for contemporary science has no truck with meaning or value.

Long ago, Aristotle (e.g., *Metaphysics,* Book I) recognized that four sorts of questions could be asked about any object or process and four "causes" or principles of explanation tendered: What is it made of (material cause)? What made it happen or how did it come to be (efficient cause)? What is its purpose or what is it for (final cause)? What is its nature or meaning (formal cause)? In Aristotelian terms, contemporary biomedicine, like all of contemporary science, concerns itself only with the efficient cause—it answers only "how" questions. And insofar as death and dying pose any of the other sorts of demands for explanation, these must be dismissed as irrelevant, spurious, or trivial. Death is *by nature* seen to be within the province of biomedicine, and the techniques of biomedicine are seen as clearly best adapted for dealing with death and with dying persons.

What this theoretical stance amounts to in practice has been well documented, and its negative effect is clearly primarily felt by aging individuals. Baldly put, it means that old persons can expect to die in hospitals. About two-thirds of the people who will die in the United States this year will be 65 or older (Fulton 1976:5). In the next decade, the number of people over 65 who will die each year will double, and 80 percent of these deaths will occur in some kind of health-care institution (Dempsey 1975:63) (currently the figure is over 70 percent). And the most cursory perusal of the burgeoning literature in thanatology indicates that dying elderly individuals will typically not experience a good death in these institutions. They are separated from friends and family, whose access to the patient is rigidly controlled (Hofmeier 1974:15; Pahier 1974:68). Correlatively, the natural expression of emotion is restricted and suppressed (Hofmeier 1974). Patients are depersonalized, treated as cases rather than individuals, and deprived of genuine and honest conversation about their condition (Dempsey 1975:70ff). Doctors and nurses play ritualized conversational games with the dying and forestall real interaction (Dempsey 1975: ch. 4; Kastenbaum 1967:21ff; Quint 1967), partially as a mechanism of self-defense against emotional pain and partially to submerge their own fear of death (Wahl 1961, Kasper 1959, Feifel et al. 1967). Dying patients often learn of their condition in harsh indirect ways (Glaser and Strauss 1965). Studies indicate an unwillingness on the part of physicians even to talk openly about impending death (Oken 1961:86ff). Further, medical staff in a sense "write off" the dying elderly, with the tacit sanction of society (Glaser and Strauss 1969:85). Nurses have been timed as responding considerably more slowly to calls from elderly dying patients than from younger, nonterminal patients (LeShan 1972:221). One survey indicated that the life of a twenty-year-old patient was proportionately more important to them in terms of expenditure of time and effort than was the life of the eighty-year-old relative to the life of a (presumably young) pet dog (Kastenbaum 1969:85). The dying elderly are often subjected to heroic, expensive surgical and medical procedures, whose net result is iatrogenic suffering. Since the financial burden of caring for the elderly is borne by society and various health insurance programs, physicians do not cavil at ordering expensive, esoteric tests and forms of treatment (Kraus 1978:C1).

These pernicious consequences of seeing the care of the dying aged as by nature a medical responsibility are well known, but even when these problems are subjected to critical scrutiny, the basic conceptual approach has not typically been questioned. Suggestions are usually made about raising the consciousness of medical personnel by taking cognizance of questions of aging and dying in the medical school curriculum, in seminars, and so forth. It is not, in fact, clear how one criticizes the delegation of death to medicine, without hubris. One sometimes feels that to do so is to fly in the face of progress, to ignore the unquestionable benefits that biomedical advance has carried in its wake, to advocate some form of know-nothing Ludditism.

Some attempts have been made to criticize the fundamental concept of medical responsibility for the aged and dying by arguments from cultural relativism and alternative cultural and historical approaches to death and dying (Kübler-Ross 1969). Couched in the terms we have used in this essay, the implicit argument seems to be that surely the medical approach cannot be natural and ultimately correct, because we have actual instances of other cultures that have not considered the dying of aged individuals to be primarily (or indeed at all) a medical question, and therefore to treat it as such is a conventional feature of our culture, not a natural truth. Though such an argument enjoys some prima facie plausibility, like many other arguments from cultural relativism, it is easily trumped. One need but point out that the existence of alternative belief systems in and of itself proves nothing, without additional arguments to show that no one belief system can be called more correct than the others. Thus, one does not refute contemporary astronomical views by pointing out that innumerable cultures have held innumerable alternative accounts of the heavens. In the same way, one might argue that the medical model is superior to alternative cultural approaches because it is *more correct*. Dying is nothing mysterious, it could be said—it is merely a biological breakdown. Contemporary biomedicine comprises the most sophisticated understanding of the human body ever achieved by mankind; therefore, dying is the natural province of biomedicine.

To criticize adequately the biomedical model, then, one must do more than show that it has unfortunate consequences and that there exist alternatives in other cultures. One must rather indicate certain conceptual incongruities and fundamental theoretical flaws in seeing the management of a dying, elderly person as the natural province of biomedical science. These flaws must undermine our confidence that death is by nature a medical problem. And one must also suggest alternatives that can be strongly grounded theoretically. This task will occupy us for the remainder of this chapter.

One obvious weakness in the biomedical approach has been suggested before but bears repeating here. In sociologese, the dying person is "a deviant in the medical subculture" (Wheeler 1976). This can be put far less ponderously and far more dramatically by pointing out that the dying elderly person makes a mockery of the medical mission—serves, in fact, as a constant reminder of medicine's ultimate failure. Though medical management of the dying is seen as natural, dying in the elderly is also seen as natural! Indeed, as I have pointed out elsewhere, what is seen as death by illness in a young person is termed "natural death" in the elderly (Rollin 1979). Note that the notion of "natural death" is in fact highly conventional—another example of the tenuous nature of the natural-conventional dualism. Further, whereas many societies value the elderly for their wisdom and experience, our culture tends to disvalue them, despite pious disclaimers to the contrary (Blauner 1976:49, 58, n.60). They are people who have no function but to wait for death and whose death is often awaited by others, for financial or emotional reasons.

On the other hand, the physician has been trained, educated, almost religiously committed to fighting death and to valuing life. Death is the ultimate enemy, and each dying aged patient is an inescapable mirror held before the face of medicine, harshly revealing its fundamental, ontological, tragic blemish. As Parsons (1976:388) has put it, "the primary meaning of death is structured as a medical defeat, either for the physician personally or for 'the state of the art' with which he is strongly identified." Whereas the death of a young leukemia victim, while tragic, may be rationalized ("In ten years, we will probably be able to control that sort of malignancy"), the death of an old person is not so easily handled, for the ultimate abolition of all death in the aged cannot reasonably be extrapolated from the current state of biomedical science. And thus the physician (or nurse) charged with managing the dying, elderly person is faced with what has been called a "performative inconsistency"—one is in the position of a person who must swear on the bible that one is an atheist or drink to the virtues of abstinence. On the one hand, one must fight death; on the other, to truly deal with the dying patient qua dying patient, one must acquiesce to its inevitability. Small wonder, then, that physicians and nurses avoid authentic contact with the dying aged.

This problem arises not only with regard to a physician's mission but also in connection with the charismatic, quasi-religious power that physicians have traditionally wielded in Western society. This power, which is an integral part of the healing process, manifests itself in physicians' ability to create illness and wellness, at least as far as the sick role is concerned, via diagnostic activity (Rollin 1979, Parsons et al. 1976). A close analysis of this ability would take us too far afield, but a similar concept is dealt with at length by Siegler and Osmand (1974) in their discussion of "Aesculapian authority." A major part of this authority derives from a patient's willingness to accept the sick role and fight death and the doctor's ability to marshall forces against it. In the case of the aged and dying, the former condition is sometimes not met, and the latter is never met. Often, the physician can do nothing at all for the dying, aged patient, especially where pain is nonexistent or easily managed, a situation more common than is usually imagined (Dempsey 1975:83). (In any case, in such instances the physician is battling pain and not death!) Under these conditions, the Aesculapian authority must break down, and the organic whole formed by doctor and patient unified in a battle that can theoretically be won is dissolved. The patient can probably no longer relate to the physician in the same way—most assuredly, the physician can no longer relate to the patient in the normal way. (Siegler and Osmond [1979] point out that a similar situation obtains between physician and patient in cases of permanent impairment.) Thus, if something like Aesculapian authority is intrinsic to the physician's function relative to a patient, and the conditions for Aesculapian authority cannot be met relative to a dying, aged patient, it is clear that in such a case, the physician has no real function. It is understandable, then, that physicians are extremely uncomfortable about dealing with dying, aged patients—they can no longer clearly relate qua physician, yet no one has absolved them of the responsibility to so relate, and, indeed, they are expected to do so.

The notion of relating qua physician leads to another tissue of less obvious but probably ultimately more important problems integral to the tendency to delegate primary responsibility for the care of the dying elderly to medicine and medical personnel. These problems arise out of the fact that in recent years, at least, medicine is viewed by the public and by medical professionals as a science, all the more so in a period where molecular and biochemical advances in medicine continue to proliferate in geometrical progression. And science, as we all know, concerns itself with the universal, the repeatable, the invariant, the general. Scientific laws are expressed as universally quantified generalizations of the form (x) $(\phi\chi \supset \Psi\chi)$, unrestricted as to time and place. While concern with individual cases (i.e., natural

history) has historically served as a prolegomenon to the development
of science (though the once popular detailed case history approach to
medical writing has all but disappeared), true science occurs only
when those particulars can be explained by general laws, which are
then deducible from more general theories. Thus, a chemist is interested, not in a particular molecule, but in the regularities exhibited
by all molecules of that sort and in explanations of why those regularities are universal. While this has been repeatedly stressed by contemporary philosophers of science like Hempel (1975) and Nagel
(1961), it is in fact as old as philosophy and is eloquently articulated
by Aristotle in his *Posterior Analytics* (book I, ch. 13), where he
tells us that it is not a brute fact that is scientific knowledge, but a
reasoned fact, i.e., one that can be shown to follow deductively from
a universal law in conjunction with a description of initial conditions.

A major corollary of this view is explicitly recognized by
Aristotle (*Metaphysics,* book VII, ch. 15) but, while implicitly taken
for granted, is not often delineated today. If all scientific knowledge
is of universals, or at least of the universal aspects of particular things,
then it follows that there can be no scientific knowledge of particulars
qua particulars (Randall 1963:32–35). One can express in a law the
essence of man in general, according to Aristotle, but there can be
no scientific knowledge of this particular man, George Washington.
(This is often expressed linguistically by saying that proper names
have no definition.) Individuals cannot be reduced to sets of laws or
bundles of general concepts, says Aristotle, and hence the study of
an individual as individual is not within the province of science. We
"know" individuals, says Aristotle (*Metaphysics,* book III, ch. 4;
Posterior Analytics, book I, ch. 18, 81b), only by perception, by
intuition, by an unutterable grasp that grows out of interaction with
the particular: "It is sense perception alone which is adequate for
grasping the particulars: they cannot be objects of scientific knowledge."

But what, one may ask, has all of this esoteric metaphysics to
do with medicine and with the dying elderly patient? Simply this—
insofar as physicians are trained in essence as scientists, they are
trained to ignore the individual as individual and to see the individual
only as an instance of some regularity or repeatable phenomenon. It
is a commonplace that physicians or nurses speak among themselves

of "the melanoma in room 22" or even of "the kidney in room 7" rather than of individuals. This is usually explained as an emotional defense mechanism on the part of the medical personnel that helps them avoid excessive psychic involvement with the fate of the patient. While there is surely some validity to this account, it is not, I think, the primary explanation. For this sort of locution stems quite naturally from a *logical requirement* of the scientistic perceptual gestalt, which sees things only in their universal aspect. If Mrs. Flotsky is undergoing acute renal failure, that is a nomic, pattern-following scientific problem; therefore there is no need to know Mrs. Flotsky in the myriad facets of her individuality. In point of fact, the entire hospital system and the incredible panoply of medical technology is set up to serve the scientific perspective and to remove those hindrances of individuality that might impede it.

We can now begin to discern the insurmountable problem that this perspective entails. While this scientization of medicine may expedite the management of a variety of patients (though even this is in some cases highly debatable), it is most assuredly irrelevant in the case of the dying, elderly patient who is beyond medical help or assistance save for perhaps requiring pain medication, which may be easily self-administered. The major needs of such a patient confronting death are ones to which medicine qua science and the physician as scientist are strictly irrelevant, for these needs are not related to the body but rather stem from one's total personhood. Elderly, dying persons are confronted with uncertainties and anxieties about meaning and value, an acute concern with the meaning of their life *in its individual particularity*. The scientific stance taken by physicians is irrelevant to these concerns, and if the physician addresses them at all, it is as a sympathetic human being, not in the physician role. The scientific stance is irrelevant, not only because there is nothing to be done and because it cannot deal with individuals as individuals, but also because current biomedical science at least purports to deal only with efficient causes ("how" causes), not with questions of meaning and value (though valuational notions are an inescapable part of biological science). "Modern medicine" says Parsons,

> has tended not to deal directly with existential issues of meaning raised
> by death. It does not claim to help patients deal with the 'ultimate'

problems associated with the . . . imminent inevitability of their deaths. Rather, it has attempted to set such matters aside in order to develop specialized means of 'treating' specific syndromes that are believed on scientific and empirical grounds to be 'treatable' [1976:384].

But it is surely questions of meaning and value that are of greatest existential concern to the dying elderly person. Is there meaning to my life? Is there significance? Has my life been of any value? Did my living and dying make a difference? These are not empirical questions, nor are they amenable to lawlike answers.

Earlier in the twentieth century, in a highly influential book, which has ramified far beyond technical German philosophy, the philosopher Martin Heidegger (1962) pointed out the connection between awareness of death and creating authentic meaning in one's life. When one becomes aware, as Heidegger picturesquely put it, of "the possibility of the impossibility of one's being," i.e., of one's death, one is pulled toward shucking off those aspects of one's life that one has fallen into, rather than authored. One is able or rather moved to tear oneself free from the influences of social pressures (what Heidegger calls "Das Mann," "the They," and what Riesman later called "other-directedness") and to authentically structure the pattern and meaning of one's own life. For Heidegger, this is a universal truth for any being capable of self-awareness and of contemplating the past and anticipating the future and whose life will someday end. Only a person who has an authentic project has genuine unity in his being, and only his life has meaning, the project being the way one deliberately shapes one's future given one's past and historical-social situation. This process continues throughout one's life.

Heidegger does not speak specifically of the dying, elderly individual, but it seems clear that for him such an individual is simply a special, dramatic case of the general human condition. For our purposes, the details of this case are significant. For an aged person whose death is imminent, the choice of project is correlatively limited, while, paradoxically, the call to authenticity and meaning creation is even more urgent and immediate. Wherein can one find this authenticity? Most plausibly, it seems, in making one's final project the finding of meaning, pattern, and unity in what has gone before, in tying one's history into an authentic, meaningful unit. This abstract insight of Heidegger's is borne out by much human experience with dying people (Kübler-Ross 1975:chs. 19, 20) has shown that there are some dying individuals who found important dimensions of meaning in their lives and were comforted with a sense of value simply by being subjects in her studies of dying patients!) All persons wish to feel that their life was of value, had meaning, and was unique.

Value, meaning, and uniqueness. We are drawn back to our insight that medicine is impotent to deal with crucial aspects of dying. Medicine can explain the efficient cause of death. But it is totally removed from dimensions of meaning and value, which we might characterize in Aristotelian terms as the final and formal causes of a person's life. Not only does medicine not deal with final or formal causes, but also it does not deal with particulars as particulars, for no science does. Yet what the dying, aged person needs is precisely help with finding the final cause, essence, (or meaning and value) of his own unique particularity. And particulars are known only by intuition, by direct acquaintance. So medicine is in a deep sense *irrelevant* to the basic problem of the dying and aged.

Can one specify in more detail the sense of meaning and value of life crucial to a good death for an aged individual? I believe this can be done with the help of concepts borrowed from philosophers. John Dewey, 1958 in *Art as Experience,* assimilates art to a more general category, which he calls "experience," in the somewhat specialized, quasi-honorific sense that we say of eating a splendid meal or of making passionate, abandoned love, "now *that* was *an experience.*" Dewey points out that life is permeated with such structured "experiences," which possess a clear beginning middle, and end, and which can be assessed as "experiences" (i.e., unified, aesthetic wholes) only after they have been completed. The idea of applying this to the unity of life is an old one, harking back to the Greeks. Aristotle, in the *Nicomachean Ethics* (book I, ch. 10), quoted Solon's dictum that one cannot count a man happy until he is dead. What this means, essentially, is that life is a whole, a unit, that can be assessed only when one looks at its totality. Hence, the completion of life (or of any "experience" of this sort) is crucially affected by what occurs at the end of the life or experience, for the conclusion of the process can crucially influence the meaning, interpretation, and value of the whole (McKee 1980–81).

This concept dovetails nicely into the Heideggerian analysis offered earlier, which makes the ultimate project of a dying individual the imposition of order, meaning, unity and pattern on life. Clearly, the very conditions under which dying, aged individuals labor to find meaning in their life will have immeasurable effect on the meaning they find in the life as a whole! (Cf. the example from Kübler-Ross mentioned earlier.) If their final days are spent in a context where their individuality is suppressed; where they are treated as scientific objects rather than as persons; where the only conversation to which they have access is trivial, inauthentic "idle chatter" or curt dismissal or patronizing reassurance, the meaning they find in life will be significantly colored. ("What does it all amount to? I'm just another wornout old cancer victim, dying alone.") If a person's final days are dominated by medical surroundings that, as we have seen, by their very nature take no account of one's individuality or one's need for meaning and value and, furthermore, inexorably suggest that one is a *medical defeat,* how is one to achieve such a sense of meaning and value?

It has sometimes been suggested, and indeed it has been the case, that clergymen, psychologists, or social workers assume the responsibility for dealing with the dying. Perhaps these areas are more suited to the recognition of meaning and value than medicine is, if only because they are less "scientific." (Kastenbaum 1969:226 has observed that the chief value of clergymen lies in the negative fact that they are *not* medical people!) But in the final analysis, these people also approach the dying person through some theoretical lenses and again do not ultimately view the person as individual. Social workers and psychologists have theoretical biases and training and, if not laws, at least a set of rules for dealing with "the dying patient," rather than with what Aristotle would call "this here concrete particular individual." And all but the most liberal clergymen are surely encumbered with theoretical theological and doctrinaire baggage. This is not to say that physicians, nurses, clergymen, psychologists, and social workers *never* help dying individuals to find meaning and value in their lives; it is rather to say that they do so as sensitive individuals rather than as physician, nurse, or whatever role for which they have been trained.

If, as I have tried to show, the care of the dying elderly is conceptually at odds with the nature of medicine, and if our tendency to see primary care of the dying as *by nature* the province of medicine is untenable, what solution can be offered? Here we can but point to a sketch of a possible answer. On the basis of what we have argued, it is clear that only a person who is prepared to look at the dying, aged individuals and their lives *atheoretically,* qua individuals, in their particularity, not as instances of a law, in terms of the internal coherence and unity of those lives, and who can help aged persons find on their own the meaningful pattern that confers value on both their living and their dying, ought to assume primary responsibility for dealing with the aged dying. Perhaps during the Middle Ages in Europe or in certain essentially theocratic countries today such a role can be filled by a priest. But in a secular society where the meaning of life is no longer sought in religious terms, this is not a tenable solution. One requires, as it were, a secular priest.

But what stance is such an individual to adopt? Can there be such an atheoretical perspective? It seems to me that such a standpoint is essentially an *aesthetic* one, in both senses of aesthetic. That is, such a person must be prepared to deal with dying persons by direct perception and interaction, for knowledge of particulars, as Aristotle said, is possible only through perception, and one must be further prepared to help these persons discern a Deweyan artistic or experiential unity in their lives. Such activity is the natural province of the arts and humanities, not of the natural sciences or even the social sciences. If anyone can do this, it is artists and humanists, whose stock in trade is the meaning and value to be found in the unique and the unrepeatable. Painters, poets, dramatists, novelists, composers, perhaps some critics, historians, and other humanistic scholars—these are people whose entire *raison d'être* is the creation or discernment of unique and individual patterns of meaning. Dying, aged individuals need someone who can help them see their life as an artistic whole, or more simply as a *well-wrought story.* Such an activity is terribly demanding, of course; it would require hours of sympathetic listening and even more hours of creative dialogue, discerning and creating patterns, here highlighting some event and there deemphasizing. The patient supplies the facts, and the counselor seizes upon the ambiguities inherent in these facts to shape them into a unity. This very process of creative interaction between the dying

person and the artist would provide a tangible concrete final project
for the dying, a sense of final significance and meaning for the end
of life that would ramify and reflect back into the meaningfulness of
the whole. (We create, as it were a living eulogy, the sort of story
that each Greek in antiquity expected would be told at his funeral and
by which he was comforted.)

What I have briefly suggested is far from utopian. It requires
no major institutional changes. Dying is likely to continue to take
place in hospitals for the foreseeable future, as long as we continue
to see death as fundamentally and naturally medical. My aim is to
mitigate the tragic effects of this distorted vision by deemphasizing
the medical aspects of dying. If the aged must die in hospitals, so be
it. But we ought not let the medical shadow obliterate individuality,
value, and meaning. Let us absolve the physicians of primary responsibility for the *person,* leaving them in charge of the body, to deal
with efficient causes. Let us leave particularity and final causation to
those whose province is value and meaning, to those whose profession it is to seek meaning and unity in particulars, to those for whom
death is a personal tragedy, not a professional threat. Here is an opportunity to do more than tender lip service to a bridge between art
and science—in caring for the dying and aged, one can effect genuine
symbiosis between the "two cultures." Let us cease to view death
reductionistically, as by nature merely biological, and rather recognize it in its total complexity as a problem that transcends the scientific and requires for its proper management the full range of human
creativity.

References

Blauner, R. 1976. "Death and Social Structure." In Fulton (1976).
Dempsey, D. 1975. *The Way We Die.* New York: Macmillan.
Dewey, J. 1958. *Art as Experience.* New York: Putnam.

—— 1960. *The Quest for Certainty*. New York: Putnam.

Feifel, H., ed. 1959. The Meaning of Death. New York: McGraw-Hill.

Feifel, H. et al. 1967. "Physicians Consider Death." In Proceedings, 75th Annual Convention, American Psychological Association. Washington, D.C.

Fulton, R., ed. 1976. *Death and Identity*. Revised ed. Bowie, Maryland: Charles Press.

Glaser, B. G. and A. L. Strauss. 1965. *Awareness of Dying*. Chicago: Aldine.

—— 1969. "The 'Social Loss of Dying Patients." Cited in Kalish (1969).

Greinacher, N. and A. Müller, eds. 1974. *The Experience of Dying*. New York: Herder and Herder.

Hempel, C. 1966. *Philosophy of Natural Science*. Englewood Cliffs: Prentice-Hall.

Heidegger, M. 1962. *Being and Time*. New York: Harper.

Hofmeier, J. 1974. "The Present-Day Experience of Death." In Greinacher and Muller (1974).

Kalish, R. A. 1969. "The Effects of Death Upon the Family." In Pearson (1969).

Kasper, A. M. 1959. "The Doctor and Death." In Feifel (1959).

Kastenbaum, R. 1967. "Multiple Perspective on a Geriatric 'Death Valley.' " *Community Mental Health Journal* 3:21ff.

—— 1969. Cited in Kalish (1969).

Kastenbaum, R. and R. Aisenberg. 1972. *The Psychology of Death*. New York: Springer.

Kraus, W. A. 1978. "Getting Costly Gadgetry out of Medicine." *Washington Post*, June 11.

Kübler-Ross, E., ed. 1975. *Death: The Final Stage of Growth*. Englewood Cliffs: Prentice-Hall.

LeShan, L. 1972. Cited in Kastenbaum and Aisenberg (1972).

McKee, P. L. 1980–81. "Consummation: A Concept for Gerontologic Theory." *International Journal of Aging and Human Development*. 12(4):239–44.

Masserman, J., ed. 1961. *Current Psychiatric Therapies*. New York: Grune and Stratton.

Nagel, E. 1961. *The Structure of Science*. New York: Harcourt.

Oken, D. 1961. "What To Tell Cancer Patients." *Journal of the American Medical Association* 175:86.

Parsons, T. et al. 1976. "The Gift of Life and Its Reciprocation." In Fulton (1976).

Pearson, L., ed. 1969. *Death and Dying: Current Issues in the Treatment of the Dying Person*. Cleveland: Case Western Reserve University.

Pahier, J-M. 1974. "Death, Nature, and Contingency: Anthropological eflections About the Postponement of Death." In Greinacher and Muller (1974).

Quint, J. C. 1967. *The Nurse and the Dying Patient*. New York: Macmillan.

Randall, J. H. Jr. 1963. *Aristotle*. New York.

Rollin. B. E. 1976a. "Natural and Conventional Meaning: A History of the Distinction." *Semiotic-Historical Studies* 3:39.

—— 1976b. *Natural and Conventional Meaning: An Examination of the Distinction*. The Hague: Mouton.

—— 1979. "On the Nature of Illness." In *Man and Medicine*. 4(3):157–79.

Schulz, R. and D. Aderman, 1976. "How the Medical Staff Copes with Dying Patients: A Critical Review." *Omega* 7:11.

Siegler, M. and H. Osmond. 1974. *Models of Madness, Models of Medicine*. New York: Macmillan.

Wahl, C. W. 1961. "The Physician's Management of the Dying Patient." In Masserman (1961).

Wheeler, A. L. 1976. "The Dying Person: A Deviant in the Medical Subculture." Cited in Schulz and Aderman (1976).

10

Nursing Care Services
for the Elderly

IRENE L. SELL

WHEN THE Senate Subcommittee on Long-term Care of the Committee on Aging in the United States began its fact finding work in 1967, the most troublesome component of the health care system was considered to be the long-term health care of older Americans. The component continues to be troublesome. Health care problems tend to increase as people grow older and 5 percent of the aged population (statistically designated as 65 and older) have health problems that require long-term institutional care. The proportion of persons requiring such care remains relatively stable, but the number of persons in need of such care grows as the population of older persons increases.

Our society tends to be death-denying. Death usually is associated with old age, so old age often is denied also (even though the alternative to not growing old is to die young). Projection upon one's own old age is unlikely to envision physical infirmity, mental deterioration, loss of home and loved ones, and the consequent need for institutional care. Yet about 5 percent of older persons face such a fate every year. In 1983, approximately 1,371,350 people will be forced by circumstance to institutionalize themselves or to have the decision made for them.* Generally, this means the final years of

*New York Regional Office of the United States Census Bureau, telephone information service.

their lives will be spent in an institution. If they are fortunate to enter a facility that provides competent, knowledgeable, compassionate care their remaining years can be meaningful and happy; if not, they may merely exist, awaiting and wishing for death.

Now, what can influence the difference of the outlook? What changes are needed to increase the likelihood that those individuals who must spend their last years of life in an institution can continue to live a meaningful life rather than a mere physical existence? How can long-term institutional care become available to those who require it? How can quality care become increased in quantity, as the numbers of people needing such care grow past the limits of our existing facilities, whether good or bad.

It is my belief that first it must be acknowledged that the care of the aged is a complex matter—that it requires competent, well-prepared, well-educated, knowledgeable, skilled, and caring people. It needs to be recognized also that the care of the ill aged is a health-care problem that predominantly requires nursing-care services, not medical-care services. Accepting the premise that nursing care is an essential component of any effort to achieve quality care for this group of patients requires clarification about the contribution that can be made by the profession of nursing, as well as a shift in thinking about the health-care needs of the people.

It is important to point out that health care and medical care are not synonymous. Health care is an all encompassing term referring to all the services available from professionals within the health field. (It is useful to visualize an umbrella or roof labelled "Health Care Field" under which the various health care professions or sciences are found.) Medical care is but one service among the many services—nursing, pharmacy, nutrition, physiotherapy, etc.—available to consumers from professionals in the health care field. For the client's particular health care need to be met, the appropriate professional service must be selected. Questions need to be raised, therefore, about whether medical care is, in general, the appropriate service for persons in long-term nursing care facilities. I suggest that the major service required by residents and patients in nursing facilities is nursing care, not medical care, and that in general mandated medical care in these institutional settings is an inordinately expensive and inappropriate service.

Nursing and the services this profession can provide are probably the least understood of all the health professions and services. Part of this misunderstanding is related to an erroneous, but popular, belief that nursing is part of medicine, rather than a distinct and unique profession in itself. While it is true that nurses and physicians must work cooperatively in the interest of patients requiring both services, the focus of nursing is different from medicine and does not necessarily require involvement of a physician. Medicine, in general, focuses upon disease. Nursing focuses upon the person with the disease or health problem; on the way in which individuals respond to and are affected by their condition; on how the health state can be influenced by person-centered nursing care.

Though nothing can be done medically to reverse a patient's arteriosclerosis, for example, much can be done from the nursing perspective to reduce the distress that may be caused by memory impairment. The care prescriptions, therefore, are based on nursing assessment, nursing diagnosis, and nursing implementation. The nursing perspective is different. The woman or man engaged in the practice of professional nursing is a colleague and peer of other health professionals and has a distinct contribution to make and service to offer. The nurse educated at the baccalaureate-degree level is prepared to engage in the professional practice of nursing, which consists of diagnosing and treating human responses to actual or potential health problems and determining care goals, nursing care focus and intervention in conjunction with the patient.

In addition to nurses with a sound basic preparation for nursing practice, an increasing number of nurses have earned advanced degrees in clinical practice specialties concerned with long-term and chronic conditions and gerontologic nursing. It is this well-prepared nurse who is interested in the long-term aspects of care to whom I refer when I ask why such nurses are not used as a majority authority for the planning, delivery, and direction of nursing in nursing, health-related, and long-term care facilities. If the mission of the long-term care field is to provide life management for residents, what profession is more qualified than nursing by preparation, by purpose, and by commitment to help residents focus on and make use of the physical, social, and emotional strengths they have? To facilitate the residents' participation in all aspects of their own care? To involve the residents

in decisions affecting their living at this institution, where almost all
will spend the remainder of their lives?

The care focus is clearly within the province of nursing. By
definition, nursing is person centered and health focused and has an
identified component of care, maintenance, and comfort goals. These
begin when former cure and recovery goals are no longer appropriate.
Care, maintenance, and comfort goals involve a focus on the person
who has the health-care problem and take into account the multiplicity of factors and situations that influence the individual's response to
his or her health state, and explores the options available in assisting
the client to arrive at decisions about care. Fulfilling care goals requires assessment, diagnosis, implementation, and evaluation of a
client's health state and nursing needs by health-care professionals
who also have the authority to direct the many kinds of nonprofessional nursing personnel who are so important in carrying out the
many technical nursing tasks and activities required by this patient
group.

Current protocols in determining the care needs of residents
in a nursing facility rarely address nursing needs. Utilization review
for reimbursement purposes demands determining the appropriate level
of nursing care based on medical diagnosis and physician prescriptions, despite the fact that the individual's reason for being in a nursing facility is to receive nursing care. The appropriateness of requiring medical diagnoses and physician prescriptions to justify a person's
continued eligibility at an institution that is providing nursing-care
services for people who need them must also be questioned. Indeed,
should not nursing diagnosis and needs be the criteria that admission
to a nursing home or facility rest upon? Why is it necessary for a
person to have a complete medical diagnosis for admission to a nursing facility? Why should people seeking nursing care for themselves
or their loved one be required to seek the permission of a physician?
Should not the public have direct access to care in nursing-care facilities, just as they have direct access to other health-care professionals?

As a growing number of nurses opt for entry into independent
nursing practice and their clientele grows, should not these nurses—
who will have clients who will need care in nursing facilities and in
long-term care institutions—have the right to admit their clients di-

rectly? Indeed, why do consumers, who have realized that their health care needs are for nursing, not have the right to direct, active admission to a nursing-care facility? Why cannot the qualified specialist in gerontologic nursing determine the admission requirements for a person seeking nursing services and requiring nursing care? Why are periodic physical assessments by physicians mandated by law at a cost to the client or taxpayer when physical assessment can be and is done by nurses, who readily make referrals to the physician when such referrals are needed?

Naturally, there will be times when nursing home residents will have medical problems requiring the services of physicians, and qualified medical care must always be available. The questions I raise require discussion, for inherent in them are answers that will require many changes in thinking, in authority, and in care emphasis. It is my belief that nursing, not medicine, is the most appropriate health-care profession to determine care needs and protocols for rendering nursing services to the institutionalized aging who are in need of relevant nursing care.

11

Medical Management
of Elderly Patients:
The Health Team Approach

DENNIS A. FRATE AND DENNIS HAFFRON

*M*UCH RESEARCH AND discussion have been devoted to describing the physical health and social welfare of the elderly. From the biomedical arena it has been well documented that the elderly have an increased likelihood of developing chronic medical disorders (Barron 1974, McGlone and Schultz 1973). On the other hand, social gerontologists have shown that proportionately the elderly have more social, psychological, and economic problems (Brody 1973, Godbole and Verinis 1974). Out of these two parallel developments has come the increasing conviction that a relationship exists between clinical disorders and nonmedical problems. As a consequence, emphasis has been placed on advocating new approaches to meeting the specialized needs of the elderly, integrating medical and social services into a holistic model or team approach (Patton 1974, Schuman and Willard 1976, Rao 1977, Berkman and Rehr 1974, Ward 1977). Although the discussion of integrating services has been common and is now an accepted concept within gerontology, there have been few empir-

This study was supported in part by a grant from the Winnebago County Board of Health, Rockford, Illinois

ical studies demonstrating the relationship between medical disorders and social, psychological, and economic problems. The purpose of this paper is to examine the relationships between chronic medical disorders and a variety of nonclinical problems and thus provide an empirical basis for advocating the health team approach in the provision of services for the elderly.

Methods

The data presented in this study were collected in late 1975 during a countywide assessment of the health status and needs of the elderly in Winnebago County, Illinois (Frate and Haffron 1976). This study was conducted by the Winnebago County Council on Aging, a local social agency charged with identifying the needs and coordinating services for area elderly, and by the Rockford School of Medicine.

The study used a mailed questionnaire sent to a sample of 1145 randomly selected households. This sample was drawn from the Council's mailing list, a composite listing of elderly households containing more than 80 percent coverage of all noninstitutionalized individuals in the county sixty years and older. Of the 1145 households surveyed, 459, or 40.1 percent, responded with usable forms; 601 individuals resided in those households. Comparing the social and demographic characteristics of the respondents to the 1970 U.S. Census revealed no major differences between the county's total elderly population and the respondents. In addition, fifty nonrespondents were interviewed, and they were characteristically similar to the study population. Thus, there is no reason to doubt the representativeness of the respondents.

Results

The health status of an individual was determined in a two-step procedure. First, to determine the prevalence of a particular condition, a list of eleven chronic medical disorders common to the elderly population was included. To be counted, an individual had to presently have the condition or to have had it within the past year. Table 11.1 shows the frequency distribution of the conditions. As indicated, two of the conditions, arthritis and hypertension, affected more than 30

TABLE 11.1. Frequency Distribution of
Medical Disorders

Disorder	Percent
Arthritis	40.0
Cancer	2.4
Dental	14.5
Diabetes	8.6
Atherosclerosis	10.3
Coronary heart disease	18.5
Hypertension	31.6
Nerves and/or tension	21.8
Prostate	4.4
Stroke	2.0
Upper respiratory disorders	10.3

TABLE 11.2. Health Index

Number of Disorders	Number	Percent
0 disorder	121	20.4
1 disorder	195	32.9
2 disorders	140	23.6
3 disorders	71	12.0
4 or more disorders	66	11.1
TOTAL	593	100.0

Mean number of disorders: 1.6

percent of the respondents, while cancer and stroke, affected about 2 percent each. Since an individual could have multiple chronic disorders, the second step of the assessment involved creation of a health index, which summed the number of conditions for each individual. As seen in table 11.2, approximately 20 percent of the elderly had none of the listed medical disorders. On the other hand, more than 11 percent had four or more of these chronic illnesses; the average number of disorders was 1.6. This health index was then examined in relationship to the respondents' demographic and economic characteristics, as well as to the presence of specific nonclinical problems.

Demographic Characteristics

The distribution of the number of medical disorders was not statistically associated to either the sex or age of the respondents. In addition, marital status, living arrangements, and rural or urban residential setting were also not related to the distribution of the number of chronic medical disorders.

Economic Indicators

Two economic measures were examined, level of income and monthly expenditures for prescription medicines. The health index was significantly related to income levels ($P < .05$). Individuals in the lower income levels, $0–3999 and $4–7999, tended to have more chronic medical conditions than higher income elderly, or those individuals in the $8–11,999 and $12,000-or-more categories. Concerning prescription drugs, those with more chronic health conditions had greater monthly expenditures for medicines ($P < .001$). The mean prescription costs per month for each health status group were:

0 disorder	$ 3.41
1 disorder	9.46
2 disorders	13.15
3 disorders	15.25
4 or more disorders	19.36

These expenditures are especially distressing since the lower income elderly have more chronic illnesses and since 87 percent of these drug costs were paid either in part or all by out-of-pocket funds within this population.

Use of Medical Care

Use rates of medical-care services were also associated with the relative health status of an individual. The mean number of physician visits during the last year increased as the number of chronic illnesses reported increased ($P < .001$). Those with no disorders visited a physician 1.8 times per year, while those with four or more conditions saw a physician 5.9 times during the past year. The mean number of physician visits by number of disorders is:

0 disorder	1.80
1 disorder	3.15
2 disorders	3.80
3 disorders	5.55
4 or more disorders	5.90

Related to physician use, a question was asked whether there was a time during the past year when an individual should have sought a physician's care for a physical disorder but did not. Not seeing a physician was significantly associated to the health index, with only 6 percent of those individuals with no conditions perceiving they should have seen a physician and approximately 40 percent of those with four or more chronic disorders feeling they should have visited a physician for a particular condition but did not (P < .001).

A significantly larger proportion of elderly with more chronic health problems participated in medical screenings outside the physician's office than did elderly with fewer chronic disorders (P < .001).

TABLE 11.3. Hospitalization

Number of Disorders	Percent Hospitalized During Past Year	Mean In-Patient Days
0 disorder	9.7	1.5
1 disorder	15.7	1.9
2 disorders	22.9	2.6
3 disorders	26.5	3.3
4 or more disorders	36.9	5.9

Screening efforts for such disorders as hypertension, diabetes, and glaucoma are included here.

As seen in table 11.3, the health index was also associated with hospitalization (P < .001). More than one-third of those individuals with four or more disorders were hospitalized during the previous year, and 80 percent of those individuals were hospitalized for one week or more.

Concomitant with higher utilization of physician services was the encountering of problems in either reaching or using a physician. The two major problems encountered by the elderly centered on cost of medical care and transportation in reaching the service. Both were significantly related to the health index, with a greater proportion of chronically ill elderly experiencing problems in medical-care costs and in transportation to the physician (P < .01).

Mobility

Individuals with more chronic health conditions were also less mobile within their home because of disabilities and also less mobile regarding transportation outside the home environment. Only 2.6 percent of those elderly with no chronic disorders needed assistance from special equipment or another person to move about the home or were bedridden, while 21 percent of those individuals with four or more disorders experienced these limitations (P < .001). A greater proportion of individuals with multiple chronic disorders needed assistance with meal preparation and with personal hygiene (P < .001 in both cases).

Concerning mobility outside the home, as shown in table 11.4, transportation difficulties to all destinations asked were also associated with increases in the number of chronic medical conditions.

TABLE 11.4. Percent Distribution of Experiencing Transportation Difficulties

Destination	Disorders					Chi-square Test of Significance
	0	1	2	3	4 or More	
Grocery store	5.1	5.8	15.2	15.7	25.4	P < .001
Drug store	3.6	5.9	12.6	15.9	22.2	P < .001
Physician	6.1	4.8	11.3	17.9	25.0	P < .001
Relatives or friends	3.8	4.1	11.2	15.8	20.7	P < .001
Church and/or recreation	4.8	5.3	11.9	18.3	22.8	P < .001

Psychological Indices

As illustrated in other studies, various psychological or emotional problems are found in association with chronic illness and may hinder an individual's adjustment in personally managing the disorder. Similar associations were present in this study. For example, an increase in the number of chronic conditions was positively associated with mental or emotional breakdowns (P < .001). As shown in table 11.5, an increase in the number of chronic illnesses was also associated with experiencing periods of acute confusion or reality disorders (P < .001). Although not necessarily a true clinical measure of reduced cerebral reserve, such experiences are a commonly documented problem of the elderly (Charatan 1976).

The last psychological variable measured was loneliness. As seen in table 11.6, an increase in the number of chronic disorders was positively associated with expressing a desire for additional companionship (P < .001).

TABLE 11.5. Experiencing Periods of Acute Confusion

	Acute Confusion			
Number of	YES		NO	
Disorders	Number	Percent	Number	Percent
0 disorder	5	4.3	110	95.7
1 disorder	27	14.0	166	86.0
2 disorders	32	23.5	104	76.5
3 disorders	21	30.9	47	69.1
4 or more disorders	21	34.4	40	65.6
Chi-square test of significance: P < .001				

TABLE 11.6. Expressions of Loneliness

	Lonely			
Number of	YES		NO	
Disorders	Number	Percent	Number	Percent
0 disorder	11	9.2	108	90.8
1 disorder	23	12.2	166	87.8
2 disorders	29	21.8	104	78.2
3 disorders	14	20.3	55	79.7
4 or more disorders	19	31.1	42	68.9
Chi-square test of significance: P < .001				

Related Medical Problems

The perceived need for new eyeglasses and for a hearing aid was also related to the relative health status of the elderly. Approximately 40 percent of the individuals with four or more chronic disorders thought they needed new glasses, while only 9 percent of those elderly with no chronic disorders reported a similar need (P < .001). Concerning the need of a hearing aid, almost 20 percent of the elderly with four or more chronic conditions expressed the need, compared with only 6 percent of those individuals with no chronic disorders (P < .01). The use of dentures and the need for new dentures were not related to the health index.

Diets and nutrition are directly related to the health status of any individual. Consequently, it was not surprising to see that the percentage of elderly on special or restricted diets, such as low salt or low saturated fat, increased as the number of chronic medical conditions reported increased (P < .001). The distribution of those on a special diet was as follows:

0 disorder	5.0 percent
1 disorder	13.5
2 disorders	22.2
3 disorders	30.0
4 or more disorders	42.9

Almost 19 percent of all the elderly were on some type of special diet, and approximately one-half of them had at least three chronic medical disorders. In addition, only 77 percent of the elderly with four or more medical disorders considered their overall diet adequate as compared with 93 percent of the elderly reporting no chronic illness (P < .01).

Discussion

The results of this study show that increases in the number of chronic medical disorders in the elderly are associated with a variety of social, economic, emotional, and related problems. Although the purpose of this paper was not to design a new geriatric medical-care delivery system, the data do empirically demonstrate the need for a coordinated, holistic approach in efficaciously managing the health and welfare of the elderly.

No doubt comment can be made on the inclusion or exclusion of specific chronic medical problems, but the association of increases of chronic disorders to concomitant nonclinical problems is clear.

Economically, the individuals who can least afford illnesses are most affected by them. Prescription costs put an added burden on these individuals and average almost $20 per month for those elderly with four or more chronic disorders. Almost 90 percent of these individuals pay for medications, at least in part, with out-of-pocket funds. Use of medical services also compounds the economic drain. The results of the use patterns are straightforward; individuals who are sick tend to see a physician more often and are hospitalized more and for longer periods of time than the relatively healthier individuals. Possibly because of their poorer health status, these individuals also exhibit more preventive health behavior as they participate in medical screening programs. Conversely, the reason 20 percent of the elderly reported no chronic conditions may be related to their lower use of all medical-care services; more than 25 percent of all elderly participating in one of the various screenings had a disorder detected that required further medical care.

Concerning transportation, it is ironic that those in most need of getting to medical services, to a grocery store, to a pharmacy, or to places for social interaction are the ones experiencing the most difficulties. Transportation is often an overlooked facet of the medical management scheme.

Problems of loneliness and periods of acute confusion are also associated within multiple chronic disorders. The presence of these problems may affect an individual's ability to adapt to chronic illness and the long-term therapy required.

These data document the magnitude and types of problems faced by a portion of the elderly population inflicted with multiple chronic diseases. Medical personnel who are confronted daily with such individuals should be aware of these nonclinical problems that may have bearing on their medical management. On the other end of the spectrum, social-service personnel would also be more effective in counseling and referral if the total range of issues facing an elderly individual were clearly identified. No doubt one of the best ways to institute such awareness is to have personnel available with expertise in both medical and social arenas. Such an approach would then be best illustrated by having a multidisciplinary health team interfacing with the elderly during their medical management.

References

Barron, J. J. 1974. "Medical Management of an Aging Population." *Minnesota Medicine* 57:623–25.

Berkman, B. and H. Rehr. 1974. "The Search for Early Indicators of Social Service Need Among Elderly Hospital Patients." *Journal of the American Geriatrics Society* 22:416–21.

Brody, S. J. 1973. "Comprehensive Health for the Elderly: An Analysis." *The Gerontologist* 13:412–18.

Charatan, F. B. 1976. "Acute Confusion and the Elderly." *Hospital Physician* 12:8–10.

Frate, D. A. and D. Haffron. 1976. "An Assessment of the Health Status and Health Needs of the Elderly in Winnebago County, Illinois: A Summary Report." Rockford School of Medicine, College of Medicine, University of Illinois and Winnebago County Council on Aging.

Godbole, A. and J. S. Verinis. 1974. "Brief Psychotherapy in the Treatment of Emotional Disorders in Physically Ill Geriatric Patients." *The Gerontologist* 14:143–48.

McGlone, F. B. and P. R. Schultz. 1973. "Problems in Geriatric Health Care Delivery." *Journal of the American Geriatric Society* 21:533–37.

Patton, S. K. 1974. "One Alternative to Institutionalization: In-Home Supportive Services." *Minnesota Medicine* 57:637–40.

Rao, D. B. 1977. "The Team Approach to Integrated Care of the Elderly." *Geriatrics* 32:88–96.

Schuman, J. E. and H. N. Willard. 1976. "Role of the Acute Hospital Team in Planning Discharge of the Chronically Ill." *Geriatrics* 31:63–67.

Ward, R. A. 1977. "Services for Older People: An Integrated Framework for Research." *Journal of Health and Social Behavior* 18:61–70.

12

The Family Physician
and Care of the Dying Aged

EDWARD B. ELKOWITZ

THE FEAR OF DEATH and dying occupies a profoundly important place in life. We are aware that man is mortal, life is finite, and we are finite with it. In the past years, man has learned to postpone death, but as we know life, man's only defense against death is to pretend to ignore Life's finitude and to think of a life beyond the one we know as mortal. We develop cultural folkways and complex taboos against death and express our death as a passing to another life.

Regardless of age, the majority of people deal with death by denying it. This is shown by society's attempts to segregate the dying elderly either by institutionalizing them or by isolation. The elderly, however, if given the choice, would prefer to live their final days in familiar surroundings, among people—family and friends—where death will not be faced alone.

When family physicians treating the elderly spend time discussing the desires and psychological complaints of the dying patient and try to understand how the elderly think and behave, they find that these patients can be arbitrarily divided into groups of young-old, middle-old, and old-old both chronologically and psychobiologically. The young-old are more anxious about and fearful of dying, while the old-old are more realistic and have an accepting attitude toward dying. The elderly, in general, do not fear death but would like to die without suffering.

The psychological pattern of the dying patient, which includes the phase of denial, may be linked to the anticipated loss of self-esteem and anticipated pain and suffering more than to the fear of death itself. There are elderly patients who desire a death that affords them the least amount of mental, emotional, and physical suffering and the maximum amount of dignity.

Helping patients die is difficult. Dying patients represent a defeat in our efforts to maintain life. But the elderly dying person's wishes to preserve life with dignity, to undergo minimal suffering, and to be viewed as a total person rather than as a disease process through the eyes of the technical machinery of our health institutions should be respected. When patient's feelings are understood and they are allowed to voice their thoughts and hopes, the approaching death is made easier. These open expressions of the dying elderly also help reduce feelings of inadequacy and guilt among the family and professional people involved. If the patients, on occasions prior to the dying state, had expressed to their physicians their feelings about death and dying and how they would wish to be treated, the physicians would then have an insight into the desires of dying elderly patients and would be able to cope with their problems, as well as be confident in the handling of both patient and family during this traumatic experience.

Discussing the seriousness of an illness or the approaching death can be cold and cruel, but it can also be merciful and gentle. Generally, the family is notified first of the seriousness of the illness, and the decision is made primarily by the family, who instruct the physician about the plan of care and thus leave the dying elderly patient in a "vacuum." This type of handling denies the dying elderly persons the right "to be able to say goodbye" to family and friends, who mean so much to them and have shared in their life.

After a while, patients develop an awareness of their situation and approaching death. Having lost faith in those around them, because of their dishonesty and secretive behavior, these patients feel alone, unable to speak to the family about problems and wishes or to the physician about the course of treatment.

Therefore, elderly persons should be told of the diagnosis and plan for treatment. This should be done in a truthful, merciful, and gentle manner, giving these patients a feeling of hope for dignity in the final stage of growth. After discussions with the physician, these patients can then decide when and how to tell the family of their impending death and thus ensure themselves a feeling of control over the final phase of life. With this type of approach, elderly dying persons are made to feel secure in the knowledge that they are free to express their wishes and have the opportunity to prepare for an orderly death. A feeling of confidence in their physician and the treatment is created, and this feeling has a reciprocal effect on physicians, who find themselves not only diagnosing and treating the patient but also reducing anguish and helping the patient to face death with dignity and to die in a dignified state.

In an earlier paper (Elkowitz 1978), I discuss the importance of the family physician in guiding family members and others in forming a team to help dying elderly patients in this life crisis so that they may have a "good death." The importance of honesty and cooperation by all those involved is emphasized, as is the patient's need to be supported emotionally and spiritually.

The family physician, in the key role, can shape an attitude toward dying that is "good enough to live with" and thus offer guidance and assistance to the dying patient and the family. Within this attitude of "good enough to live with," the family physician can inject hope. For it is hope that will keep the dying patient living while alive and help fight off the despair that accompanies a "waited death."

The physician's attitude should be one of caring and active interest, which instill hope. Hopelessness is often a precipitator of death. Although hopelessness is considered a part of the depression syndrome, it has been seen to arise outside this depression as well. It is often this type of hopelessness that can hasten the death of the elderly patient, particularly one suffering a severe illness.

Hopelessness has been associated with the high incidence of death occurring within thirty days of an elderly patient's birthday. To the elderly, a birthday may be associated with the nearness of the end of life, while to the young a birthday signifies maturity and hope and offers encouragement to live.

Visits to the physician by the dying patient, or the physician's visits to the dying who cannot get around, can offer a great amount of hope to the patient. A simple statement by the physician, "I'll see you next week," can be instrumental in keeping up the patient's hope.

The family physician, with years of experience, should caution the family about the detrimental effects produced by avoiding physical contact with the dying person. It is sad to watch anything die. Too often, there is a repulsion toward dying objects. But it is at this stage that physical and emotional contact must be maintained to lift the spirits of the dying patient. Family members who spend time with the patient in an unhurried manner, whether it be active or passive, can offer the patient reassurance that someone cares.

The physician should talk honestly to patients about the extent of their illness and what they can expect. Telling patients honestly of the state they are in alleviates suspicion on their part. Once suspicion is aroused, patients lose trust in the physician and family members, and this loss of trust can trigger unforeseen difficulties and make them feel uncomfortable within their own familiar environment.

The physician should be honest with the family members also, advising them of the progression of the illness or disease, the psychological makeup of the dying person, what problems they can expect, and how to cope. Once the family members have been told of the phases the dying patient may be expected to go through, they can assist the physician in a team effort to administer to the needs of the patient.

The physician should also encourage patients to keep active in their life role, rather than wallow in self-pity, and should instruct the family members in the importance of their cooperation.

Some elderly patients fear death, and the skilled physician can coax the patient to discuss these fears and eventually to acknowledge them. Once this step has been achieved, the physician, although probably unable to allay the patient's fears, can assure the patient that the fears are natural. It has been shown that most dying patients welcome the opportunity to discuss their fears. The family physician can act as a release valve by allowing the patient to vent emotions. Once the anxieties and fears have been brought out into the open, they can be dealt with realistically, affording the patient a more psychologically comfortable and dignified death.

For the elderly patient and the family, the fear of death and the dependent needs of the dying patient have a great psychological impact. Too often, dying and death are taken out of the family's hands and given over to institutions. At times, this may occur because of the family's inability to face the problem of death or because of the vain hope of prolonging the patient's life. Thus, the patient's wish to die in familiar surroundings becomes thwarted, not because of the insensitivity of family members but because of ignorance about the personal needs of the dying patient and the lack of communication between patient and family.

Within the confines of the institution, the goals are to maintain and preserve life, regardless of the patient's wishes. The psychological and emotional stress this places on patient and family would make it preferable and more humane to allow elderly patients who are dying to be kept out of institutions and to remain in familiar surroundings where their personal wishes may be carried out and they can be assured of dignity in their final days of life. This can be accomplished with the help of the family physician, who can give palliative treatment and comfort to the dying person and offer advice and assistance to the family members in caring for the patient.

However, there are times when elderly persons should be institutionalized. If they do not want to burden the family, or if they have a medical debility of such a nature that home care would be impractical, institutionalized care should seriously be considered. Hospices, which cater to the needs of the dying, are specially equipped for this purpose. The patients are given sympathetic understanding and proper medical treatment by well-trained personnel. The environment is kept cheerful, and there is an atmosphere of caring. Here, the patient, not the disease, is the center of attention.

In summary, it must be reemphasized that physicians must make the dying elderly patient aware during each phase of the illness that they know what is happening and continue to care. Physicians must give reassurance and hope, because elderly patients fear the process of dying and do not want suffering and an undignified death. Thus, physicians must plan each step of the treatment with care, humanity, and understanding for the elderly patient and the family.

Primary-care physicians, particularly if they are the family physician, know the patient and family and should play an active, authoritative role. They should show compassion and concern not only to the patient but also to the family. With this type of direction, death, instead of being a negative, guilty, and angry experience, can be a positive, accepting one.

References

Ashkenazy, E. 1975. "Reflections on Accepting Death." *Progressive* 39:20.

David, R. H. and M. Neiswender, eds. 1973. "Dealing with Death." Monograph published by Ethel Percy Andrus Gerontology Center, University of Southern California, Los Angeles.

Elkowitz, E. B. 1978."Death and the Elderly Patient." *Journal of American Geriatrics Society* (January) 26:36–38.

13

Psychotherapeutic Approaches and Techniques in Treatment of the Terminally Ill Patient (1950-1975)

DAVID B. KASSOFF

Introduction and Background

*F*ROM 1950 TO 1975, various medical and psychiatric authors ventured to suggest approaches of care for individuals regarded as terminally ill, with differing views on the matter. The object of this paper is to review various psychotherapeutic approaches and techniques in the treatment of the terminally ill patient from this historical perspective.

Definition of "Terminally Ill"

Young (1960:103) defines the dying patient as "a subgroup of the living made up of those whose death is known to be imminent and relatively predictable," because of various concurrent events. This is usually a fatal illness or occasionally an external force such as criminal, political, or military sentence. In this paper, *terminally ill* refers to those whose death is impending because of a fatal illness.

Psychotherapy of Patients with Terminal Illness

Techniques Relative to Informing the Patient

Various authors have commented on the question "Should patients be informed of the nature of their terminal disease, and if so, under what circumstances?"

Eissler (1955:143) believed that it is immaterial whether patients consciously know that death is impending; the assumption is that somewhere within them there is such knowledge. This rather enigmatic explanation is demystified by Roose (1969:391), who asserts that patients know the truth through a variety of iatrogenic factors, most notably the doctor's silence or evasions. However, he feels that the therapist must be honest about the knowledge, because the immediate confrontation by patients with the truth enables them to develop trust in the therapist. Roose believes this will eventually permit patients to live out a more fundamental transference wish, which will demand complete trust in the therapist. He states that later the truth may be redenied by the patient.

In contrast, Eissler (1955:170) and Joseph (1962:24) feel that the deception of telling patients that they have a benign disease may be justified because it is an "unavoidable step to spare the patient mental pain." Aronson (1959:253) addresses this problem by explaining that one should be guided by the principle of permitting and helping patients to keep as much as possible whatever roles are important to them.

Cramond (1970:389) has written about experiences with patients in chronic renal failure. Because of the overt manifestations of their pathological conditions, all were forced to consider their own ultimate demise; most were able to discuss their feelings and beliefs with awareness and relief. He states that only a small number used denial. He concludes that seriously ill patients can and do consider death as a possible outcome and may welcome the opportunity to talk about their feelings. He points out that sharing this fear with the physician is therapeutic and promotes a more comfortable communication. At the same time, he cautions that this fear should be discussed only when the relationship between patient and doctor is sufficiently close. In addition, he warns that clues for the patient's readiness to discuss this subject should be left to the patient (rather than directly prompted by the psychotherapist). In one instance, however, he feels that the physician must confront the issue; for example, where time is short and business affairs must be settled. Finally, Kübler-Ross (1973) claims that most of the patients interviewed in her study appreciated a physician who was honest with them or made them aware of the seriousness of their condition, provided the doctor expressed two points:

      1. "I will stay by you as long as is needed no matter what happens."

      2. "There is always hope."

      Early research (Kelly and Friesen 1950, Samp and Curreri 1957) tended to support the idea that the great majority (85 to 90 percent) of cancer patients and healthy people preferred to be told of their disease. This is a far greater percentage than the average physician would estimate. Most physicians surveyed did not tell as a policy (70 to 90 percent) (Fitts and Ravdin 1953, Rennick 1960, Oken 1961). According to Oken (1961), this decision is based on the personal opinions, beliefs, convictions, and emotional justification of physicians rather than on clinical observation. Presently, we still do not have adequate data on the consequences of telling patients they have a terminal illness.

Techniques Dealing with the Fears Connected with
Death and Dying

      Fears that the terminally ill patient has regarding death and dying are frequently the first problem that confronts the professional.

      Pattison (1974:691–94) and other authors (Cramond 1970, Norton 1963, Rosenthal 1957) have listed and described these fears as follows:

      • Fear of the unknown.

      • Fear of loneliness and isolation (this includes the fear of abandonment and separation from family and friends).

      • Fear of loss of the body and loss of self.

• Fear of loss of self-control (connected with this is the fear that courage will fail if the process goes on too long. It may also be associated with the fear of losing one's sanity).

• Fear of pain (both psychic and physical).

• Fear of the loss of identity in the face of forces of dissolution.

• Fear of regression, perhaps to the extent to which one retreats from the outer world of reality into a primordial sense of being, a selfless state of nonbeing.

• Fear of the loss of power over one's destiny.

• Fear of dependency (this may include fear of an increasing dependency on others and of being a nuisance).

Pattison (1974) deals with each of the fears by suggesting specific approaches for each one. For example, regarding the fear of loss of family and friends, the professional can help patients mourn these impending losses. The fear of loss of self-control can be approached by allowing dying patients to retain whatever authority they can; they can be sustained in retaining control over doing daily tasks and making decisions, with avoidance of shame for failure of control.

Rosenthal (1957:631–32) feels that one way to diminish patients' fear of death is to rearouse creative impulses (for example, artistic activity). In her view, this may ensure that life can still have meaning. In addition, she encourages the patients to be aware of their fears instead of repressing or suppressing them.

Cramond (1970:390), in dealing with fear, or more specifically its expression in the form of anxiety, suggests that the more distressing and troublesome aspects of anxiety can be dealt with by the use of major tranquilization (for instance, chlorpromazine or thioridizine). He feels that it may also be of value to give the patient the chance to discuss spiritual matters and turn to a minister, priest, or rabbi for help.

Use of Interpretation and Insight

An outspoken proponent of the use of insight in the psychotherapy of the terminally ill patient is Rosenthal (1957). She feels that "when insight is gained on the threshold of death, the frustrated patient will almost invariably perceive his life as not having been wasted" (p. 631). As was already stated, she encourages patients to be aware of their fears instead of forgetting them. She warns, however, that "obviously such therapy must be confined to those who in their last phase of life are still amenable to such insight" (p. 633). With regard to insight psychotherapy, she goes on to say that "the patient's guilt feelings are one of the most potent elements behind his fear of death and should be the primary concern. . . . Psychotherapy, by dealing with dynamic sources of guilt feelings, can bring insight and help resolve guilt. Without some degree of insight, guilt feelings, although they may be repressed, are likely to remain active and potent sources of continuous anxiety" (pp. 628–29). In contrast, other authors (Cramond 1970, Norton 1963, Eissler 1955, Roose 1969) refer to uses of insight or interpretations in their therapy with terminally ill patients but do not attempt to support techniques or examine them in detail.

Support of Denial

Roose (1969) refers to denial as an important defense. He suggests that denial is not pathological as an adaptation to death and dying and therefore should not be torn down. He feels that denial facilitates regression to varying depths, ultimately to a "state of reunion" (p. 392). Kostrubala (1963) sanctions the patient who has what he terms "scientific delusions" (p. 546). For example, the incurable patient with metastatic carcinoma may believe that hope and cure are in sight.

Creation of Positive, Authoritarian Transference

Eissler (1955) believed that "the patient must obtain from the very beginning of contact the impression that he can rely totally on the psychiatrist, and that there are no limitations to which the psychiatrist will go in order to assist him" (p. 126). Eissler stated that in the psychotherapy of the dying, the assignment of a substitute is essentially out of the question. The relationship with one primary therapist must not be diluted (p. 196).

Eissler (1955) felt that the technique of treatment of the dying patient must center on the "gift situation." He believed that the "psychiatrist must create at the proper time the correct situation in which to give the right gift" (p. 126). Examples of the "gift" may be the extended availability of the therapist or lack of fee for services rendered. Eissler (1955:126) further stated:

> The gift can have a beneficial effect only if it occurs at a time when it is experienced by the patient as a symbol, when he has formed a strong positive transference. To a certain extent, the patient must learn that the psychiatrist knows better what the patient wishes than the patient himself. Then the gift will be experienced by the patient as the physician's giving him part of his own life, and the dreadful stigma of being selected for death while life continued outside will be converted into a dying together, greatly reducing the sting of death or transferring it into an impending rebirth which may convert the reality of death into its opposite.

Aronson (1959) views the gift from the physician "as evidence of sublimated love, reinforcing the waning testimony of the internal good object against the isolating agony of death" (p. 256).

With regard to the terminally ill patient's working through of mourning, Norton (1963:557) encourages a gradual decathexis from objects in the environment with a recathexis to the therapist. This formula suggests that the patient can grieve the loss of the therapist shortly before death.

Eissler (1955) theorizes what the essential psychotherapeutic technique in the treatment of the terminally ill patient should be. He states, "It is conceivable that through an approach which mobilizes the archaic trust in the world and reawakens primordial feelings of being protected by a mother, the suffering of the dying can be reduced to a minimum, even in the case of extreme physical pain and psychological pain" (p. 119). Young (1960) states this more simply: the "therapeutic factor" is a "satisfaction of dependency needs given freely and without guilt provocation, enabling the patient to re-experience something akin to a successful infancy" (p. 108). As Roose (1969:393–94) describes, the therapist becomes the "benevolent, omnipotent, and archaic mother" (p. 393). He attempts to show that denial and regression facilitate development of a fantasy of reunion (in this state there is peace and calm in the face of death).

> In reunion there is life-immortality. There can be no anxiety about the future in reunion—suicide no longer exists as a possibility, pain is comforted. Also regression to the point of reunion cannot be

associated with guilt or anxiety since the patient's superego is merged with that of the all-giving and powerful archaic mother in the form of the therapist who has encouraged and facilitated this goal.

Eissler (1955) explained that in the establishment of this reunion, there is no separation between external reality and internal reality (p. 197). Furthermore, he believed that the primary function of the psychiatrist in this clinical situation is "to provide the optimal libidinal accretion to the patient" (p. 85). Eissler stated that with regard to transference, it is not viewed in this setting as a psychotherapeutic tool but rather as an end in itself (p. 197).

Existential Approach to Psychotherapy
LeShan and LeShan (1961) feel that psychotherapy with the dying patient is valuable if it focuses on the patient's strengths and positive qualities and what has blocked their full expression, rather than on "pathology." They feel that in this way patients can come away with more to value and thus will accept themselves and their fate. They see patients often alone and isolated and consider that therapists, by their presence and interest, give meaning through warm human contact. The therapist's focus is on life rather than on death, which these authors feel considerably diminishes the patient's fear of death. They believe that what is important is to search for values and meanings in life.

In this approach, it is important to recognize that there can be positive aspects of facing death. These aspects are primarily existential. The acceptance of death may forcibly remind an individual of the limited amount of time available. This, in turn, may become an incentive for the patient to make the most of life.

The Handling of Countertransference
The terminal patient's imminent death can unleash anxiety in the doctor about his or her own death. It can incur deep wounds to the physician's narcissism and feelings of omnipotence. Feifel's (1955:122) report of physicians' counterphobic stance toward death may be reflected by their choice of medicine as a career. Then, having reached the point of practicing physicians, they are often expected to be less fearful and emotional than others when faced with

a dying individual. Physicians who have not resolved their conflicts regarding death may be faced with anxiety and disillusionment in such a situation (Kasper 1959).

Pattison (1974:697) feels that before clinicians can master the therapeutic technique of helping the dying patient, they must first confront death within themselves. Eissler (1955), in keeping with his already mentioned approach to psychotherapy with the terminally ill patient, believed that the therapeutic emphasis is far less on what is done and said than on what the psychiatrist feels and can make the patient feel. Eissler (1955:143–44) has written of the "split attitude" the psychotherapist must have:

> On the one hand, the magnitude and the gravity of the situation must be fully recognized, acknowledged, and accepted by the psychiatrist. . . . On the other hand . . . the psychiatrist must not waver in his conviction that the patient is ultimately immortal. The resultant behavior of the therapist must be contradictory, but strangely enough it is not experienced as such by the patient. Just the opposite seems to be true. . . . The patient wants to obtain reassurance that no harm will befall him, but simultaneously he wants to be treated in conformity with the gravity of the situation.

In a close look at the literature, various approaches to treatment of the terminally ill patient become apparent. The multiplicity of dynamic understandings, goals of treatment, and treatment techniques presented by the authors reveals differences not only in their general approach to therapy but also in their individual subjectivity. The variety of approaches very probably represents the way these different professionals view their own death. As such, their own attitudes and feelings about the dying patient are of great importance.

In the most usual way, death is experienced as a loss—a loss for both the dying person and the survivors. However, the loss is not experienced in the same way for the survivors as it is for the person faced with imminent death. First of all, for the survivors, it is the loss of another individual, not of themselves. Second, clinical observation prompts the reflection that for many individuals, the perception of death from a temporal distance and when it is personally near may be quite different situations. Professionals must be careful not to confuse their own feelings with those of the dying patient. In this context, it is important, in the treatment setting, to suspend any judgments derived from one's personal point of view be they ethical or religious or related to medical or psychiatric standpoints. Such viewpoints have the danger of looking down with pity or horror upon anyone to whom dying occurs. As Binswanger (1944) has written (regarding the feeling about death on the part of one of his patients), "we must neither tolerate nor disapprove of it nor trivialize it with medical or psychoanalytic explanations, nor dramatize it with ethical or religious judgments" (p. 292). He stated further that "the true ground of understanding can be grasped in imagination whenever the human steps out of the perspective of judgment, condemnation, or even acquittal" (p. 292).

The point here is that if therapists are going to assist the patient to accept the reality of death, they must abandon their own prejudices, traditional beliefs, and imposing emotions, so that they can begin to see death through the eyes of the patient. A disregard for this approach is likely to result in the erection of psychological barriers between the person treating and the dying patient that cause the previously mentioned isolation of the patient. The practice of withholding from the patient information of impending death may also derive from these psychological obstacles.

Additional Suggestions Regarding the Psychotherapy of the Terminally Ill Patient

Given the fact that there are a great number of individuals who are terminally ill, the question arises, "Whom does the psychotherapist treat?" Perhaps the easiest way to answer this inquiry is by way of exclusion. Eissler (1955) felt that the people who do not need psychiatric care are "those patients who have integrated the idea that death is the matrix of life and that in dying one fulfills life's primary law" (p. 142).

A converse of Eissler's formulation reads, "Those people who *do* need psychiatric care are those patients who *have not* integrated the idea that death is the matrix of life and that in dying one fulfills life's primary law." From the standpoint of natural law, this statement is of great significance. It recognizes that death is inevitable and that the individuals who suffer are the ones who have not accepted the reality that they must come to a physical end that takes precedence over their symbolic (human) world—that is, that they are going to die. However, this account falls short. It recognizes death strictly as a concrete end to a biological existence and disregards what the meaning of that end might be for the individual who has given abstract meaning to life. In Eissler's treatment approach to the terminally ill patient, if the goal of therapy is to assist patients in achieving the maximum individuality and dignity of which they are capable in the face of imminent death, it can hardly be accomplished by maximum regression with the subsequent loss of ego boundaries and identity. Rather, directness and an acceptance of the patient as a mature adult are paramount. With this in mind, the question arises: "How can the professional help the terminally ill patient?"

> The secret of all helping, thus Kierkegaard expresses it, lies in the fact that he who wishes to lead a person to a special aim must realize with great precision to look for the person needing help there where he really is, and to begin there where he is found. This means: to help is before everything else to put oneself in the other's place, to man one's home in his existence, to learn to know the world in which he lives (Van Den Berg 1955:102).

The problem facing terminally ill patients in need of psychiatric assistance is temporal relative to other people. They are faced with the same problem each individual has, but their dilemma is that they cannot avoid it as easily. They know when they will die and how much time they have left. They are under greater pressure to face death and incorporate it into the meaning of their lives so that it is acceptable as the inevitable end to their existence. Having accomplished this end, dying patients may then live out the rest of their lives with a minimum of emotional suffering.

This, then, raises a problem concerning the meaning of life and of death and their integration. Just as the meaning of life differs from person to person, so does the meaning of death. The research accomplished thus far attests to the fact that death can mean different things to different people (Feifel 1959). For some it means the end of physical life but leads to spiritual transcendence. For others, it is the end of existence and as such is the measure of whether or not their lives have been worthwhile. Other examples can be offered. What is important, however, is that different perspectives of death transform the lives of those who hold those perspectives. At the same time, one's perspective of death is the result of one's life experiences. Feifel (1959:126) has written: "Death is a multifaceted symbol the specific import of which depends on the nature and fortunes of the individual's development and his cultural context."

There are multiple examples of how death represents various idiosyncratic meanings for different people based on their various cultural, religious, and philosophical preferences. This is in addition to other important factors such as age, individual socioeconomic conditions, family situation, differences in personality, extent of education, early life experiences, severity and mode of organic processes, and attitudes of the physician and others, which mold the individual's attitudes toward death. This area requires concepts that attempt to integrate biological, psychological, and social dimensions.

As Barton and Hollender (1973:22) have written, "An approach must be developed which studies and elucidates but does not simply re-reduce the subject to impersonal research protocols." More specifically, professionals must respect the beliefs of terminal patients so that they can meaningfully integrate the concept of death into their lives. The patients must be offered the right to choose what meaning life has for them and in this way to die with dignity. One must be careful not to force one's own ideas, one's feelings and solutions on the patient. The content of the therapy should be guided by the needs and desires of the patient. Patients must sense that their own ways of dealing with death are acceptable to the therapist or physician and that this person is available to help them look at alternatives if they wish. Since religious beliefs may be involved, physicians should be willing to seek or accept the help of the clergy. It will not be surprising to find that in some cases a specialized chaplain or rabbi can establish trust and confidence more easily than the medical staff (Carey 1975).

Before concluding this discussion, it is necessary again to stress the importance of mourning and fear for the terminally ill patient. In this regard, all terminally ill patients who are aware of their impending death share a common ground. They all experience mourning, as well as fear, as death approaches. In view of this, the professional must offer them support in their mourning and help them find the courage to face their fears in a meaningful and human way.

Conclusion

The object of this paper has been to present and examine various psychotherapeutic approaches and techniques in the treatment of the terminally ill patient.

Among the conclusions drawn from the discussion are the following:

1. We do not yet have adequate data on the consequences of telling people they have a terminal illness.

2. There are a variety of approaches in offering psychotherapeutic assistance to the terminally ill patient. The multiplicity of treatment goals and techniques reveals differences not only in the general approach of professionals to therapy but also in individual subjectivity. The variety of approaches very probably represents the way these professionals view their own death. The author believes that professionals must be careful not to confuse their own feelings with those of the dying patient. Such a personalized viewpoint has the danger of looking down with pity or horror upon anyone to whom dying occurs.

3. The author suggests that the goal of therapy should be humanistic in approach—that is, to assist patients in achieving the maximum individuality and dignity of which they are capable in the face of imminent death. This involves assisting terminal patients to incorporate the reality of death into the meaning of their lives so that it is acceptable as the inevitable end to this existence. More specifically, professionals must respect the beliefs of these individuals and offer them the right to choose what meaning life and death have for them and in this way to die with dignity.

4. Mourning and fear are an important part of the experience of the terminally ill patient. In view of the fact that such individuals experience mourning and fear as death approaches, the professional must offer them support in their mourning and help them find the courage to face their fears in a meaningful and human way.

Finally, it is important to recognize that aspects of this problem have been left untouched. These include working with the families and other survivors, the use of groups, and the possibilities of benefit from somatic treatments (in particular the use of medications).

References

Aronson, G. J. 1959. "Treatment of the Dying Person." In H. Feifel, ed. *The Meaning of Death,* pp. 251–58. New York: McGraw-Hill.

Barton, D. and M. H. Hollender. 1973. "Death Takes a Holiday—Reconsidered." *Pharos* (January) 36:20–22.

Binswanger, L. 1944. "The Case of Ellen West, An Anthropological-Clinical Study." In R. May, ed. *Existence,* pp. 247–364. New York: Simon and Schuster, 1958).

Carey, R. G. 1975. "Living Until Death: A Program of Service and Research for the Terminally Ill." In E. Kübler-Ross, ed. *Death: The Final Stage of Growth,* pp. 75–86. Englewood Cliffs, New Jersey: Prentice-Hall.

Cramond, W. A. 1970. "Psychotherapy of the Dying Patient." *British Medical Journal* 3:389–93.

Eissler, K. R. 1955. *The Pychiatrist and the Dying Patient.* New York: International Universities Press.

Feifel, H. 1959. "Attitudes Toward Death in Some Normal and Mentally Ill Populations." In H. Feifel, ed. *The Meaning of Death,* pp. 114–30. New York: McGraw-Hill.

Fitts, W. T., Jr. and I. S. Ravdin. 1953. "What Philadelphia Physicians Tell Patients with Cancer." *Journal of the American Medical Association* 153:901–4.

Joseph F. 1962. "Transference and Countertransference in the Case of a Dying Patient." *Psychoanalysis and Psychoanalytic Review* 49:21–34.

Kasper, A. M. 1959. "The Doctor and Death." In H. Feifel, ed. *The Meaning of Death.* pp. 259–70. New York: McGraw-Hill.

Kelly, W. D. and S. R. Friesen. 1950. "Do Cancer Patients Want to Be Told?" *Surgery* 27:822–26.

Kostrubala, T. 1963. "Therapy of the Terminally Ill Patient." *Illinois Medical Journal* 124:545–47.

Kübler-Ross, E. 1973. "Death and Dying." Videotape. Division of Educational Communications in Cooperation with Department of Nursing, SUNY Upstate Medical Center, Syracuse, New York.

LeShan, L. and E. LeShan. 1961. "Psychotherapy and the Patient with a Limited Life Span." *Psychiatry* 24:318–23.

Norton, J. 1963. "Treatment of a Dying Patient." *The Psychoanalytic Study of the Child* 18:541–60. New York: International Universities Press.

Oken, D. 1961. "What to Tell Cancer Patients." *Journal of the American Medical Association* 175:120–28.

Pattison, E. M. 1974. "Help in the Dying Process." In S. Arieti, ed. *American Handbook of Psychiatry,* 2nd ed. 1:685–702. New York: Basic Books.

Rennick, D. 1960. "What Should Physicians Tell Cancer Patients?" *New Medical Material* 2:51–53.

Roose, L J. 1969. "The Dying Patient." *International Journal of Psychoanalysis* 50:385–95.

Rosenthal, H. 1957. "Psychotherapy for the Dying." *American Journal of Psychotherapy* 11:626–33.

Samp, R. J. and A. R. Curreri. 1957. "Questionnaire Survey on Public Cancer Education Obtained from Cancer Patients and Their Families." *Cancer* 10:382–84.

Van Den Berg, J. H. 1955. *The Phenomenological Approach to Psychiatry.* Springfield, Illinois: Charles C Thomas.

Young, W. H. 1960. "Death of a Patient During Psychotherapy." *Psychiatry* 23:103–8.

Behavioral Neurology
and the Right to Refuse Treatment

PAUL HARDY and MARTIN ALBERT

COMPETENCY IN SENILE dementia—the right to refuse treatment in this mental state—is a study in itself. Over the past 15 years, medical ethics has developed and expanded exponentially. Dominant concerns have ranged from abortion to euthanasia, from human and fetal experimentation to population policy, from truthtelling to the allocation of scarce medical resources. In addition, the notion of health care as a basic human right has received extensive attention both in the interdisciplinary community of people concerned with ethical issues in health care and in legal and legislative circles. The right to refuse health care and treatment has been less well enunciated.

Interestingly enough, the courts have led the way in shaping ethical and social policy in this manner through such landmark decisions as *Harrison v. Gilgard,* New York Supreme Court, 1962. This case concerned the denial of an application from a hospital administrator to administer blood to a member of the Jehovah's Witness faith. The rights of the terminally ill to refuse treatment have, in recent years, been enunciated by the clergy and laity, by medical personnel, and by some legislators. Most notable in this vein have been the California Natural Death Act and similar legislation passed in other states. However, the right of the elderly patient, who may be experiencing senile mental deterioration, to refuse treatment has not been adequately explored to date, despite the fact that this is an issue of everyday concern. The reasons for this lack of exploration are undoubtedly complex. On the surface, one can say that in Western society there has been a cross-disciplinary neglect of the demented patient. For the medical community, only during the past ten years have clinicians begun to understand the spectrum of clinical presentations of dementia, not to mention the neuropsychological natural histories of the dementias.

In May 1978, the Massachusetts Appeals Court overturned a lower court ruling in *Lane v. Candura* and stated that a 77-year-old woman with diabetes had a right to refuse amputation of her gangrenous right foot and lower leg despite "fluctuations in mental lucidity and occasional losses in her train of thought." This ruling would appear to stand as a landmark not only for the legal community but, more important, for the medical community and the interdisciplinary community of people concerned with ethical issues, such as this one in health care. The court, in the process of fact-finding, noted that Rosaria Candura was born in Italy, emigrated to the United States in 1918, was married, and had a daughter and three sons. She lost her husband in 1976 and had been depressed and unhappy since that time. Her relationship with her children had markedly deteriorated.

In 1974, she had had an infection in a toe, on her right foot, which became gangrenous. It was discovered at that time that she was diabetic. The toe was amputated. In late 1977, she bruised her right leg while getting onto a bus. The bruise developed into gangrene, which necessitated an operation in November 1977 in which a portion of her right leg was excised. At that time, an arterial bypass was done to decrease the likelihood that gangrene would recur. She had to give up her house, and she went from the hospital to a rehabilitation center, where she remained until April 1978. She then returned to the hospital, and it was found that she had gangrene in the remainder of her foot. Her attending physicians recommended that the leg be amputated without delay. She originally agreed to the amputation of the leg but withdrew her consent on the morning of the scheduled operation. She was discharged on April 21 and went to her daughter's home but returned to the hospital within a few days. Around May 7, responding to the persuasions of a doctor who had known her for many years, she consented to have the operation but then again refused to go through with it. Her daughter, believing that her mother was becoming senile and incompetent to make a reasonable decision, filed for a decision in the probate court, seeking appointment of herself as temporary guardian with the authority to consent to the operation on the behalf of her mother.

This petition was awarded in the probate court, for the judge thought the mother to be incompetent. The patient's sons, however, appealed the decision before the county court of appeals. The court of appeals overturned the probate judge's ruling after finding the patient to be competent despite periods of irrationality. The determination of competency in this demented patient was thus fundamental in the appeals court's analysis. In rendering their decision, the judges noted that the lower court did not adequately establish the fact that the patient was incompetent. In addition, they noted that the probate judge had misinterpreted the facts that had been placed before him.

Now let us turn to a brief discussion of competency in American law. In American common law, an individual is considered competent until determined otherwise by a judicial process. Historically, the assessment of mental competency to stand trial in criminal proceedings has been in the forefront of law and medicine. This area has been the stimulus for the development of the whole subspecialty of forensic psychiatry. During the early decades of this century, psychiatrists began to assume an active role in aiding the courts by serving as consultants and expert witnesses in criminal proceedings, because they were deemed to have the greatest degree of expertise in assessing one's mental state.

The role of the psychiatrist first became formalized in statutory law in this country in 1921 with the enactment of the so-called Brigg's Law of Massachusetts. This law, named after its chief psychiatric advocate Brennan Briggs, was the first statute to establish an automatic pretrial psychiatric examination of certain classes of criminal defendants. It was intended primarily to eliminate the battle of the experts, which even in those early years had become a spectacle of public scorn and professonal uneasiness in criminal trials involving psychiatric issues. By having two psychiatrists appointed by the state department of mental health, it was expected that the examiners would be impartial and that their findings and opinions would be accepted by both sides. However, this has been far from the case, as has been well documented by such leading scholars as William J. Curran, professor of legal medicine at Harvard, and L. D. Friedman, a noted forensic psychiatrist.

On the surface, the association of psychiatry and law would appear to be a natural one. And legal connotations of the phrase *psychological competence* would appear to be similar to psychiatric connotations. However, the semantic implications are not exactly identical, and much confusion has, therefore, frequently arisen.

In the legal sense, when the phrase *psychological competence* is applied to the criminal, it refers to whether the individual demonstrates a degree of mental soundness sufficient to stand trial. Identical criteria are used without regard to the offense. When applied to civil proceedings, civil responsibility is judged in terms of the degree of mental competence appropriate to the particular act in question—such as writing a will, making a contract, refusing medical treatment, or assuming guardianship. Traditionally, the criteria for determining competency have varied with the act. For example, the criteria for determining whether adults are competent to be the guardian of a child are more demanding than the criteria for determining whether they can dispose of their own possessions by making a will. Friedman has noted how difficult the assessment can become in frequent situations where allegations are made of "senile deterioration, chronic psychosis, mental retardation or incapacitating chronic alcoholism." In these diseases, the psychologist has particular difficulty answering two fundamental questions: whether the patient understands the nature of the specific act in question and whether the patient is aware of the duties and obligations connected with the act.

Analysis of the psychiatric testimony in the Candura case provides a poignant example of the potential confusion that can arrive in determinations of competency in brain-damaged individuals. In turn, it highlights the limitations of contemporary forensic psychiatry, especially when carried out from a psychoanalytic perspective. The first psychiatrist stated in his testimony that in his opinion, Mrs. Candura was incompetent to make a rational choice. His views were based on three inferences derived from his examination of her. First, as noted in the appeals court record, he inferred from her unwillingness to discuss the problem with him that she was unable to focus on the problem or to understand that her refusal constituted a choice. Second, he characterized her as suicidal. Third, he felt that there may have been a possibility that her mind was impaired by toxicity caused by her gangrenous condition. Particularly, it is interesting to note that the court of appeals refuted the last inference, because it could not be substantiated by clinical evidence. Relying heavily on these psychiatric observations, the probate judge concluded that

> without necessarily finding the ward to be mentally ill for all purposes, she is incapable of making a rational and competent choice to undergo or reject the proposed surgery to her right leg. In this context at least, her behavior is irrational. The court finds that her confused mental condition resulting from her underlying senility and depression warrants the excise of the jurisdiction of this court.

A second psychiatrist found that the patient was competent despite her forgetfulness and disorientation in time. His examination of her revealed the following reasons for her refusal of the surgery: (1) she had been unhappy since the death of her husband; (2) she did not want to be a burden to her children; (3) she did not believe that the operation would help her, for the first bypass operation had failed to arrest the advance of gangrene; (4) she did not want to live as an invalid or in a nursing home. In testimony, she also indicated that although she ultimately wanted to get well, she felt that this was no longer a realistic possibility. Thus, she did not fear death but welcomed it.

The subjectivity and limitations of the presumed expert psychiatric testimony are strikingly highlighted in the court's investigation into the conflicting testimony. When asked to explain why his opinion differed from that of the first psychiatrist, the second psychiatrist answered, "I think it is just a personal philosophy type of thing where I believe that the person himself ought to be given the benefit of the doubt as to what he or she wants to do with his or her life. Whereas, I suppose, he is protective, I cannot really speak for him, but his general philosophy is different from mine." Likewise, a portion of the first psychiatrist's testimony is of interest. He said, "You know, it really comes down to a philosophical difference. I hope that there is no psychiatric argument in this case. It is the right of the patient to decide if he wants to die. I spend all my life trying to keep people alive, so I take quite a different view.''

Does not such conflicting expert testimony raise questions about the methodology and the theoretical foundation of forensic psychiatry? Does it not generate a professional uneasiness for those of us concerned with interdisciplinary issues in thanatology as they are affected by law and ethics?

We have seen in the preceding account that on the basis of facts attained in the case, two psychiatrists and two courts reached different conclusions regarding Mrs. Candura's mental competency to refuse medical treatment. Although several explanations might be offered for this, the most important one is that the methods of contemporary forensic psychiatry, especially when carried out from a psychoanalytic perspective, are inadequate for collecting clinical data concerning mental functioning in organically impaired patients. Second, the methods of contemporary forensic psychiatry are inadequate for organizing the data into a coherent conceptual framework in order to evaluate the facts subsequently.

The application of recent advances in the clinical subspecialty of behavioral neurology would seem to offer a means of improving the collection and organization of data into a conceptual framework based on clinical phenomena as they occur in nature. In addition, behavioral neurology appears to complement uniquely the Anglo-Saxon common-law notion of competency appropriate to the act in question. Behavioral neurology is that branch of clinical neurology concerned with the analysis of human behavior and intellectual functioning through the discipline of human neuropsychology. Human neuropsychology, in turn, is based on a systematic analysis of disturbances of behavior following alterations of normal brain activity by disease, damage, or experimental modification. In addition to systematic observations of abnormal behavior, neuropsychology offers the possibility of determining cerebral localization of mental functioning, and thus correlates the components of intellectual functioning to specific areas of the brain.

Behavioral neurology attempts to analyze human behavior and intellectual functioning in terms of seven parameters or states: (1) arousal and attention, (2) emotion and the differentiation of mood from affect, (3) language, (4) cognition, (5) memory, (6) praxis and constructional ability, and (7) thought content. Behavioral neurology uses a detailed but flexible battery of bedside and complex neuropsychological tests to determine each of these parameters of mental functioning in a far greater degree than present-day forensic psychiatry does. More important, however, it attempts to interpret the facts in light of its constantly evolving theories of the neurobiological basis of human mental activity and behavior.

In behavioral neurology, there is a constant tension between attempts to localize mental functioning and behavior to specific areas of the brain; this science attempts to understand how these specific functions and behaviors correlate with such localization and how the localizations are integrated and interdependent. For example, behavioral neurology, through its study of disease states, has found that disorders of memory can exist relatively independently of language, praxis, emotion, and cognition. In turn, disorders of memory can exist relatively independently of one another. In Korsakoff's syndrome, for example, immediate recall and remote memory can be intact while recent recall and the ability to learn new information are profoundly impaired. A further example is that the ability to abstract can be preserved in the face of disorders of memory. Mrs. Candura's case of senile dementia illustrates this. Although she was found to be "irascible, disoriented to time, forgetful as to time, and to have a wandering train of thought," the court of appeals noted that she "exhibited a high degree of awareness and of acuity when responding to questions concerning the proposed surgery." Thus, the court of appeals noted, and certainly behavioral neurology would argue—justifiably so—that "senile symptoms in the abstract may of course justify a finding of incompetence, but the inquiry must be more particular." Behavioral neurology thus provides a powerful tool for aiding that particular inquiry for brain damage in demented patients by improving the collection of neuropsychological data and fitting them into a coherent framework of mental functioning based on disease status.

Finally, we turn to one ethical and legal implication of behavioral neurology. The import of behavioral neurology does not lie just with its methodology and theoretical groundwork. Potentially, it has significant implications for our understanding of human nature. In turn, it may have implications for general theories of ethics and for particular issues in medical ethics with respect to demented people and brain-damaged people such as stroke victims and the retarded. Specifically, behavioral neurology has implications for our understanding of the important legal and ethical notions of personhood. Historically, Anglo-Saxon philosophy and law have given man's cognitive capacity an edge over emotional capacity. In this tradition, the emotions have been considered untrustworthy and often animal-like for reasons that distinguish us from other animals on the phylogenetic scale.

However, modern-day neurobiology's understanding of the anatomy, physiology, and methodology of the emotions strongly indicates that man's emotional capacities are unique and not to be equated necessarily with animal instincts. Man's emotions and will should be considered an integral part of what it means to be human and to have personhood.

There exist in clinical neurology specific syndromes that affect the rationality more than the emotional capacity and integrity. Senile dementia prior to the onset of apathy, as exemplified by Mrs. Candura, is one such clinical, pathological entity. In such individuals should not our ethical and legal deliberations give as much recognition of and protection to this aspect of one's personhood? In the compromised individual, should not the avoidance of one's pain and prolonged suffering, organized and controlled by frontal and perhaps right hemispheric functioning, be given as much recognition and perception as rationality? Pascal once wrote, ''The heart has its reasons, which reason does not know.'' Translated into contemporary neuropsychological framework, Pascal's wisdom might read, ''The frontal limbic system has its justifying value, which reason cannot know.''

15

Lung Cancer:
A Challenge and New Hope

RICHARD A. MATTHAY,
DONALD H. MAHLER,
WILLIAM W. MERRILL, DARRYL C. CARTER,
LAWRENCE W. RAYMOND, JACOB LOKE,
and FRANK Y. REYNOLDS

AFTER DISEASES of the heart, lung cancer is the second leading cause of death in adults and is the number-one cancer killer ("Cancer Statistics" 1978). It was estimated that more than 100,000 people would die of this disease in the United States alone (Cohen 1978, Meigs 1977). The incidence of lung cancer in the male population is highest about age 65 and about age 75 in the female population, indicating that this is a disease of the elderly (Chahinian and Chretien 1976). In fact, the mortality rate continues to increase with age. In contrast, lung cancer is rare before the age of 40, those under 40 accounting for approximately 2 percent of all cases (Chahinian and Chretien 1976).

In the last 50 years there has been a steady rise in the incidence of lung cancer, primarily among males ("Cancer Statistics" 1978, Chahinian and Chretien 1976). Unfortunately, there is no evidence that the incidence of carcinoma of the lungs is decreasing; in fact, we face an ever-increasing epidemic of cases (Mittman and Bruderman 1977, Matthay 1978). Furthermore, evidence indicates that correlated with changing patterns of cigarette smoking, the mortality trend for females is beginning to look similar to that of males, with a steep and dramatic recent rise ("Cancer Statistics" 1978, Stoller 1977). Young women, particularly teenagers, are beginning to smoke cigarettes at an earlier age than in the past and are smoking more heavily (United States Department of Health, Education, and Welfare 1977).

Etiologic Factors

The 60 to 90 square meters of respiratory epithelium in human beings are an ideal target for atmospheric pollutants, including carcinogens carried by the 12 cubic meters of ambient air breathed daily by the average person (Matthay 1978). Generally speaking, the risk is proportional to the quantity of tobacco consumed (Chahinian and Chretien 1976, Hoover 1978). With equal tobacco consumption, other factors influencing the risk are inhalation of the smoke, earlier initiation of smoking, speed of combustion, and number of puffs per cigarette (Chahinian and Chretien 1976). Additional agents of proven or suspected carcinogenic risk include asbestos, arsenic, chloromethyl ethers, chromium mustard gas, nickel, and radiation (Chahinian and Chretien 1976, Frank 1978).

Diagnosis and Therapy

Approximately one-half of patients with lung cancer are inoperable when the diagnosis is established because regional or systemic tumor extension has already occurred (Cohen 1978). For the remaining patients, some are found to be technically inoperable at surgery and others are candidates for only a palliative resection. Only 30 to 40 percent of presenting patients, in fact, have a potentially curative resection in which the lesion can be clearly extirpated. Of these latter patients, 25 percent survive five years (Cohen 1978, Meigs 1977, Selawry and Hansen 1973). Thus, the five-year survival for the entire group of lung cancer patients is less than 10 percent (Mittman and

Bruderman 1977). Unfortunately, conventional surgery, radiotherapy, and chemotherapy have not altered these statistics markedly. Since surgery is the only known curative therapeutic modality for significant numbers of patients, the tumor must be detected early while it is still localized in the lung.

Screening for Early Diagnosis

Several studies in this country and in Europe have evaluated the efficacy of chest radiographic screening at four- to five-month intervals in the early detection of bronchogenic carcinoma (Cohen 1978, Nash et al. 1968, Brett 1969, Boucot et al. 1970, Weiss et al. 1973). High-risk individuals (cigarette smokers above age 40) were studied. The results of these studies have been disappointing, with only moderate improvement in survival. In studies reported by Nash et al. (1968) and Brett (1969), only 18 and 15 percent, respectively, of individuals with lung tumors detected by mass chest radiography survived for more than four years. For control patients, less than 10 percent survived five years. A study conducted by the Philadelphia Pulmonary Neoplasm Research Project was not able to confirm even these moderate survival benefits. Of 6,136 men screened, 94 proven cases of bronchogenic carcinoma were found. The overall five-year survival of these patients was only 6 percent (Boucot et al. 1970, Weiss et al. 1973). Only 37 percent of the 94 cancers were resectable at diagnosis, and even in this group the five-year survival rate was only 18 percent.

There are at least two reasons for only the modest survival gain by mass radiographic screening. First, a lesion must generally be about one-half inch in diameter to be seen on chest x-ray (Carbone et al. 1970). Such a tumor is already relatively advanced, representing approximately 30 mitotic divisions or doublings of an initial single tumor cell in a natural history that may encompass approximately 40 doublings (Collins et al. 1956). Second, it is often difficult to detect malignant lesions radiographically (Cohen 1978, Weiss and Boucot 1974). Such lesions may be obscured by preexisting nonmalignant x-ray abnormalities or by normally opaque structures on chest x-ray, including ribs, diaphragm, and heart.

A more promising method of early diagnosis is serial examination of sputum cytology specimens in high-risk individuals (cigarette smokers above age 40) (Cohen 1978, Saccomanno et al. 1974, Erozan and Frost 1974). The basis of this approach is the fact that lung cancer patients shed cells with increasing degrees of cytologic atypia for long periods of time before the diagnosis of bronchogenic carcinoma is established (Saccomanno et al. 1974). Collection of five daily sputum samples is optimal. The detection rate increases from 45 percent with a single specimen to 86 percent for three sputums and to 95 percent when five sputums are evaluated (Erozan and Frost 1974).

A major limitation of this screening method is the prohibitive cost of screening multiple sputum samples. Studies are under way in the United States to evaluate the cost-effectiveness of this approach. Serial examination of sputum cytology appears most useful in detecting epidermoid (squamous cell) and small-cell anaplastic carcinoma, since these cell types generally grow into the bronchial lumen (Cohen 1978). Since small-cell anaplastic carcinoma is generally not considered to be a surgical disease, the main benefit of cytology detection program will be for patients with epidermoid carcinoma.

If a positive sputum cytology is obtained and a chest radiograph does not reveal a lesion, the tumor can usually be localized by fiberoptic bronchoscopy (March et al. 1974, Sanderson et al. 1974, Pearson et al. 1974) and/or tantalum bronchography (Stitik and Proctor 1975). Stitik et al. demonstrated that since mucosal neoplasms interfere with mucociliary clearance, there is delayed clearance of tantalum at the tumor site following bronchography (Stitik and Proctor 1975, Baker et al. 1975). At The Johns Hopkins University four out of five patients with radiologically occult malignancies had their tumors localized by tantalum bronchography (Baker et al. 1975).

Other New Approaches: A Role for Immunotherapy?

Since conventional surgery, radiation therapy, and chemotherapy have all failed to increase survival in lung cancer markedly, improved modalities of treatment for this disease are urgently needed. There are reasons for believing that immunotherapy may have a profound impact on this grim situation (Hersh et al. 1977). First, tumor antigens and tumor immunity have been identified in patients with lung cancer (Hollinshead et al. 1974). Second, in many patients with lung cancer severe immunodeficiency exists (Steward 1973), and patients receiving radiotherapy experience additional and often prolonged compromise of their cellular immune system (Thomas et al. 1971). Immunotherapy offers hope of restoring immunocompetence in lung cancer patients to assist in eradicating tumor.

During the last ten years there have been major advances in immunotherapy both in animal models of malignancy and in human malignant disease. In animals, several types of experimental tumors metastatic to the lung have responded to various immunotherapeutic approaches (Hersh et al. 1977). Finally, during the last few years there have been several positive trials of immunotherapy of lung cancer itself, both after resectional surgery and for metastatic disease (Hersh et al. 1977).

Studies in patients with far-advanced, unresectable lung cancer suggest that systemic immunotherapy with (1) Bacille Calmette Guerin (BCG), an attenuated form of *Mycobacterium bovis* (Villasor 1965; Khadzhiev and Kavaklieva-Dimitrova 1971, Edwards and Whitewell 1974, Yamamura et al. 1976); (2) BCG cell wall skeleton (Yamamura et al. 1976); and (3) *Corynebacterium parvum,* a nonspecific immunotherapeutic agent (Israel and Halpern 1972) is associated with prolonged survival. However, the most promising data have been generated in the area of regional immunotherapy. McKneally and co workers in Albany published positive results of a prospective randomized trial of intrapleural BCG immunotherapy for lung cancer (McKneally et al. 1976: a,b), Following resectional surgery for carcinoma of the lung, McKneally and his colleagues injected 10^7 viable organisms of BCG through the chest tube draining the pleural space. Results after a 36-month median follow-up were as follows: tumor recurrence was noted in fifteen of 35 control subjects and in only three of 30 BCG-treated subjects (personal communication, McKneally). The difference between the two groups is statistically significant ($p < .001$). Presumably BCG, a nonspecific stimulator of both cellular and humoral immunity, is taken up by regional lymphatics and lymph nodes. It is likely that both BCG-activated macrophages and lymphocytes at these sites function as effector cells in tumor destruction (Zwilling and Campolito 1977). BCG was well tolerated with minimal side effects. Most patients developed an influenza-like syndrome with a low-grade fever, which was treated successfully with antipyretics (McKeally et al. 1976a,b). Dissemination of BCG organisms was prevented by Isoniazid therapy for 12 weeks, starting two weeks after BCG injection (McKneally et al. 1976a,b). Unfortunately, these positive results have not been confirmed by other studies, and there is no evidence that patients with advanced unresectable disease benefit from this therapy.

Also, in a preliminary study, Holmes et al. (1977) described the results of preoperative injection of BCG through a fine needle inserted across the chest wall into the lung tumor in nine patients. Four patients developed a small pneumothorax, but none required a chest tube. Four developed mild fever (none above 102° F). At the time of surgery, two to three weeks after BCG injection, the pleural space was free of significant adhesions, and a granulomatous reaction was noted in the injected tumor nodule and regional lymph nodes. All patients remain free of disease after a mean follow-up of five months.

At Yale University School of Medicine, with support by the National Cancer Institute, a study has been conducted to evaluate the efficacy of intratumoral BCG in prolonging survival of lung cancer patients. BCG is injected directly into the tumor via a fine needle inserted through the fiberoptic bronchoscope (Matthay et al. 1982). Previous studies in other cancers have shown that for best results BCG should be administered directly into the tumor or at a site close to the tumor (McKneally et al. 1976a, b; Holmes et al. 1977). For this reason, intratumoral injection of BCG was chosen for the Yale study. To date, 43 patients in this study have received intratumoral BCG through the bronchoscope. The procedure has been well tolerated. All patients developed a fever (average temperature 102.6° F) lasting two to three days, and in most cases a peritumor infiltrate was noted within three days of injection. At resectional surgery two to three weeks later, the lung tumor and tumor-bearing regional lymph nodes were infiltrated with BCG organisms, and a marked lymphocytic and granulomatous reaction was noted. To date, however, there are no data that survival is prolonged.

Summary

Lung cancer remains the major cancer killer in human beings. This disease is most common in individuals over age fifty-five, and the incidence rises progressively with age. Recently, associated with increasing cigarette smoking, there has been a marked rise in cancer of the lung among females, such that now the incidence is similar to that in males.

Although surgery remains the most definitive therapy for this disease, more than 50 percent of patients are unresectable at presentation. The five-year survival in this disease is less than 10 percent, and conventional surgery, radiotherapy, and chemotherapy have failed to alter these statistics markedly.

Recent efforts to improve the outcome in this disease have been directed to early diagnosis and immunotherapy combined with surgery. Attempts to detect lung tumors while they are still resectable—namely, serial chest radiographs and sputum cytology screening—in high-risk individuals are expensive and appear only moderately helpful. A promising therapeutic approach is regional or intratumoral immunotherapy. Presumably immunotherapeutic agents, such as BCG, nonspecifically stimulate the immune system to eradicate tumor burden remaining following surgical resection. However, the single most important need is to decrease cigarette smoking or to make cigarettes free of carcinogenic properties.

References

Baker, R. R., F. P. Stikik, and B. R. Marsh. 1975. "The Clinical Assessment of Selected Patients with Bronchogenic Carcinoma." *Annals of Thoracic Surgery* 20:520–28.

Boucot, K. R., D. A. Cooper, and W. Weiss. 1970. "The Philadelphia Pulmonary Neoplasm Research Project. Survival Factors in Bronchogenic Carcinoma." *Journal of the American Medical Association* 216:2119–23.

Brett, G. Z. 1969. "Earlier Diagnosis and Survival in Lung Cancer." *British Medical Journal* 4:260–62.

"Cancer Statistics." 1978. *Cancer* 28:17–32.

Carbone, P. P., J. K. Frost, A. R. Feinstein, G. A. Higgins, and O. S. Selawry. 1970. "Lung Cancer: Perspectives and Prospects." *Annals of Internal Medicine* 73:1003–24.

Chahinian, A. P. and J. Chretien. 1976. "Present Incidence of Lung Cancer: Epidemiologic Data and Etiologic Factors." In L. Israel and A. P. Chahinian, eds. *Lung Cancer: Natural History, Prognosis and Therapy*, pp. 1–22. New York: Academic Press.

Cohen, M. H. 1978. "Diagnosis, Staging and Therapy." In C. C. Harris, ed. *Pathogenesis and Therapy of Lung Cancer*, pp. 653–700. New York: Marcel Dekker.

Collins, V. P., R. K. Loeffler, and H. Twey. 1956. "Observations on Growth Rates of Human Tumors." *American Journal of Roentgenology* 76:988–1000.

Edwards, F. R. and F. Whitwell. 1974. "Use of BCG as an Immunostimulant in the Surgical Treatment of Carcinoma of the Lung." *Thorax* 29:654–58.

Erozan, Y. S. and J. K. Frost. 1974. "Cytopathologic Diagnosis of Lung Cancer." *Seminal Oncology* 1:191–98.

Frank, A. L. 1978. "Occupational Lung Cancer." In C. C. Harris, ed. *Pathogenesis and Therapy of Lung Cancer*, pp. 25–51. New York: Marcel Dekker.

Hersh, E. M., G. M. Mavligit, and J. U. Gutterman. 1977. "Immunotherapy and Lung Cancer." In M. J. Strauss, ed. *Lung Cancers: Clinical Diagnosis and Treatment*. New York: Grune and Stratton.

Hollinshead, A. C., T. H. M. Stewart, and R. B. Herberman. 1974. "Delayed Hypersensitivity Reactions to Soluble Membrane Antigens of Human Malignant Lung Cells." *Journal of the National Cancer Institute* 52:327–38.

Holmes, E. C., K. P. Ramming, J. Mink, W. F. Coulson, and D. L. Morton. 1977. "New Method of Immunotherapy for Lung Cancer." *Lancet* 2:586–87.

Hoover, R. 1978. "Epidemiology: Tobacco and Geographic Pathology." In C. C. Harris, ed. *Pathogenesis and Therapy of Lung Cancer*. New York: Marcel Dekker.

Israel, L. and G. Halpern. 1972. "Le *Corynebacterium Parvum* dans les Cancers Advances." *Nouvelle Presse de Medicin* 1:19–23.

Khadzhiev, S. and Y. Kavaklieva-Dimitrova. 1971. "Treatment of Bronchial Cancer Patients with a Water Saline Extract of BCG." *Vopr. Onkologie* 17:15–57.

McKneally, M. F. Personal communication.

McKneally, M. F., C. Maver, and H. W. Kansel. 1976a. "Regional Immunotherapy of Lung Cancer with Intrapleural BCG." *Lancet* 1:377–79.

McKneally, M. F., C. Maver, H. W. Kansel, and R. D. Alley. 1976b. "Regional Immunotherapy with Intrapleural BCG for Lung Cancer." *Journal of Thoracic Cardiovascular Surgery* 72:333–38.

Marsh, B. R., J. K. Frost, Y. S. Erozan, and D. Carter. 1974. "Role of Fiberoptic Bronchoscopy in Lung Cancer." *Seminal Oncology* 1:199–203.

Matthay, R. A. 1978. "Editorial—Lung Cancer: Unwanted Equality for Women." *New England Journal of Medicine* 297:886–87.

Matthay, R. A., D. A. Mahler, M. S. Mitchell, et al. 1982. "Intratumoral Immunotherapy with BCG Prior to Surgery for Carcinoma of the Lung." In W. D. Terry and S. A. Rosenberg, eds. *Immunotherapy of Human Cancer*. New York: Excerpta Medica, pp. 69–79.

Meigs, J. W. 1977. "Epidemic Lung Cancer in Women." *Journal of the American Medical Association* 238:1055.

Mittman, C. and I. Bruderman. 1977. "Lung Cancer: To Operate or Not?" *American Review of Respiratory Diseases* 116:477–96.

Nash, F. A., J. M. Morgan, and J. G. Tomkins. 1968. "South London Lung Cancer Study." *British Medical Journal* 2:715–21.

Pearson, F. G., D. W. Thompson, and N.C. Delarue. 1974. "Experience With the Cytologic Detection, Localization and Treatment of Radiographically Undemonstrable Bronchial Carcinoma" *Journal of Thoracic Cardiovascular Surgery* 54:371–82.

Saccomanno, G. V., V. E. Archer, O. Auerbach, R. P. Saunders, and L. M. Brennan. 1974. "Development of Carcinoma of the Lung as Reflected in Exfoliated Cells." *Cancer* 33:256–70.

Sanderson, D. R., R. S. Fontana, L. B. Woolner, P. E. Bernatz, and W. S. Payne. 1974. "Bronchoscopic Localization of Radiographically Occult Lung Cancer." *Chest* 65:608–12.

Selawry, O. S. and H. H. Hansen. 1973. "Lung Cancer." In J. F. Holland and E. Frei III, eds. *Cancer Medicine,* pp. 1473–1518. Philadelphia: Lea and Febiger.

Steward, A. M. 1973. "Tuberculin Reaction in Cancer Patients. 'Mantoux Release' and Lymphosuppressive-Stimulatory Factors." *Journal of the National Cancer Institute* 55:625–32.

Stitik, F. P. and D. F. Proctor. 1975. "Delayed Clearance of Tantalum by Radiologically Occult Lung Cancer." *Annals of Otolaryngology* 84:589–95.

Stoller, P. D. 1977. "Editorial—Lung Cancer: Unwanted Equality for Women." *New England of Medicine* 297:886–87.

Thomas, J. E., P. Coy, H. S. Lewis, and A. Yeun. 1971. "Effect of Therapeutic Irradiation on Lymphocyte Transformation in Lung Cancer." *Cancer* 27:1046–50.

United States Department of Health, Education, and Welfare. 1977. "Human Health and the Environment: Some Research Needs" (DHEW Publication No. NIH 77-1277). Washington, D. C.: National Institute of Environmental Health Sciences.

Villasor, R. 1965. "The Clinical Use of BCG Vaccination in Stimulating Host Resistance to Cancer: Phase II. Immuno-chemotherapy in Advanced Cancer." *Journal of the Philippine Medical Association* 41:619–32.

Weiss, W. and K. R. Boucot. 1974. "The Philadelphia Pulmonary Neoplasm Research Project. Early Roentgenographic Appearance of Bronchogenic Carcinoma." *Archives of Internal Medicine* 134:306–11.

Weiss, W., K. R. Boucot, and D. A. Cooper. 1973. "The Philadelphia Pulmonary

Neoplasm Research Project. Survival Factors in Bronchogenic Carcinoma.'' *Journal of the American Medical Association* 216:2119–23.

Yamamura, Y., I. Azuma, T. Taniyama, K. Sugimura, D. Hirao, R. Tokuzen, M. Okabe, W. Nakahara, D. Yasumoto, and M. Ohta. 1976. "Immunotherapy of Cancer with Cell-wall Skeleton of *Mycobacterium Bovis.*" *Annals of the New York Academy of Sciences* 277:209–27.

Zwilling, B. S. and L. B. Capolito. 1977. "Destruction of Tumor Cells by BCG-Activated Alveolar Macrophages." *Journal of Immunology* 119:838–41.

16

Living Before Death
with Chronic Cancer

WILLIAM A. NELSON, L. HERBERT MAURER,
and PETER Q. HARRIS

*I*T HAS BEEN said frequently and accurately that the word *cancer* causes a feeling of dread and horror in the hearts of all. Why must this word be so terrifying? The answers are multiple and complex, and three seem most common.

First, cancer is viewed as incurable. The diagnosis of cancer for many people is viewed as tantamount to a death sentence. The execution may be prolonged for an extended period, but in the end, "it" will get you. Second, cancer is viewed as a disease that causes extreme pain and suffering, not only to the patients but also to the families. Even the treatment modalities are commonly interpreted as being almost as agonizing as the disease itself. The third factor is that cancer presents an overwhelming threat to an individual's feeling of control. People with cancer believe that there is little they can do on their own behalf once the diagnosis is made. The feeling of hope, which surrounds other diseases, becomes a feeling of hopelessness with cancer. Dr. Cassell (1976:43–44) has emphasized this societal characterization of the disease: *"The Cancer Ward* by Alexander Solzhenitsyn, uses the cancer wing of a Soviet hospital as an allegory for authoritarianism, repression, and exile. The universal concept of cancer in the metaphor makes clear the striking effect of an illness, without hope, in removing man from control of his own life.''

There is little doubt that health professionals are struggling to overcome the first two factors that have contributed to the dread of cancer. The American Cancer Society has attempted to present to the lay public a more realistic understanding of what it means to have cancer. Educational programs strive to diminish the thinking that cancer is noncurable. Major advancements have been made in a number of malignant conditions. Yet fully two-thirds of patients who die of cancer still have to cope with the ongoing nature of the disease and the ultimate reality of death. New treatment modalities developed through individual and cooperative group research studies have indeed given cancer patients increased hope and a longer life expectancy. But not infrequently that longer life is overshadowed by the continued presence of cancer. The disease may be ''controlled'' better by the new technologies, but the patients' feelings of the loss of control over themselves are also prolonged. Living longer with cancer as a chronic illness in the midst of the loss of control creates a greater vulnerability to psychosocial disturbance.

In this paper we describe how promoting the quality of life of cancer patients who suffer from a chronic illness rests on the thesis that the patients' feelings of self-control are paramount. We describe how this is possible, the basis of our work with cancer patients. We believe the feeling of control can and should be facilitated, especially for those patients whose cancer is incurable. Such a feeling is promoted mainly within the framework of a patient-doctor relationship.

Control is a goal in life that all people seek. We desire control over ourselves from our earliest infant state. From our first walk, through tieing a shoe, to going off to school, we strive for mastery and independence over ourselves. We continually strive for control of our lives. The psychoanalyst Erik Erikson (1964:119) has described several basic human qualities. One characteristic he lists is ''will,'' which ''is the unbroken determination to exercise free choice as well as self-restraint.'' To possess free choice along with self-restraint is to struggle for control. It is to decide as a unique individual the nature and course of one's own life.

The world of the cancer patient is a life of decreasing control. Patients feel a surrender to a disease, to an institution, and to a health care team. Preliminary results from a research study comparing coping styles of patients who have suffered their first myocardial infarction and patients with lung cancer indicate a dichotomy in attitude toward their disease. Heart patients seem to respond to their illness in a defiant, challenging manner. They feel that by acting on their own behalf through a change in diet, activity, and work they can affect their disease. Cancer patients appear to be passive, dependent, and submissive as a result of their diagnosis. They feel that they can do little on their own behalf, other than follow the "doctors suggestions." The cancer becomes the controlling element in these patients' lives. Not only does the patients' response to cancer cause the loss of control, but also the physiologically disabling aspects of the specific form of cancer compound the sense of loss. The patients may be impaired to such an extent that they can no longer work and be active. They see themselves as no longer the person they were before the diagnosis of cancer. Their low self-esteem is frequently augmented by the notion that cancer may be contagious or an act of God. Friends and relatives often react to these patients as though they are modern-day lepers.

Closely related to the loss of control to a disease is the feeling that the hospital now is in control. Patients realize that to be treated means to go to a hospital or a physician's office. They feel very small and lost in these institutions with the massive technology, special language, unique style of communication, and complex hierarchy. In large teaching hospitals, patients are unclear about the differences between interns, residents, and oncologists. To patients, a doctor is a doctor and a nurse is a nurse. Their life is placed in the hands of others. In such an institution, the commitment is to the diagnosis and treatment of disease. Within the framework of this medical model, medical treatment refers to cure, which also means relief from suffering, pain, and physical distress. For patients with chronic cancer, this is often impossible. Thus, both the staff and patients are deprived of the "usual" reward in medicine—health—and this thereby further stimulates the patients' sense of isolation. Also, the patients' sense of isolation often stems from the treatment itself. They must go alone to radiation therapy. They must be isolated so that their physical deterioration does not upset others. The patients frequently get their chemotherapy at night when friends and family are away.

The patients may not like this loss of control and isolation, as can be manifested in their depression, anxiety, and anger, but they accept it. The patients are placed in a human and physical environment geared for the treatment of a disease and for the convenience of the health care team. The unique values, life styles, and cultures of the patients are set aside to treat the disease.

While these factors can increase the sense of loss of control, it must be realized that the feeling is propagated by the attitude and style of care provided by the patients' physician. It has been noted that "one aspect of the student's socialization into the physician's role is the understanding that the doctor-patient relationship must be controlled by the physician. Having control over who directs (the physician) and who is subordinate (the patient) is considered beneficial to patient care" (Gerber 1977:75). The physician is trained to exercise control by orchestrating the manner of care. "Patients are told in countless subtle ways that the inconveniences, embarrassments, nudity, menus, routines, and personal questions are normal. They are not to worry; they are to let the staff do its work and all will be well" (Mills 1977:204). Chronic cancer patients realize that all will not be well, but the staff, led by the physician, continues to take away the patients' sense of self-mastery. Even though the sense of self-control is so needed by chronically ill patients, control is rarely shared.

We are not attempting to demean physicians, hospitals, and their staffs. The task of the hospital in providing efficient health care is essential. Our concern is that too limited a view of health care is often applied; we neglect the nonphysical needs of the patient with chronic cancer.

The traditional medical model emphasizes efficient treatment and health. One must question whether this is appropriate for chronically ill cancer patients in whom the primary goal is often to promote quality of life. If the sense of control is an intrinsic desire for all people, then it seems only logical that the removal of such a desire would detract from the patients' quality of living.

While most patients accept the fact that they have cancer and realize that they may eventually die from this disease, they seek to live as they have in the past within their own identity and values. One of the primary goals that must be strived for within the physician-patient relationship is not only to control the disease but also to support the patients' desire to determine their own standards. One may choose many anecdotal experiences to illustrate how this can lead to a successful outcome. For example, we were confronted by an avid horse rider who had breast carcinoma metastatic to the bone. A fall would likely result in her becoming permanently bedridden. Should we forbid the activity? Should we "strongly discourage" the activity? Or should we accept the fact that the ability to ride a horse was such an integral part of this woman's life that the risks (that she was aware of) were truly outweighed?

There are two pertinent points that need to be made about this example. The first point is more obvious in that, making the decision, the physician must weigh both the importance of the woman's desire to ride as a means of enhancing her control and life quality and the potential medical complications. The second point is more subtle and yet very important. The woman must be seen as the one making the decision. It is not a matter of the physician's "allowing" or "forbidding" her to ride. By accepting the use of words like "allow" or "forbid" are we not covertly depriving the patient of a considerable measure of self-control? It seems to be a sad commentary on medicine that such questions are generally raised in terms of what should "we" do.

The patient should decide what she ought to do in a particular situation. That the decision about whether the woman should ride is a medical matter to be decided by a physician is problematic. Similarly, the concept that decisions pertaining to patient care "are medical decisions to be made by one trained in medical science rests on the confusion between technical or scientific questions in the medical context, which one trained in medicine should be able to answer, and ethical or other value questions in the medical context for which in principle they have no special expertise" (Veatch 1976:2). It is the confusion between deciding a patient's diagnosis, treatment options, and prognosis that is based on medical knowledge and assertions about what the patient ought to do with such knowledge.

It is the role of the physician to describe and interpret the technical information necessary for the decision. The physician then can create a discussion pertaining to the information being presented.

During the discussion the physician is not, and cannot be, value free. The discussion is a cooperative and sharing process. Yet throughout it the physician must avoid dominating the deliberation in such a way as to undermine the patients' right to determine their own fate. As Dr. Melvin Krant once stated in a lecture, "Maybe the bravest thing a doctor can say to a patient is, I can't tell you what to do."

We realize that patients do frequently press for the physician's opinion. We feel it is certainly responsible to respond to such questions as long as the patient is afforded a reasonable opportunity to make the final decision. We believe that such a decision-making process is morally appropriate in that it promotes patient autonomy and is therapeutic for promoting life quality.

In our own center we have implemented several programs to deal with the issue of patients' self-control. Patients are permitted considerable freedom of choice when they are hospitalized. Families (including young children) may visit at all times. Spouses or friends may sleep in the room with the patient. Passes are liberally given, and patients are not forced to "stay in pajamas, be in bed and wait." Tests are scheduled around meals and visits rather than through them. Personal preferences with regard to examinations by medical students, favorite nurses, blood drawing, analgesia, and so forth are solicited and accepted. Outpatient visits are scheduled to accommodate rather than inconvenience. A "hostel" has been established in the community where outpatients receiving radiation therapy may stay at low cost near the hospital with their family. Patient and family support groups are available and provide a forum for the exchange of feelings and thoughts in living with cancer. All these procedures tend to reestablish a sense of mastery of one's life. Nurses are also provided group experiences to help them deal with their own feelings of helplessness and thus understand and assist their patients.

We have made several observations about cancer patients that show that the major issue in coping with the disease is not the fear of death but rather how well and how long the patient will be able to live with the presence of continued disease. In studies of two different types of cancer, breast cancer and mycosis fungoides, we found that the patients' sense of control over the cancer contributed to their life quality.

In one research project the psychosocial and functional status of women with breast cancer was studied (Silberfarb et al. 1978). This is a most difficult oncologic disease to manage, for it is a chronic illness with long periods of quiescence followed by rapid exacerbation and disability. It affects 6 percent of women, many of whom are at the most active period of their lives. In addition, for the physician, there are many therapeutic options at each stage in the disease that make it very complex to treat. For the patients, it creates physical disabilities, i.e., loss of important organs. Much has been written about the mastectomy patient and problems immediately thereafter, but little has been recorded about the problem of continuing disease.

As part of a rehabilitation project for the New Hampshire Breast Cancer Network Demonstration Project, 146 patients with breast cancer completed an extensive functional status survey that analyzed levels of physical functioning and problems created by the disease or its treatments, as well as emotional problems. Several important findings have come from this study. First, the time of greatest anxiety, depression, and other severe emotional problems occurs at the first recurrence (where there are still multiple therapeutic options) and not during the postmastectomy period or during the far advanced or preterminal stages of the disease. There was, in addition, no correlation between physical disability, which increased with each stage of the disease, and the level of emotional disturbance.

More importantly, it was at the time of first recurrence that more anger toward health care providers, concern about continued suffering, and a sense of loss of control over the life situation were observed. Apparently, the first recurrence forces patients to realize that they must continue to live with cancer and all the phenomena of the disease that is dominating their life. This reality stimulates the anger/depression.

To further indicate how the issue of control can affect quality of life, we describe the findings from a second study, a psychiatric pilot project on mycosis fungoides. Mycosis fungoides is a rare form of skin cancer usually occurring in the fifth or sixth decade. In the early stages it can usually be well maintained with topical chemotherapy or radiation therapy. In the final, tumor stage, the average life expectancy is reduced to one to three years. We conducted psychiatric evaluations on 20 individuals at varying stages of this disorder. As a group, patients with mycosis fungoides accepted their illness and tolerated their treatment very well despite the complications of weakness, nausea, and vomiting associated with cancer therapy. Most of the patients maintained a high level of functioning at home. We attribute this remarkable degree of quality of life to several factors: the physician-patient relationship, visibility of the disease, and active involvement of the patient in his care.

The physician responsible for the treatment of the patients has an active concern about this particular disease and is excited and enthusiastic about the work. Patients feel that the physician is strongly interested in them and that they have something to offer. The physician takes the time to get to know something about their personal lives, and this reduces their sense of isolation. Although we noted a pattern of depression and anger when the disease progressed to the terminal stage, the earnest effort of the physician's ability to keep fighting without being overly optimistic was well tolerated and appreciated.

The visibility of the illness made a significant difference. It made denial almost impossible. It also provided a patient with clear evidence of the progress of the disease. The patients saw that the chemotherapy or radiation therapy worked and were not bothered by fantasies that the disease was slowly growing somewhere deep inside. The patients knew immediately when they had a relapse, which usually (though not always) resulted in their seeking further treatment. There was little question about whether or not the physician was withholding information about the stage of the disease.

The third factor we identified involves the patients' participation in the treatment. One of the common treatment modalities was twice-a-day self-painting of the entire body with nitrogen mustard. This is a tedious process taking one and a half to four hours per day. Almost all patients were compliant, and most took a certain degree of pride in their task. It became evident that the daily ritual afforded them an opportunity to fight the disease themselves. They obtained considerable satisfaction from applying poison to the tumor cells rather than passively swallow an oral agent. Patients felt strongly that they were acting on their own behalf.

Discussion

The primary goal in cancer management is to cure and then rehabilitate the patient. Frequently this goal is unachievable, but advances in medical technology do allow the patients to live for years despite the presence of cancer. Thus, a secondary goal of palliation is sought when cancer is recurrent or chronic. Together, the patient and physician must establish what gains are to be achieved; that is, pain relief, improvement in performance status, or treatment of potential complications. The expanding life expectancy of these patients makes them more vulnerable to the emotional and physical problems that accompany the chronic illness of cancer. The possibility of these problems can necessitate changes in life-style and hence in their quality of living. We feel that, along with the medical goals, the whole health care team must struggle to promote the patients' quality of life despite the presence of cancer.

A major tactic that should be employed in the promotion of such a goal is to provide patient self-control. While death and dying may be discussed (if the patient so desires), the patients' concerns are more focused on their living and family and how they can regain control over a life that is dominated by one element, cancer. Patients want and need control, not only over body functions such as walking, bladder and bowel elimination, and food intake, but also over their human and physical environment. Simply, patients need to feel in control of their lives. The health care team should be cognizant of these desires and not spend excessive time worrying about whether the patient is going through various "stages of dying." This process will occur naturally, slowly in some instances, rapidly in others, and occasionally not at all. Focus should be on quality of living, which means helping the patient retain control over bodily and emotional functions.

We believe the basic ingredient of a chronic cancer patient's life quality is the maintenance of control over life. Our studies and experience indicate that within the framework of the staff (especially the physician) and patient relationship, patient control can and should be fostered by (1) allowing patients to maintain personal identity and family role functions, (2) promoting patients' ability to act on their own behalf, (3) seeing patients as shared partners in all decision-making, and (4) understanding patients' personal values of self-mastery within the constraints of the disease.

References

Cassell, E. J. 1976. *The Healers' Art*. New York: Lippincott.

Erikson, E. H. 1964. *Insight and Responsibility*. New York: Norton.

Gerber, I. 1977. "The Making of a Physician: The Socialization Process and Medical Care of the Dying Patient." In D. Peretz, N. Lefkowitz, A. H. Kutscher, D. Hammond, N. Huber, and M. Kutscher, eds. *Death and Grief, Selected Readings*. New York: Health Sciences Publishing Corp.

Mills, L. D. 1977. "Issues for Clergy in Care of the Dying and Bereaved." In D. Barton, ed. *Dying and Death*. Baltimore: Williams and Wilkins.

Silberfarb, P., M. D. Maurer, L. Herbert, and C. Crouthamel. 1978. "Psychosocial Aspects of Neoplastic Disease: I. Functional Status of Breast Cancer Patients During Different Treatment Regimens." *American Journal of Psychiatry* 137:4.

17

Mortality Among the Bereaved

DWIGHT N. McNEILL

"So I, too, pined away, so doom befell me, not that the keen-eyed huntress with her shafts had marked me down and shot to kill me; not that illness overtook me—no true illness wasting the body to undo the spirit; only my loneliness for you, Odysseus, for your kind heart and gentle counsel, gentle Odysseus, took my own life away."

—Homer

*I*T HAS LONG been a common theme among writers of prose and poetry that an individual may die from grief. As early as the eighth century B.C., Homer wrote in the *Odyssey* about a woman dying from the grief caused by the loss of her son. "Griefe" was listed as a cause of death in the mortality tables for the city of London in the seventeenth century. These deaths were characterized by rupture of the auricles and ventricles and were attributed to a "broken heart."

During the last 20 years, a relatively small number of investigators have explored the causal connection between bereavement and mortality. This study confirms previous reports (Young, Benjamin, and Wallis 1963; Parkes, Benjamin, and Fitzgerald 1969; Rees and Lutkins 1967) that the risk of dying among conjugally bereaved males is significantly increased during the first six months of bereavement. This is the first study to show that conjugally bereaved females have a significantly increased mortality experience during the second and third six-month periods of bereavement. This study supports previous suggestions in the literature (Kraus and Lilienfeld 1959) that the relative risk of dying during bereavement is inversely related to age. The cause-specific mortality experience of the recently widowed is assessed, as well as the relationship between the cause of death of the deceased spouse and the relative risk of dying among the bereaved.

Materials and Methods

The design was a retrospective cohort study. The cohort was of 9,247 widows and widowers whose spouses died in 1965 and who were less than seventy-three years of age and resident in Connecticut. The widowed had to have been recorded on their spouses' death certificate for inclusion. A state health department file including all deaths between 1965 and 1968 was scanned for the death certificates of the widowed cohort members. A computer was programed to match the death certificate of the widowed spouse with that of the deceased spouse if they matched appropriately on name, sex, and marital status.

There are methodological limitations that underestimate the true number of widows and widowers who died. Incorrect recording of marital status, sex, or name on the death certificate would obscure a match. Also, out-of-state migration and remarriage of the widowed spouses would preclude a match because of an inability to follow each widowed spouse. Because those who were not matched were assumed alive throughout the study, this produced an analysis biased against the hypothesis that there is an increased mortality among the bereaved.

The mortality experience of the widowed cohort was compared with that of the married Connecticut population of the same age and sex. The cohort was stratified into five 10-year age groups, and the annual cause-specific death rates of the married population for each age group were calculated for the years 1965 to 1968.

The underlying cause of death, as defined and recorded on tape by the Connecticut vital statistics department, was used in the analysis. This cause of death was what the physician who signed the certificate considered to be the one that was most important in bringing about the demise of the individual. The categorization of the causes of death and the ICD numbers used in the analysis are presented in table 17.1.

The age of each widow or widower had to be assumed from the age of the deceased spouse, because the cohort members were ascertained from the death certificates of the spouses, and death certificates do not list the age of the decedent's spouse. We assumed that the widows who died, whose ages were recorded on their own

TABLE 17.1. Categorization of Causes of Death and International List Numbers, Seventh Revision

Cause	Code
Infective and parasitic disease	1–138
Malignant neoplasm, including neoplasms of lymphatic and hematopoietic tissues	140–205
Diabetes mellitus	260
Mental, psychoneurotic, and personality disorders	300–326
Vascular lesions affecting central nervous system	330–334
Arteriosclerotic and degenerative heart disease	420–422
Other diseases of the heart and hypertensive heart disease	430–443
Diseases of the arteries	450–456
Influenza, pneumonia, bronchitis	480–502
Cirrhosis of the liver	581
Accidents and suicides	800–962, 970–979

death certificates, were exactly as much younger than their husbands as were the widows who did not die. Similarly, we assumed that the widowers who died were exactly as much older than their wives as were the widowers who did not die. The average age difference between deceased widows and their husbands and between deceased widowers and their wives was found to be three years. We therefore assigned each widow an estimated age of exactly three years less than that recorded for her husband, and each widower an estimated age of exactly three years more than that recorded for his wife.

The significance of the difference between observed and expected number of deaths was assessed by assuming those values follow the Poisson distribution and by then testing to see whether the

observed number of deaths fell within two or more standard devia-
tions of the expected.

Results

Age and the Relative Risk of Dying During Bereavement

In figure 17.1 the incidence of conjugal bereavement (in 1965
in Connecticut) by age group is plotted along with the relative risk of
dying during the high-risk period of bereavement. The incidence of
bereavement tends to increase exponentially with age, whereas the
relative risk of dying during bereavement decreases with age from
seven in the 20 to 29 age group to 0.9 in the 65 to 69 age group. No

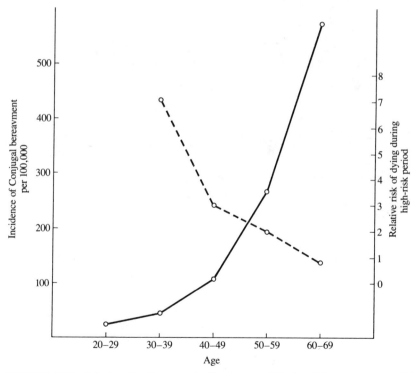

FIGURE 17.1. Relationship Between the Incidence of Conjugal Bereavement (solid
line) and the Relative Risk of Dying (broken line).

other study concerned with mortality among the bereaved has demonstrated this decreasing relative risk with age, although one study indicates the possibility of this trend (Kraus and Lilienfeld 1959).

The High-Risk Period of Increased Mortality: Sex Differences

The risk period of increased mortality during bereavement is distinctly different between the sexes. In figure 17.2 it can be seen

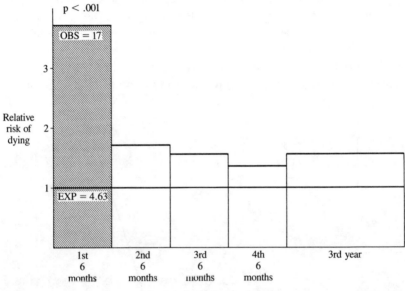

FIGURE 17.2. The Relative Risk of Dying According to the Duration of Widowerhood Among Widowed Males Less than 60 Years of Age.

that the relative risk of dying during the first six months of bereavement is 3.7 greater for males (under 60)—a difference between the observed and expected number significant at the .001 level. Throughout the rest of the study period the relative risk remains greater than one, though the increased mortality does not attain statistical significance. This finding has been replicated in two previous studies (Young et al. 1963; Rees and Lutkins 1967).

It can be seen in figure 17.3 that the risk of dying among recently widowed females is almost twice as high as among married females during the second and third six months of bereavement. The

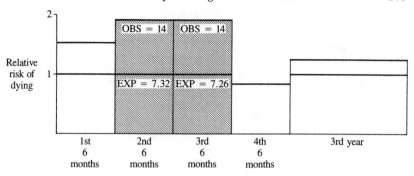

FIGURE 17.3. The Relative Risk of Dying According to the Duration of Widowhood Among Widowed Females Less than 60 Years of Age.

excess mortality during this period is significant at the .001 level. During all other periods of the study the mortality experience of bereaved females is not significantly different from that of married females. This study confirms a previous suggestion in the literature (Cox and Ford 1964) that females have a distinctly different high-risk mortality period than males do.

Cause-Specific Mortality Patterns

The different high-risk periods for bereaved men and women may be attributable to the cause-specific mortality patterns. For bereaved males (see table 17.2) the highest relative risk of dying during the first six months was from "suicide"—a relative risk of 12.1; $p <$

TABLE 17.2. Causes of Death Where the Observed Number Is Greater Than the Expected Number Among *Widowers* Less Than Sixty Years of Age During the First Six Months of Bereavement

Cause	Observed Number	Expected Number	Relative Risk	p Value
Suicide	4	0.33	12.1	.0001
Arteriosclerotic and degenerative heart disease	9	1.93	4.7	.0001
Vascular lesions affecting the central nervous system	1	0.22	4.5	NS*
Other	3	2.15	1.4	NS
Overall	17	4.63	3.7	.0001

*NS = not significant.

.0001. Durkheim (1951) first emphasized the association between widowhood and suicide, and McMahon and Pugh (1965) confirmed the association. The other cause of death significantly increased among bereaved males with a relative risk of 4.7 is "arteriosclerotic and degenerative heart disease." This finding, the "broken heart," was replicated by Parkes et al. (1969).

For bereaved females (table 17.3) a rather different constellation of causes accounts for the excess mortality during the high-risk

TABLE 17.3. Causes of Death Where the Observed Number Is Greater Than the Expected Number Among *Widows* Less Than Sixty Years of Age During Second and Third Six Months of Bereavement

Cause	Observed Number	Expected Number	Relative Risk	p Value
Liver cirrhosis and alcoholism	6	0.93	6.5	.0001
Arteriosclerotic and degenerative heart disease	6	2.59	2.3	.05
Malignant neoplasms	11	5.59	2.0	.05
Suicide	1	0.80	1.2	NS*
Other	4	4.67	0.9	NS
Overall	28	14.58	1.9	.001

*NS = not significant.

period. The highest relative risk was for "liver cirrhosis and alcoholism" (RR = 6.45). Other causes of death showing a significantly elevated mortality were "arteriosclerotic and degenerative heart disease" (RR = 2.3) and "malignant neoplasms" (RR = 2.0). No other studies have investigated the cause-specific death patterns for bereaved females. Bereaved males also show a significantly increased mortality from "liver cirrhosis and alcoholism" during the second year, and bereaved females show a significant excess of deaths from heart disease during the first six months of bereavement.

Relationship Between Cause of Death of Spouse
and Increased Mortality Among the Bereaved

Bereaved males who died during the first six months of bereavement are 5.6 times more likely to have had their wives precede them in death through suicide relative to bereaved males who died after the high-risk period (p < .01). Similarly, bereaved males who die during the high-risk period are 3.3 times more likely to have had wives precede them in death from "vascular lesions affecting central nervous system" (p < .05) and are two times *less* likely to have had wives die from cancer (.05 < p < .1). These data seem to indicate that the suddenness of a spouse's death may modify the mortality risk for the remaining spouse. These data tend to support previous studies (Gerber, Rusalem, Hannon et al. 1975; Clayton et al. 1973) that have indicated that prolonged terminal illness in the spouse may permit the survivor to prepare himself through anticipatory grief.

TABLE 17.4. Causes of Death Among Deceased Female Spouses That Impart a Significantly Higher/Lower Risk of Dying to Bereaved Males During the First Six Months of Widowhood

Causes of Death of Deceased Wife	(1) Widowers Who Died During First 6 Mos.		(2) Widowers Who Died After First 6 Mos.		Ratio	
	No.	%	No.	%	1:2	p-Value
Suicide	4	23.5	48	4.2	5.6	.01
Vascular lesions affecting the central nervous system	4	23.5	83	7.2	3.3	.05
Malignant neoplasms	3	17.6	433	37.9	0.5	.05 < p < .1
All other	6	35.2	564	49.4	0.7	NS*

*NS = not significant.

Discussion

Limitations of the study include the determination of cause of death from death certificates and the approximation of the age of the widowed cohort members. It is plausible that the widowed are more likely to be given less desirable causes of death (such as suicide or liver cirrhosis) than are the married, although no evidence exists to substantiate this. It is also possible, but not very probable, that the widowed who died were systematically older than the widowed who did not die and that this would produce an artificially elevated mortality experience for the assigned age groups. However, the results of this study are very consistent with previous published reports, and it is therefore unlikely that these limitations detracted from the study in any significant way.

One may infer that the excess mortality is due to the deleterious effects of bereavement. The death of one's spouse usually represents the loss of a person's most meaningful source of interaction and support. The ensuing process of grief, which may last from a few weeks to a few years, is an unhealthy state that involves suffering and impairment characterized by loneliness, despair, role confusion, relative poverty, sexual frustration, and alienation (Parkes 1972).

Possible mechanisms whereby mortality is increased among the bereaved include physiologic changes that may increase the vulnerability to disease (Schmale 1973); psychological changes (such as depression) that may lead to suicide; changes in health practices of the survivor, such as a failure to detect and seek help for cancer early; neglect of the management of chronic diseases, such as diabetes and hypertension; and other changes, such as increased alcohol consumption (Jacobs and Ostfeld 1977) and the absence of care that was previously provided by the deceased, who may have been the medically responsible person in the marriage (Shepherd and Barraclough 1974; Jacobs and Ostfeld 1977).

Alternative hypotheses that may explain the increased mortality are homogamy (the "unfit" marry the "unfit") and joint unfavorable environment; however, these probably explain only a small part of the risk (Kraus and Lilienfeld 1959; Jacobs and Ostfeld 1977; McNeill 1973).

Preventive efforts should be directed toward educating clinicians about the mental anguish and high risk of morbidity and mortality among the recently bereaved.

References

Clayton, P. J., J. A. Halikas, W. L. Maurice, and E. Rubins. 1973. "Anticipatory Grief and Widowhood." *British Journal of Psychiatry* 122:47–51.

Cox, P. R. and J. R. Ford. 1964. "The Mortality of Widows Shortly after Widowhood." *Lancet* 1:163.

Durkheim, E. 1951. *Suicide: A Study in Sociology.* New York: The Free Press.

Gerber, I., R. Rusalem, N. Hannon, et al. 1975. "Anticipatory Grief and Aged Widows and Widowers." *Journal of Gerontology* 30:225–29.

Jacobs, S. and A. Ostfeld. 1977. "An Epidemiological Review of the Mortality of Bereavement." *Journal of Psychosomatic Medicine* 39:344–57.

Kraus, A. S. and A. M. Lilienfeld. 1959. "Some Epidemiological Aspects of the High Mortality Rate in the Young Widowed Group." *Journal of Chronic Disease* 10:207–17.

McMahon, B. and T. F. Pugh. 1965. "Suicide in the Widowed." *American Journal of Epidemiology* 81:23–31.

McNeill, D. 1973. "Mortality Among the Widowed in Connecticut, 1965–1968." Masters thesis, Yale University.

Parkes, C. M. 1972. *Bereavement: Studies of Grief in Adult Life.* New York: International Universities Press.

Parkes, C. M., B. Benjamin, and R. G. Fitzgerald. 1969. "Broken Heart: A Statistical Study of Increased Mortality Among Widowers." *British Medical Journal* 1:740.

Rees, W. D. and S. G. Lutkins. 1967. "Mortality of Bereavement." *British Medical Journal* 4:13.

Schmale, A. M. 1973. "Adaptive Role of Depression in Health and Disease." In J. P. Scott and E. Senay, eds. *Separation and Depression: Clinical and Research Aspects.* Washington, D.C.: American Association for the Advancement of Science.

Shepherd, D. and B. M. Barraclough. 1974. "The Aftermath of Suicide." *British Medical Journal* 2:600–3.

Young, M., B. Benjamin, and C. Wallis. 1963. "Mortality of Widowers." *Lancet* 2:454.

18

The Day Hospital Psychiatrist
as *Grief Facilitator*
in *Elderly Veterans*

STANLEY E. SLIVKIN

THE PSYCHIATRIC DAY Hospital of the Boston Veterans Administration Hospital was established in April 1970 to serve as an alternative to inpatient admission. As part of a multifaceted approach to the biopsychosocial problems of the aging veteran population, the Day Hospital psychiatrist has been involved actively in developing innovative roles to facilitate grief work in the elderly veteran. The only limiting factors have been the requirements that the patient should have a caring family member or friend at home to supervise the home-care environment and that he should be able to commute to the Day Hospital.

In my experience the Psychiatric Day Hospital offers a unique opportunity to integrate the levels of medical and psychiatric assessment required to facilitate this grief work. This is especially true since we are a part of the general hospital milieu and we are able to mobilize the suppliers of medical, surgical, social service, nursing, pastoral, and psychiatric support, which are necessary to meet the needs of aging patients and their families. I have pointed out in previous papers (Slivkin 1977a and b) how the availability of multidisciplinary support systems increases the likelihood that the patient, family, and staff will be encouraged to deal realistically with the requirement for necessary grief work in anticipation of the termination of living.

A major force in development of the Day Hospital program has been the realization that the general hospital can foster growth in delivery of psychiatric services to the elderly patient, especially if channels are opened to increase communications between the various professional disciplines. Much new ground has been broken in the dissemination of knowledge so as to coordinate meaningful treatment plans. I have encouraged development of improved consultation and liaison services, ward conferences, hospital workshops, and individual or group supervision of multidisciplinary hospital staff members. The multidisciplinary orientation has been found an integrating factor in planned delivery of services. In the past there has been a cleavage in adequate health-systems care when there is a split between helpers, patients, and families. Successful grief work in the elderly requires a unified, purposeful relationship between these interdigitating systems.

The resistance in the medical delivery system to attempts to break down hierarchical roles is incredible. Each discipline struggles to maintain its "turf." Staff members responsible for the overall treatment of patients tend to resist the obvious benefits of a truly multidisciplinary approach. I have found myself, at times, in a tempestuous struggle with fellow professionals who resist efforts to make them look at the total picture of the patient's physical and mental health. The importance of the nutritional state in maintaining a more nearly adequate life-style for elderly patients is denied, at times, without adequate examination of the totality of the elderly patient's needs. Often a "benign neglect" is visible in the behavior of inadequately sensitized professionals. The Day Hospital psychiatrist in a general hospital setting finds himself in the role of advocate for the elderly patient in a process where consensus is possible only after meaningful communication and negotiation between patient, family, and professional staff. He is also able to mediate in situations where inappropriate countertransference responses of staff interfere with grief work of patients or families.

Throughout all endeavors, it is important for the psychiatrist to maintain an essentially nonthreatening posture so that the needs for psychological support are not denied too massively by patients, families, and professional staff alike. A healthy sense of humor and a capacity to avoid being entangled in the manipulative efforts of all interested parties are of great importance if the therapist is to maintain objectivity and neutrality in a frequently emotionally supercharged atmosphere.

The credibility of the psychiatrist as a caring person is lost easily when he is manipulated by any of the involved groups. To function profitably in the role of thanatologist, the professional requires exquisite sensitivity to the nuances and implications of behavior by all persons involved in the grieving process. Although the psychiatrist is not unique in possessing the qualities of empathy, understanding, and caring, he certainly does possess the potential to play an important role in orchestrating the interdigitating needs of all participants in an important area of human growth.

Case Reports

Case 1: A 73-year-old World War I veteran had been admitted to the medical service for treatment of gastrointestinal bleeding caused by an acute gastric ulcer. He responded well to medical management initially but became gradually withdrawn, suspicious, anorexic, and finally demented over a period of several weeks. His personal hygiene was nonexistent at this point and the difficulties of coping with his behavior became overwhelming to the professional staff. A psychiatric consultation was requested during which I resisted staff pressure to transfer the patient to the inpatient psychiatry service.

I met with the patient's two daughters, the nursing staff, and the patient's attending physicians. It became clear that an inordinate amount of anxiety was being introduced into the treatment system by the patients' two daughters, both of whom had borderline personality organizations. An agreement was negotiated whereby the daughters would talk on a regular basis with me, and I would help them deal with what, at times, was an almost psychotic frenzy of anxiety, demandingness, grief, and depression. They worked through many of their unresolved feelings about the loss of their mother many years earlier and their fears of losing their father.

The father had been placed on moderate doses of thioridazine, and a program of reality-based stimulation was introduced. Nurses were encouraged to repetitively tell him the date, time, and weather and to talk about his daughters and their need for him to be well. The patient was seated in a Barcalounger chair in front of a television set during periods when the nursing staff was busy elsewhere. In about 48 hours, the patient was in contact again, and was able to discuss with me his wish to "fade away into nothingness and to die in peace." He was angry that he was improving both physically and psychiatrically, since that meant he would be "torn apart" by the struggle of each daughter to control his life. It became clear that the oedipal and sibling rivalrous struggles of his daughters were behind the development of his gastric ulcer and his later dementia.

Since the patient's hospital discharge, he and his daughter have maintained Day Hospital follow-up. His daughters are less rivalrous and more supportive of him in his efforts to live a more reasonable life. The patient himself has become reinvolved in his previous profession as a dealer in rare books.

Case 2: A 69-year-old World War II veteran was seen in psychiatric consultation by me on the medical service because of psychotic depression secondary to pulmonary malignancy with metastasis to the brain. The patient had lost considerable weight over a period of several months, primarily because of his refusal to eat. Total parenteral nutrition had been considered by professional staff, but the patient's family objected strenuously to efforts to maintain life because of the poor prognosis. However, the patient's family became disturbed sufficiently over his psychotic depression and anxorexia to be willing to meet with me and other professional staff. I was informal chairman at a meeting during which family and treating staff discussed their feelings of helplessness in coping with the disturbing turn of events. It became clear that the family was now willing to cooperate in supporting any treatment plan that might restore even limited function in the patient so as to be able to deal more effectively with their grief.

The patient was transferred to the inpatient psychiatry service, where a brief series of four electroconvulsive treatments was given at my recommendation. The patient responded well, began to eat once again, and was discharged to the care of his family. The patient's wife and children made a number of visits to see me in the Day Hospital during his final days and were able to deal successfully with his death.

Case 3: A hypertensive cardiac 70-year-old veteran sustained a "blackout" while driving his wife home. The resulting loss of control over his automobile caused a crash into a tree. As a result of this accident, his wife was killed instantly. These events overwhelmed him emotionally and he developed a severe depression with a recurrent wish for suicide. No amount of medical explanation that the accident was the result of events beyond his control would ease his guilt.

This aging patient was admitted to the Psychiatric Day Hospital as an alternative to inpatient admission because it was feared that he might give up completely if some independence could not be maintained. He wept constantly in groups sessions, raged at younger patients who did not seem to be sympathetic enough, and improved steadily. Despite his expressed feelings that he should be punished for his dereliction, he was gradually able to deal with the meanings of his loss and his excessive guilt about survival. He has found many advocates among the Day Hospital population and has permitted himself to become closer to his children. Following the accident, he had withdrawn from his children as part of his self-inflicted punishment. Active involvement in a caring outpatient environment resolved his crisis.

Discussion

Marmor (1974:xii) has postulated the importance of the dynamic interactions in which every person is enmeshed from birth, both with the environment and with other people, all of whose inner processes have been shaped and altered by their own interactions with a wide variety of systems. Nowhere is this dynamic process more evident than in the intricacies and shadings of feelings related to loss or grief. There is clearly a multiple-system involvement whenever serious loss is threatened—including patient, family, and a plethora of multidisciplinary helpers. The major stumbling block to successful grieving appears to be a lack of clear communication among the multiple systems and of joint acceptable decision making by all participants in the thanatology process. It is in this area of relatedness that the Day Hospital psychiatrist in a general hospital setting can perform yeoman service. The psychiatrist's skills and role as constant object often turn dysphoria in any component system into a successful intervention. Krant (1975) has noted the difficulty grieving individuals manifest in seeing themselves as psychiatrically disturbed and their hesitation in acknowledging the need for help in dealing with the process of grieving.

Sampson (1977) has pointed out that events surrounding death can be enriching and rewarding if the dying person can be relieved of fear and can be in familiar surroundings and if the people who are close are not deprived of doing all that they can. Feelings of helplessness in family and staff are translated quickly into evidence of hopelessness, whatever the realities may be. Verbal or nonverbal communication of these feelings by family members or helpers leads patients to withdraw from cooperation with efforts to maintain meaningful relatedness. This withdrawal from interaction with significant family members and professional staff leads to severe interpersonal problems and important communication breakdowns.

Abrams (1966) has described in considerable detail the difficulties inherent in maintaining important communication outlets between the cancer patient and significant others. Poorly developed systems of sharing feelings lead to wide separation in any grief process. Saunders (1973) has noted the wide gulf that develops between patient and family because of unshared knowledge and the immense sense of relief when improved sharing occurs. This need for sharing affects the entire community involved in the system described as the hospital milieu. Miller (1971) has described the importance of recognizing that therapeutic decisions affecting patients are never made in a vacuum. All manners of helpers are involved in implementation of such decisions—physicians, nurses, social workers, chaplains, dietitians, and housekeeping personnel. For many years, when a commonsense explanation was not available to detect what was going on with a particular patient, I have queried housekeeping personnel. When all other staff members are too involved to know what is troubling a patient, it is refreshing to know that the person to whom the patient relates at a comfortable level is the person no one asks for information—the person who cleans the patient's room. Many a seriously ill patient has received the greatest comfort from such resource people, who are not always seen as such by the "trained professional."

I have noted with considerable interest what appears to be a shift in emphasis from the youth cult to the more pressing concerns about older citizens in this country. In part, these concerns appear to be related to such widely politicized problems as the fears of bankruptcy of the social security and welfare systems because of increasing longevity. In my opinion, such fears can only support constructive reexamination of our attitudes about aging, illness, and the destructive physical and emotional effects of unresolved grief. Evidence that this constructive reexamination is taking place is manifested by the increasing numbers of professionals who have become interested in the broader issues of the aging process, including degenerative illness and death. However, these developments are somewhat threatening to those professionals who have not dealt resolutely with their own feelings about personal aging and eventual death. Those among us who cannot contemplate our own mortality find it extremely difficult to deal with any patient's feelings about impending separation from everything of value to the individual person. How can professionals deal both intellectually and emotionally in a mature manner with feelings in a patient when they cannot tolerate those feelings in themselves? It seems clear that what is indicated is more education in this area rather than less. In my dealings with professionals in other specialized areas of medicine, I am troubled most often by their continuing need to deny suffering, grieving, and dying. It seems to bear out the contention that many seek expertise as a mechanism to help them cope better with their own anxieties related to sickness and death.

Conclusions

It has been my experience that the Day Hospital psychiatrist in a general hospital setting has a unique role as facilitator of grief work in the elderly patient. The psychiatrist is admirably suited to play the role of coordinator of patient, family, medical, surgical, psychiatric, social service, nursing, pastoral, and dietetic efforts to sustain interest in preserving meaningful life for the elderly patient. Grief and loss are major disturbers of psychological homeostasis, but coordinated efforts by all interested parties offer an opportunity for patients and significant others to take their leave with enhanced dignity and empathy in a difficult situation.

Shneidman (1975) has stated that "for the survivor or spectator the death of another person is an event. He lives through that event with emotions ranging from joy and equanimity to anguish and grief.'' The psychiatrist can facilitate the grief work of survivors by helping them to feel less guilty about their relationships with significant others whom they lose. Not only is psychological support essentialy to the aging and potentially terminal patient, but also it must be extended to survivors for as long as required. Prophylactic intervention with survivors may obviate pathological mourning or psychosomatic illness based on pathological identification with the deceased. In my Day Hospital work, I encourage survivors to maintain a support relationship with staff members. This type of support is especially helpful through the first anniversary of the death of significant family members. In my experience those survivors who have mourned successfully rarely need support beyond the first anniversary, although some need brief reassurance at the significant anniversary time for a number of years.

Finally, I would like to comment briefly about case 2. Many professionals tend to avoid looking at the quality of the life remaining to an obviously terminal patient. In this case there were those who might have been content to allow the patient to remain psychotically depressed, anorectic, and uninvolved. However, because of the emotional pain his situation caused to family and staff, a reasonable decision could be made by all parties concerned to use brief electroconvulsive therapy and thereby help the patient to become available for successful grief work once again. His return to participatory living allowed the working through of grief, which he clearly had not been able to tolerate previously. It led to a second chance to work through the unthinkable for a very ill patient, and his family was grateful for the openness of the discussions preceding the decision to employ electroconvulsive treatment, and they appreciated being privy to all communications. This was another case where open lines of communication permitted the successful mourning of a loved one.

References

Abrams, R. D. 1966. "The Patient With Cancer: His Changing Pattern of Communication." *New England Journal of Medicine* 274:317–22.

Krant, M. J. 1975. "A Death in the Family." *Journal of the American Medical Association* 231(2):195–96.

Marmor, J. 1974. *Psychiatry in Transition*. New York: Brunner/Mazel, p. xii.

Miller, M. B. 1971. "Decision-making for the Death Process of the Ill Aged." *Geriatrics* (May) 26:105–16.

Sampson, W. I. 1977. "Dying at Home." *Journal of the American Medical Association* 238(22):2405–6.

Saunders, C. 1973. "A Death in the Family: A Professional View." *British Medical Journal* (January) 1:30.

Shneidman, E. S. 1975. "On the Deaths of Man." *Hospital Physician* (June) 28–31.

Slivkin, S. E. 1977a. "Death and Living: A Family Therapy Approach." *American Journal of Psychoanalysis* 37:317–23.

—— 1977b. "Psychiatric Day Hospital Treatment of Terminally Ill Patients." *International Journal of Psychiatry in Medicine* 7(2):123–31.

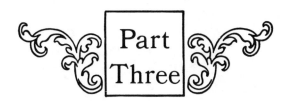

Ecological Issues
in Geriatric Care

19

The Elderly and the Ecology of Death: Issues of Time and Space

CAREL B. GERMAIN

"You would know the secret of death.
But how shall you find it unless you
seek it in the heart of life?"
—Kahlil Gibran

*D*EATH, LIKE LIFE itself, is an ecological process involving the interaction of biological, social, cultural, psychological, temporal, and spatial forces. Ecology is the study of the relations of organisms and environments within a view of the organism and its environment as interdependent, complementary parts of a unitary system. Each can be understood only in relation to the other, and each shapes the other in continuous reciprocal processes of adaptation. Ecology is a useful metaphor for the helping professions because it raises the social and physical environments to the foreground of attention, along with the more customary focus on the person. An ecological metaphor leads us to examine what the environment must furnish for optimal human development and functioning over the life cycle, including the personal and social tasks of aging and of death as part of life.

Adaptation

The central concept in ecology is adaptation: the cultural, social, psychological, and biological processes by which human beings change themselves to conform to environmental pressures and demands or change the environment so that it is more responsive to human needs and aspirations. Born with complex DNA coded in the genes, each individual has the potential for many different lives. Each realizes individual potentialities only as they are released by the particular environmental circumstances, involving some degree of free choice in the selection of environments (Dubos 1974, Dobzhansky 1976). Many segments of the population, however, live in environmental circumstances that stifle the potential, inhibit optimal functioning, and provide little or no freedom of choice. These include the poor and many aged persons.

Even in the best of circumstances, any inherent harmony between people and their environments must be disclaimed. Environments are constantly changing, and people's needs and goals are constantly changing. While people and environments, in general, strive toward an adaptive balance that is good for both, people sometimes damage environments and environments sometimes fail to provide the needed resources. Thus life being what it is, the adaptive interchanges between people and environments are marked by periods of stress. Some stress is zestful and sought after, some is manageable within the usual adaptational processes of the person, and some is unmanageable, being perceived as beyond one's adaptive limits or usual coping capacities. What is perceived and experienced as difficult and unmanageable stress varies with age, sex, genetic endowment, previous experience, cultural norms, vulnerability to particular kinds of stress, and the state of the person.

The stress of terminal illness in the aged person poses adaptive tasks pertaining to internal biological changes, psychological pain or fears, and external forces within the social and physical environments. The latter may include, for example, changes in physical setting, emotional withdrawal of staff or family members, and difficult medical procedures.

Coping refers to the capacities and skills that people use to eliminate stress, or to reduce it, or to mitigate its impact. These include motivation; problem-solving skills of planning, judgment, and anticipation; securing and using information about the nature of the stress and the coping tasks; a degree of self-esteem and self-confidence; and sufficient defense against anxiety and depression or other threatening affects that problem solving can proceed (Mechanic 1974, White 1974). Successful coping leads to the mastery of the stress or at least to its reduction. Less successful coping results in the persistence or even the increase of stress.

Successful adaptation throughout life draws upon and contributes to the sense of identity and self-worth; the sense of cognitive, emotional, and social competence in the cultural and historical contexts of one's environment; a sense of inner freedom (self-regulation) that permits relative autonomy from both internal and external demands; and the sense of human relatedness—the capacity to care for and be cared for, to be appropriately dependent or independent as situations require (Germain 1979). Whether these adaptive achievements appear and flourish depends in large measure upon environmental circumstances. Whether they are sustained through the massive stress posed by terminal illness and death is, in part, a function of the social and physical environment of family, health care organization, and community. They are important attributes for successful coping.

Professional practitioners tend to focus primarily on coping behavior and to overlook its environmental context. The problem-solving skills referred to above depend on adequate preparation by society's institutions of the family, school, hospital, and so on. Yet none of the institutions of our society has prepared people for the coping tasks involved in dying or in bereavement. The culturally acceptable solution to the stress evoked by death has traditionally been the use of denial and social isolation. Certainly the present cohorts of elderly have had no training for skills in coping with death and bereavement. One can assume that the courses on death and dying now appearing in high school and college curricula may change this; they may represent an important form of primary prevention in health and mental health.

Attention is not often given to the institutional or even the family environment in regard to whether coping efforts are rewarded so that the elderly person is motivated to continue active adaptive and coping efforts instead of sliding into a state of helplessness and hope-lessness. Some institutions find it easier to dampen the patient's ef-forts to secure information, maintain some degree of control, and participate in planning by staff indifference, forced inactivity, and reliance on medication. Kalish (1968) refers to the category of self-perceived social death, where the elderly person feels he is as ''good as dead'' and ''may as well be dead.'' Such a self-perception may be precipitated by a terminal diagnosis, or by feelings of isolation and helplessness, or by anxiety over increasing dependence. The aged person's loss of statuses and roles, the many personal losses, and the indignities suffered all affect the motivation to cope with the stress of illness and death and may well provoke feelings of being ''better off dead.'' This kind of social death may be reversible with appro-priate nutriments from the environment, such as increased human in-teraction, cognitive stimulation, and opportunities to function as a mature and responsible adult in whatever ways are still possible: se-curing information; making decisions, however modest in extent; par-ticipating in planning; and so on.

Successful coping requires minimal control of depression and anxiety and some maintenance of self-esteem. For many dying el-derly, the social supports that play an important part in psychic com-fort are missing because of the loss of close attachments, loneliness and social isolation, and the lack of statuses and roles that integrate one into a social structure. Thus the patient may slip into depression and despair, become extremely anxious or agitated, or withdraw into pseudo-senility or other maladaptive states. Kalish (1968) describes a category of psychological death in which the comatose, completely drugged, or senile patient is no longer aware that he *is*. Even such extreme states as these may sometimes be reversible through sensory stimulation, increased human interaction, and reinstitution of aspects of the adult role.

Since social death and psychological death are, in varying degrees according to the individual, reversible, practitioners working with the aged need to become aware of how to achieve reversal or, better still, prevention of the condition in the first place. Such a statement implic-itly assumes that time and personnel are available, and that the elderly and the terminally ill still deserve to utilize as completely as possible the life still available to them (Kalish 1968).

And finally, adaptation and successful coping depend on adequate time and space—literally and figuratively—for the exercise of self-regulation and the development of adequate coping maneuvers. Yet the social structure of family, community, or institution may not provide freedom of time and space required by the dying elderly person for the adaptive tasks and may not be able to provide for choice among such options as disengagement versus interaction. Human beings present a wide range of diversity, and to support their adaptive potential requires a matching environmental diversity, particularly in the areas of time and space and free choice.

Time

Auerswald (1971) has described ecology as the study of life and death over time and space. While he does not delineate this interesting statement further, one may assume he is referring to the development of the human species over evolutionary time and across the space known as the average expectable environment of the hunter-gatherers of the Stone Age. Such evolutionary development occurred as processes of genetic mutation and environmental selection increased the "fit" between the human species and their environmental niche. Organic evolution of human beings ceased for the most part when cranial and brain development, language structures, and symbolization made possible a new and more rapid form of social evolution that largely replaced organic evolution.

But life and death at the individual level are also played out over time and space. In the examination of aging, biological features are often given primacy, including sensory decline, diminished strength and vigor, and, perhaps, chronic illness or disability. Major attention is given to social features, including the impact of the loss of work and family roles, shrinkages in the social network, reduced income, poor housing, and the bureaucratized impersonality of services and institutions. Cultural factors are carefully noted, including stereotyped negative images of the elderly and the value placed on youth, productivity, achievement, and attractiveness. Psychological features receiving attention include cognition and memory, personality characteristics, and attitudes toward self and others and toward the aging process. In comparison to the interest in these factors, relatively little attention is paid to issues of time and space. Still, some suggestive materials are now available.

Attitudes toward time and the use of temporal resources are affected by previous life experience, physical and psychological states, and cultural orientations (Germain 1976). Despite individual diversity, however, it seems clear that time is as significant a feature of the life space for the elderly as it is for those at other points in the life cycle. Indeed, it may also have a special meaning for the elderly since it has long been connected to issues of change and permanence, creativity and final limits, and beginnings and endings.

It is believed that the elderly experience time's passage as speeding up, and this is said to be due to lowered metabolic rates and the slowed oxygen consumption by the brain as the years advance. On the other hand, some elderly persons experience time as hanging heavily over them as a pall. These are persons whose time is empty of meaningful or valued activity and who are often described by others as sitting in place and waiting to die. So one must say there is a qualitative experience of time's passage. In general, it is believed that the elderly shift their temporal orientation quantitatively from "time already lived" to "time left to live." In doing so, they relinquish a former emphasis on future time, so characteristic of the wider culture, in favor of the present and relish each day for itself. Some may also find a new pleasure in past time through reminiscence and life review (Butler 1964). Less adaptively, others may turn to the past in order to ward off the unpleasantness of the present or the fears of the future. In so doing, they become less related to the environment and lose the capacity for autonomy, and then the sense of identity, the sense of competence, and the quality of human relatedness are diminished as well.

For some, social time may become difficult as the schedules of family or institutional life or of bureaucratized services do not mesh with biological rhythms, previous temporal habits, or culturally patterned responses to time. The preferred tempo of events may change as biological rhythms slow down. Many elderly persons are very sensitive to even slight changes in schedules and temporal routines and are impatient of delay, waiting, and postponement. Waiting is justifiably regarded by many people, and not only the elderly, as a reflection of their devalued status. In extreme situations of bland environments that offer little sensory/perceptual stimulation, elderly residents may become disoriented temporally with respect to the year, month, and day.

Much can be done by family and staff members to avoid delay or postponement in planning and action and unnecessary changes in routines and schedules. Where possible, giving the terminal elderly some sense of control over temporal arrangements restores the sense of autonomy and competence instead of undermining it. Such patients can be helped to sustain or regain an orientation to time through the presence of clocks, calendars, and the staff's or family's explicit references to time of day, week, month, and year in their social interchanges. Temporal structuring of the home or institutional situation and careful scheduling in which the elderly person participates to the degree possible may also reawaken motivation and coping efforts. Help in organizing time and in pacing activities can improve and support the sense of competence.

For the dying elderly, time is running out. Death of an elderly person is on schedule in the life cycle and more expectable than shocking as in the case of a young person's dying. Yet for the elderly person or the family, the pain of loss may be intense, and perhaps more so in Western than in Eastern societies. In the traditional cultures of India and China, time was cyclical and all things returned in their proper time. One's present life was the consequence of how one had lived one's past life, and it was but a stage of preparation for the next life. The cycles continued until Nirvana was reached. In Western thought, both secular and religious, time is linear and unidirectional (Germain and Gitterman 1979). For some the religious belief in the immortality of the soul is comforting in the face of death or bereavement. For those who do not hold this belief, the adaptive task is to deal with the notion of the ending of time—the total extinction of the self. This is a difficult task on many levels, but especially since it is all but impossible for the present perceiving self to imagine the nothingness of the ultimately nonperceiving clay. Many may have a wistful wish to know "how history is all going to turn out," yet find solace in an evolutionary view that they have participated in the cosmic rhythm of life, which continues although individual manifestations terminate. For most terminally ill elderly, the acceptance of the ending of time may be a somewhat lighter task if one has led a life of some satisfaction. The task may be onerous for those who look back upon an unhappy or a disappointing past with anger or regret. Three general types of responses to the task of facing the time left to live have been specified by Peak (1977).

1. Most elderly persons face the prospect of death and handle it by active means within their capacity. They accept dying as part of being old and as part of life itself. Their mastery of its threat implies that they feel in control of their situation, based on a minimal amount of denial. Most have worked out the acceptance of time's ending long before the terminal phase, and many have made plans for their death or are ready to do so. The extent of such preparation apparently increases with education, although it is greater among whites than blacks regardless of education (Lipman and Marden 1966). Sufficient resources, including education, may make possible this kind of anticipatory socialization to the final stage of life and its associated tasks.
2. A small group of elderly persons appear to block out the idea of death completely. This prevents their making the plans and preparations that might lead to a sense of closure and peace. When such excessive denial is extended to serious illness or disability as well, there is danger that death may be hastened.
3. A still smaller group comprises those elderly who are greatly disturbed by ideas of death—their own or the death of those close to them. They spend time and energy avoiding the associated fears. Some may become preoccupied with their own body functions and state of health and may turn away from the environment.

Such inward perceptions close off the nutritive interchange needed to maintain the sense of identity, competence, autonomy, and relatedness. Some may "give up," becoming the helpless and hopeless group described earlier in the phenomena of social or psychological death. Others may surrender through suicide. Persons over sixty-five contribute a disproportionate share of the nation's suicides (25 percent), and most suicides among the elderly appear to take place in the context of serious illness (Bock 1972).

While these are ideal types, which do not describe any individual aged person who is dying, they are suggestive of helpful approaches. Not all are afraid to die, and many can be helped to express their feelings and questions and to make their plans. Many seek information about the nature and extent of the final illness and what to expect and are much more fearful of dying alone or in pain. The practitioner who is in tune with his own feelings, as well as those of the patient, can help the patient deal with the information and to feel involved and in control appropriate to the patient's capacity and interest. As death approaches, helping the patient to reduce activity, to decrease interaction with the important friends or family, and to disengage is important. "The feeling that there is a plan of treatment carried out by those who care for them, in itself, will produce comfort and knowledge that they will be cared for when the time comes" (Peak 1977).

Some elderly individuals may be anxious in the terminal phase not so much because of the imminence of death itself but because of unwelcome changes in their social or physical evironments. Changes in spatial location against their wish are dangerous to the health and well-being of the institutionalized elderly, whether the change is within the institution itself or from institution to institution. Such spatial issues force new adaptive tasks on the elderly that may be beyond their limits. Where such moves are necessary, residents should be included in all stages of planning for the new facility and the arrangements in moving, with ample support following upon the move.

Space

Social and physical space are as critical as the temporal factors in the ecology of death. Not only the stability of location but also the particular ecological qualities must be considered. Like time, space has received minimal attention from practitioners and program developers. It has, however, been the object of research among the environmental psychologists, and interesting findings are available (Germain 1978).

Social interaction among residents and between residents and staff depends in large measure on the arrangement of space and of the furniture within it. Chairs placed in a row against a wall is an arrangement that is likely to discourage interaction. Conversational groupings of chairs around small tables invite interaction (Sommer 1970).

Human beings, like many other forms of life, arrange themselves spatially with respect to intimate, personal, social, and public zones of distance. The size of each zone depends largely on culture, although the size is also mediated by age, sex, experience, the particular situation, and the particular persons within the situation (Hall 1969). With sensory decline, the elderly person's zone of personal distance appears to contract and even to fuse with the intimate zone (DeLong 1970). This is because visual, olfactory, tactile, and auditory cues important to communication are now received less clearly. In general, younger persons such as staff in geriatric institutions and in hospitals have larger zones of personal distance. They therefore tend to regard the spatial behavior of the elderly as intrusive, as transgressing into the zone of intimacy. Thus they may seek to hold the elderly person at arm's length, to pull back from him or her literally and figuratively. Such behavior is interpreted by the elderly as coldness and impersonality.

Voice loudness is also a characteristic of spatial distance. Within the intimate zone, most American adults whisper. In transactions with the elderly whose hearing may be impaired and who use the intimate zone for the personal zone, the use of loudness alters the context. The message is changed either to "anger" or to speaking to someone who does not comprehend clearly. This results in a shift in linguistic style involving syntax, vocabulary, and tone to one more typically used when speaking to a small child. DeLong (1970) suggests that this shift leads the speaker to conclude that the elderly are childlike and to treat them as if they are children. Such distortions in communicating with the elderly are not conscious or purposive. They are patterned spatial behaviors that occur outside awareness. These notions suggest that the staff be given knowledge about the spatial zones of the elderly and how these differ from their own in order to increase their understanding and tolerance of the elderly person's behavior. DeLong suggests that the staff selection might consider the differing cultural groups whose zones of personal distance are more similar to those of the aged and who rely on greater sensory involvement in interpersonal relations.

Such findings also suggest the need for a much higher level of sensory input in the physical environment if the elderly are to function at an optimal level. Environments must be diverse with respect to providing visual, auditory, tactile, olfactory, thermal, and kinetic stimulation, as landmarks for orientation and as nutriment for the sensory/perceptual apparatus needed to maintain autonomy, identity, competence, and relatedness. Also because of high levels of sensory involvement in their interpersonal transactions and their need for tactile involvement with the environment, many elderly persons tend to dislike large, empty spaces. They prefer space that younger family members or staff members perceive as cluttered with objects or people. For the elderly, cluttered space provides a sense of closeness by reducing the distance between objects to arm's length.

This matter of objects is also important. From the transitional objects of infancy to the treasured objects of adulthood, objects can be important parts of one's sense of identity. Their loss can be a source of stress, even of grief. This is just as true at the final stage of life. Yi-Fu Tuan (1977:187–88) writes,

> Objects anchor time. They need not, of course, be personal possessions. We can try to reconstruct our past with brief visits to our old neighborhood and the birthplaces of our parents. We can also recapture our personal history by maintaining contact with people who have known us when we were young. Personal possessions are perhaps more important for old people. They are too weary to define their sense of self by projects and action; their social world shrinks and with it the opportunities to proclaim fair deeds; and they may be too fragile to visit places that hold for them fond memories. Personal possessions— old letters and the family settee—remain as accessible comforts, the flavor of times past hovering about them.

How important, then, that the aged person facing death have the comfort of treasured objects at arm's length.

Many elderly persons commonly fear nursing homes and other geriatric facilities out of recognition that this may be the last nonhospital home they will have and that they are, indeed, entering the place where they will die (Kalish 1968). Programmatically, the growing emphasis on home health care offers the hope that the place to die is becoming as important to consider as the time to die. The natural life processes of birth and dying seem increasingly to be regarded as once again functions of the family rather than of the hospital or of the hospital alone. In order for the terminally ill elderly to be able to die at home—if this is their wish and the wish of their family—home health care and respite for family members must be further developed. Still another place to die is the hospice, designed to provide comprehensive services to the dying person and to the family, including extensive home care. Wherever the space to die is located, and whenever the time to die is upon one, the greatest comfort of all may be to not die alone. "Death itself is a human experience of relatedness, its interpersonal quality often being distorted as greatly by the withdrawal of the living as of the dying" (Will 1959).

Summary

Humanizing death so that the final adaptive tasks are achieved has received increasing attention in the literature and among practitioners. Emphasis is placed on communication between patient and family, patient and staff, and family and staff and on mobilizing and sustaining natural support systems for all three. This paper has been concerned, in particular, with protection of the adult role of the dying elderly to the greatest degree possible. This includes sustaining their involvement and participation—in human interaction, in planning and decision-making, and in physical and mental activity—consonant with capacity, interest, and cultural orientation. If what is done with and for the dying elderly person reawakens or sustains the sense of identity and self-worth, competence, autonomy (self-regulation), and human relatedness, then the reciprocal adaptive tasks of patient, family, and staff may be more readily achieved. The elderly person's ability to cope with these tasks is not a function of personal strength alone. It depends, also, on the diversity of the family or institutional environment, on the opportunities for choice and action, on the comfort and support provided, and on the structuring of time and space.

References

Auerswald, E. H. 1971. "Families, Change, and the Ecological Perspective." *Family Process* (September) 10(3):263–80.

Bock, E. W. 1972. "Aging and Suicide: The Significance of Marital, Kinship, and Alternative Relations." *The Family Coordinator* (January)21:71–79.

Butler, R. 1964. "The Life Review: An Interpretation of Reminiscence in the Aged." In R. Kastenbaum, ed. *New Thoughts on Old Age*. New York: Springer.

Coelho, G. V. et al., eds. 1974. *Coping and Adaptation*. New York: Basic Books.

DeLong, R. 1970. "The Micro-Spatial Structure of the Older Person: Some Implications of Planning the Social and Spatial Environment." In Pastalan and Carson, eds. (1970).

Dobzhansky, T. 1976. "The Myths of Genetic Predestination and Tabula Rasa." *Perspectives in Biology and Medicine* (January) 19(2).

Dubos, R. 1974. *Beast or Angel?* New York: Scribner.

Germain, C. B. 1976. "Time: An Ecological Variable in Social Work Practice." *Social Casework* 57(7):419–26.

—— 1978. "Space: An Ecological Variable in Social Work Practice." *Social Casework* (November) 59(9).

—— 1979. "Ecology for Social Work." In C. B. Germain, ed. *Social Work Practice: People and Environments*. New York: Columbia University Press.

Germain, C. B. and A. Gitterman. 1979. *The Life Model of Social Work Practice*. New York: Columbia University Press.

Hall, E. T. 1969. *The Hidden Dimension*. New York: Doubleday.

Kalish, R. A. 1968. "Life and Death: Dividing the Indivisible." *Social Science and Medicine* 2:249–59.

Lipman, A. and P. W. Marden. 1966. "Preparation for Death in Old Age." *Journal of Gerontology* 21(3):426–31.

Mechanic, D. 1974. "Social Structure and Personal Adaptation: Some Neglected Dimensions." In Coelho et al., eds. (1974):32–44.

Pastalan, L. A. and D. H. Carson, eds. 1970. *Spatial Behavior of Older People*. Ann Arbor: University of Michigan Press.

Peak, D. T. 1977. "The Elderly Who Face Dying and Death." In D. Barton, ed. *Dying and Death: A Clinical Guide for Caregivers*, pp. 210–19. Baltimore: Williams and Wilkins.

Sommer, R. 1970. "Small Group Ecology in Institutions for the Elderly." In Pastalan and Carson (1970):25–39.

Tuan, Yi-Fu. 1977. *Space and Place: The Perspective of Experience*. Minneapolis: University of Minnesota Press, pp. 187–88.

White, R. W. 1974. "Strategies of Adaptation: An Attempt at Systematic Description. In Coelho et al. (1974):47–68.

Will, O. A., Jr. 1959. "Human Relatedness and the Schizophrenic Reaction." *Psychiatry* (August) 22(3):205–23.

20

Toward Terminal Care
of the Aged at Home:
Practice, Problems,
and Implications for Care

VIRGINIA W. BARRETT

*H*ISTORICALLY, there has been a shift in Western attitudes about death from acknowledgment of the finality of death, although never simply accepted, to less acceptance, to the denial of death as part of our lives. It has been reported that death was recognized and acknowledged in the past by dying persons and those around them, and much attention was paid to preparations in keeping with their wishes, as influenced by the culture and social status. With a few exceptions, death was usually publicly experienced, as evidenced in woodcuts and paintings portraying deathbed scenes attended by children, relatives, friends, and neighbors (Aries 1975).

The change in attitude about death and dying developed gradually. With the approach of the nineteenth century, there was a shift of responsibility for death preparation from the individual to the family, and a developing belief that the dying person needed to be isolated and insulated against open acknowledgment of the terminal process. With the twentieth century, the place of dying was moved out of the home and into the hospital, where it could be fought against and generally avoided and depersonalized (Aries 1975).

The woodcut or oil painting of death in the 1970s would certainly portray a different scene: the dying person, perhaps, would now be in a hospital bed and gown, identified only by a plastic strap on the wrist, removed to the space farthest from the doctor and nurses' station once death was deemed no longer preventable, and surrounded by equipment. This picture is substantiated by reports based on studies showing greater distance put between staff and terminal patients and less time spent with patients once a terminal diagnosis is made (Shusterman 1973, Glaser and Strauss 1965). If the dying person is over 65 years old, this isolation is magnified.

There are several influences that will, in the future, change this picture. These include statistical studies of death among the aged, economic aspects of terminal care, increased awareness of the physical and psychosocial aspects of terminal care and geriatrics, and the development of home health agencies and hospices in the United States. Finally, shift of chronic care and terminal care away from the hospital is suggested. With the hospital bed use regulations now in effect and the high cost of institutional care, a study of the alternatives for this care available in the community is appropriate. Nursing homes that provide long-term chronic care, when affordable, are generally not able to provide terminal care in a specialized and comprehensive manner. It is the position of this paper that the practices and problems of care for the terminally ill elderly need to be studied, especially as they apply to the home environment. In conclusion, the implications for care will be discussed.

Statistically, prior to 1900, the leading cause of death was communicable diseases, but with longer life expectancy, there is an increase in occurrence of degenerative disease. According to the 1975 U.S. Health Statistics, the life expectancy for men is 68.7 years and for women 76.5 years. There has also been gradual growth in the percentage of the population over 65 years of age in the United States, approximately 20 million at present. The population over 65 years of age spends more for health care than any other part of our society, has a limited use of health services, and has the largest incidence of multiple chronic conditions.

According to the Mortality and Morbidity reports of 1974 (Erhardt and Berlin 1974), one-fourth of the elderly live in households below the poverty line and have been helped only somewhat by Medicare and Medicaid, especially when custodial care is needed as opposed to acute care. Ninety-six percent of people over 65 years old live in the community.

The leading causes of death for people over 65 in the United States in 1975 were heart disease, cancer, strokes, respiratory disease, accidents, arteriosclerotic heart disease, diabetes mellitus, and circulatory disease (of these deaths, 23 percent of the males and 18 percent of the females over 65 died of cancer).

The economics of death has been the subject of very few studies. Feasibility studies of hospices report some of the costs of the physical aspects of terminal care, but one needs only to experience a death in the family to be aware of other financial burdens. These include will arrangements, estate tax, investment decisions, insurance arrangements, gifts, necessary paper and telephone communications, and the funeral. The cost of physical care for the cancer patient over the course of illness, between $5,000 and $50,000 (Rose 1976), and the cost of estate settlement, $500 to $10,000 or more, occur at a time when the family is emotionally and physically weakened. The emotional and physical expense of death to the survivors is an area in need of investigation (Grollman 1974).

Because medical insurance programs are institutionally oriented, the cost of patient care at home, although substantially less than in the hospital, is often more burdensome to the family. The insurance requirements of periodic rehospitalization in order to obtain reinstatement of home-care services for the chronically ill is often an accepted practice even when the medical need for hospital readmission is absent. Medical insurance programs, and those proposed under the National Health Insurance bills, do little or nothing to cover cost of care for the terminally ill aged at home.

For the past forty years the majority of elderly have died in hospitals. Although it is believed that the trend in terminal care in the future will be away from the hospital, it is advisable to review the hospital's role.

Aged, homebound people are among the medically unreached, and often the first contact that the older person has with the physician is in the hospital setting, in a crisis situation. Acute-care facilities give their highest priorities to cure and disease control, with recovery as the goal. Medical insurance plans share this priority. With the aged, in particular, the point will come where if there is a chronic degenerative disease present, recovery as a goal will not be possible (Dobihal 1974).

In the hospital, as elsewhere, the elderly are often thought of as homogeneous and without diverse needs. Death in the hospital is viewed to some degree as failure on behalf of the staff to reach the goal of recovery, although this is much less the case with older patients than younger ones (Burnside 1973, Kübler-Ross 1975). The hospital is frequently viewed by the dying elderly patient as "a place to die" and, in the main, is seen as overwhelming, aggressive, and alien (Brickner 1975). More money is spent by the government on health institutions than on community programs.

But now we must ask: "When is a person dying?" Glaser and Strauss (1965) reported that dying usually refers to the expectation of death during a present hospitalization. Dying is further explained as the point at which the individual's declining condition can no longer be stabilized by medical intervention. With the introduction of hospice, however, the term *terminal* has been defined as "expected to die within a six-month period."

Physical considerations of caring for the dying patient at home are many and diverse, depending on the composition of the family and the needs of the patient. The problem of physical care also depends on the length of the illness and the resulting increasing rate of dependence on others. The duties to the family of cooking, cleaning, laundry, and so on are increased with the dependence of a patient. If the dying person is confused, unsafe, or anxious, arrangements have to be made to have someone present in the home at all times. Heavy patients are very difficult to lift, and if there are not enough family members or friends around to assist with lifting, a hydraulic lift or support poles may be needed. Equipment of this type, plus bedpans, wheelchairs, hospital beds, walkers, commodes, intravenous medication poles, support rails, and oxygen tanks, require space, and if the house or apartment is small, it is often not possible to accommodate what was considered advisable when the patient was in the hospital.

Arrangements for transportation to clinics and doctor's offices can require much time, money, and coordination. The responsibility for medication, although legally that of the patient, becomes the concern of the family. A change in the noise level in the house, with unfamiliar equipment, irregular sleep patterns of the patient, and disease- or drug-related outbursts, can all add to the lack of sleep frequently reported by families as a major problem with caring for a dying patient at home (Keywood 1974). The prevention of pressure sores and the care associated with incontinence are necessary and time-consuming parts of terminal care. Disposal of the equipment used in this care can be an added legal problem in some communities.

To understand the psychosocial aspects of death it must first be considered that one is a future-oriented being and that it is impossible to imagine nonexistence. As a result there are several attitudes—philosophical, religious, and scientific—that develop in the society to assist in explaining and experiencing death. With a shift of terminal care away from the public experience, the fears and misunderstandings about death can grow and may explain the depiction of death as malignant and catastrophic in the media today. Of course, it is also seen in the media as punishment, reward, escape, entertainment, status, social control, and an expression of love (Vernon 1970).

How the aged person interprets the dying process is highly individual, and the acceptance of death is related to the interpretation of one's cohort's experience with death, one's own problems, and one's sense of contribution to the lives of others. Among the people caring for the dying person, there is an insecurity that grows out of attitudes about their own deaths and lack of knowledge about the condition of the patient. Changes in condition are perceived and responded to in different ways and can produce conflicts among the staff, family, and friends (Vernon 1970). The person dying does not do so in a structured way and may, at different rates and intensities, experience the different stages identified by Kübler-Ross (1969): shock and disbelief upon first contemplating the approaching death, anger and crying with further awareness, restitution with bargaining, resolution with the expression of sadness and depression, and acceptance with a withdrawal from verbal contact. These stages, which can fluctuate greatly, are also experienced at different rates and intensities by the family, friends, and professional and nonprofessional staff in attendance. Because of these fluctuations on both sides of the care relationship, it is understandable why conflicts arise in spite of the best intentions. If the elderly dying person, for example, mentions fear of death to a relative or staff member who has not emotionally accepted that eventuality, the caregiver may react by retreating. Depression and anxiety are more debilitating than the illness to both caregiver and care recipient.

Death in the home has an element of intimacy that is unique, and the feelings of approaching loss and the loss itself are experienced to a greater degree in small groups than in larger, impersonal settings. The social system of the home is disrupted during the terminal-care process, and each one of the physical-care considerations previously mentioned evokes a reaction, or series of reactions, that can be incompatible with the social system or a source of strength to the people within it. However, considered to be at risk emotionally are those situations where the elderly person lives alone or with a frail spouse, the primary caregiver is an active parent of several children, and where there is already discord in the home (Keywood 1974). To this list should also be added the situation quite typical of this society, where the elderly person, prior to the terminal phase of illness, has not lived with the family for many years. Moving back in with children may be viewed by all involved as a dependence in an independent, mobile society.

Resentment over the high cost of care and guilt over the feelings of resentment are not uncommon in families. Feelings of guilt over feelings of positive anticipation of the death of the elderly family member are also not unusual for families to experience. Fatigue and anxiety interfere with learning or carrying out patient care and may lead to a profound emotional burden and hopelessness. Among families of terminal patients in the home, the areas of needed help include nutrition advice, drug information, sleep, money, child care, physical assistance with transportation, and emotional support (Rose 1976). Grieving, so often associated with the postdeath period, is a death-preparatory function as well and affects the family.

Pain, when present, is interpreted differently by each dying person and can have the effect of eliminating feelings of self-control and self-respect, freedom and independence (Kübler-Ross 1975). "Death with dignity," a popular phrase used to describe a goal of

terminal care today, would hardly be applicable to the situation where
pain is experienced frequently and over an extended period of time.
Pain and isolation are the two most frequently expressed fears of the
dying (Dobihal 1974).

The cultural influences on the behavior of the dying elderly
person and the family as they seek and accept treatment, respond to
professional personnel, interpret pain, prepare for death, and express
emotions are often unrecognized by health workers (French and
Schwartz 1973). The dying patient needs to discuss feelings of anxiety and depression, to have a sense of self-respect and identity, to
have a sense of control over the decisions being made about care,
and to have a role in this final, significant event of life. The fulfillment of these needs is often denied (Buckingham et al. 1976).

Finally, compounding these problems, dying elderly patients
may have burdensome feelings if those around them expect courageous and cooperative behavior at a time when their need for independence, control, and self-respect is satisfied only through emotional outbursts, touchiness, irritability, complaining, arguing, and
refusing physical-care intervention. Negative behavior is often an
outward sign of a person's feelings of inadequacy and guilt connected
with the dependence of terminal illness. The combination of advanced age and illness decreases the individual's capacity for assuming past responsibilities and making careful decisions. The resulting
feelings of shame and insecurity, if unrecognized and untreated, can
be seriously detrimental.

Three Case Studies

Case A

Mrs. A, a black female widow, died in the hospital from a
cerebral vascular accident at the documented age of 100 years and 9
months in 1977. The interview concerning her terminal care was conducted with Mrs. A's daughter. Mrs. A had lived in her daughter and
son-in-law's private home for thirty years. Two grand-nephews also
reside there. Mrs. A had been in excellent health until two months
following her one hundredth birthday. At this time she developed a
weakness in her leg and had difficulty walking. No medical attention

was sought until she was unable to walk six months later, and the family decided that she was not going to improve.

The physician, whom the daughter called, was unfamiliar with Mrs. A and refused to examine her outside the hospital. Once admitted to the hospital, she deteriorated rapidly and the family reported that they felt that the hospital staff did not make an effort to treat her, because of her advanced age. The daughter wanted physical therapy and other treatment measures begun and felt frustrated at the lack of communication. She was never told that her mother was dying. Mrs. A's daughter said that she had not been with her and was not ready to "let her go" at the time Mrs. A died.

This case represents a situation where health intervention and emotional support could have prevented a great deal of anxiety and frustration. Mrs. A's daughter's refusal to contact a physician for six months and the desire for therapy in the hospital represent a denial of her mother's progressive deterioration. If this had been identified by terminal-care-oriented professional staff, upon the admission to the hospital, Mrs. A's daughter could have received supportive counseling, been taught required care techniques, been actively involved in the care plan, and assisted in examining and implementing alternative arrangements such as home care. Since the hospitalization lasted a little over three weeks, all expenses were covered under Medicare and Medicaid.

Case B

Mr. B, a white male, was 83 when he died of cancer in his home in 1975. Mrs. B, his wife, in her seventies, cared for him during the year and a half before he died. During this year and a half Mr. B, who was obese, weak, and confused, gradually deteriorated, and Mrs. B was told by their physician that he had cancer and would not recover. Mr. B was bedridden for the last eleven months of his life and could not be left alone. He was incontinent of urine and feces. Mrs. B borrowed a hospital bed and received help from her friends and neighbors in changing his sheets and position. A full-time maid in their employ for many years assisted in his care. Medical supervision, the administration of pain medication, and Foley irrigation were provided by professionals who were neighbors.

Mr. B was admitted to the hospital for one week, a month

before he died, but he refused to stay, and Mrs. B brought him home again. When Mr. B was lucid, he appeared to Mrs. B to know that he was not going to recover, although death was never talked about openly between them. When Mr. B died, Mrs. B felt positively about her decision to support his request to be at home and about her ability to care for him. Mrs. B was interviewed three years later.

It is obvious that this experience was unusually positive. Since they were financially secure, they did not have an economic burden. They had lived in their community for their entire lives and had established close relationships with people who were willing to take part in this care and to lend support to Mr. B's decision to remain at home. It is hard to imagine that this experience would have been as successful without the many supporting features. Mrs. B had many women friends who were also widows and was able to resume her activities quite successfully, an example of positive adjustment more frequently seen with women than with men. Finally, the passage of three years may have contributed to Mrs. B's positive recollections.

Case C

Mrs. C, a white female, was widowed for one and a half years prior to her death at the age of 87 in 1977. Mrs. C had lived all her life in England, but following her husband's death, she was unable to care for herself and her home and moved to the United States to live with her daughter. After living with her daughter for 9 months, Mrs. C developed symptoms of drowsiness and an unsteady gait, was admitted for two weeks to a local hospital, and was diagnosed as having terminal cancer. With the exception of a 2-week hospitalization at another hospital with another physician for a fecal impaction removal and catheter insertion, Mrs. C remained in the daughter's home until her death 10 days after hospital discharge. Mrs. C had no pain throughout her illness.

Mrs. C's daughter, son-in-law, two teenage grandchildren, a school-age grandchild, and church members all took part in her care, although the daughter did the largest portion of it. Mrs. C enjoyed activity around her. The teenagers felt some resentment in having to stay alone with her, but otherwise her presence did not change their activities. The son-in-law was concerned about the negative effect the dying experience would have on the children.

Mrs. C's daughter reported that there were several problems

during the last hospitalization, which included lack of a medical insurance plan; inattentiveness to her mother by the staff, which she attributed to her mother's being a good patient; and a lack of preparation by the staff of what was to be expected and the care needed as the deterioration progressed. Mrs. C and her daughter never spoke of her condition as terminal, but her daughter promised her in the hospital that she would go back to the daughter's home and remain there. The home care department of the hospital arranged for a visiting nurse, who was a great help to the family. Mrs. C's daughter is content with her decision to have her mother die at home and derived satisfaction from providing her mother with love and care at the end of her life.

Case C represents a positive experience, although it was not without problems. Two of the aforementioned risk factors were involved: separation for many years and the primary caregiver's also caring for several children in addition to being occasionally employed. Mrs. C's family could have benefited from supportive communication, instruction in technical care skills, and financial advisement. The last hospital admission might also have been avoided. Cases C and A had physicians previously unfamiliar with the dying person and their families, and a lack of communication is present in both instances.

There are very few statistics available to indicate use of terminal home health agency care by people over the age of 65, and none that indicate the location in which this population dies—hospital, chronic-care facility, nursing home, private residence, and so on.

There are private organizations that also offer services to the homebound terminally ill aged, but in this report the services available through hospice and other home health agencies are discussed. Although home care has been administered through the city and state health agencies for years in the past, official home health agencies, as they are called today, have been in existence for more than a decade. These agencies provide coordinated, physician-directed services at home. They are centrally administered, usually hospital based, and provide care for selected patients who do not need hospitalization and cannot attend outpatient facilities. Most recipients of this type of care need a variety of services—medical, nursing, physical therapy, social service, housekeeping, and so on. The patient's suitability for home care is dependent on the needs present and on a suitable physical and psychological home environment. For the person over 65, Medicare will cover one hundred nursing or therapist visits a year and 80 to 100 percent of the cost of equipment, which is usually rented. When these visits are used up, a hospital readmission may be needed to reactivate Medicare coverage. Other coverage depends on the policy of the insuring organization. No service is usually available at night, and a limited amount on weekends. Medical visits are scheduled according to the individual physician's practice.

The hospice concept planned for and established in the United States today is modeled after some twenty-five hospices in Britain, the most well known being St. Christopher's. The Connecticut Hospice in Branford, Connecticut, founded in New Haven originally, is the prototype for others in this country.

Hospice programs are designed specifically to provide services to the terminally ill and their families. Depending on the facility, this can be inpatient or home care or both. Ideally, this service is interdisciplinary, with a staff dedicated to the maintenance of a quality of life satisfactory to the patient. The hospice philosophy supports the concept of 24-hour availability of service, existence of a support system for the patient and family, a program of effective pain relief as needed, and ongoing work with the bereaved. In addition to the home health agency team described before, the hospice team includes a pastoral counselor and professional and nonprofessional volunteers (Kutscher et al. 1983).

Those who are advocates of home care and hospice generally support terminal care in the home. The exception to this would be situations where the home environment does not allow for this or where the patient rejects the idea. The shift of chronic care away from the hospital and the high cost of institutional care suggest a need for reevaluation of the home as a place to die.

Summary

In this report I have explored some of the influences that should be considered as they apply to the terminally ill at home: statistical, financial, physical, social, and psychological. Three case studies were reported as examples of the unique nature of terminal care of the aged at home, and some existing services for home care have been described.

Several problems are present, and with the overview, their interrelationships can be seen. Cost is always at the base of health care and determines who receives what and where. The elderly terminal patient, although a recipient of Medicare, is limited in what care can be received. Hospice usually requires a diagnosis of cancer, which is not the predominant cause of death among the elderly. Home health agencies require a cooperating physician, cannot provide 24-hour service, provide fragmented care with a lack of consistency of caregivers, and are not specifically oriented to terminal care. There is no third-party coverage for care during the bereavement period. Transportation to health-care services is always a problem, if it is available at all. The society in which the terminally ill aged live does not consider their physical and emotional needs a priority.

Ideally, the individual should be in control of the death environment, but this is not realistic in our society at present. Therefore it is up to the families and other caregivers to provide as much support as possible to assist the elderly dying person in maintaining an acceptable quality of life in whatever setting is required. To obtain this patient-centered goal, the following are offered for consideration by caregivers and care coordinators:

1. If the patients are in the hospital, make sure that they and their family are part of the care plan. Involve the family in the actual physical care so that they are prepared if discharge is being considered. The family should be told what to expect and what to do in an emergency. Provide them with information and support. Be aware of the patients' and family's concepts of the priority of needs.
2. At the time of transfer to the home, assess the home environment prior to discharge, physically and psychosocially. Will needed equipment fit? Is it safe? Is the family aware that increased caution is needed with the elderly patients' diminished environmental awareness? At what times of day or night is the most care needed? Can these needs be met in a consistent manner to provide a sense of stability to the patient and family? Does the care plan respect the family's daily routine?

3. Is there unresolved discord in the home? An understanding of the cultural behavior patterns, long-existing tensions, and family conflicts can help predict, prevent, and solve problems. Assess the past patient and family reactions to crisis and the patterns of resolution.

4. Creativity is needed in providing an atmosphere appealing to the patient's interests and conducive to meaningful interaction. Humor where appropriate can be beneficial, and knowing when to be quiet is essential.

5. Make sure that the patient maintains a sense of independence and freedom of communication. Adjustment to terminal illness can be impeded by closed communication, feelings of isolation and desertion, preoccupation with one's losses, and fears connected with dependency.

6. Make sure that supportive patient care does not encroach upon those care procedures that the family may have been using before or may wish to use now. Physical contact between the family and patient can be an important source of nonverbal communication.

7. Make appropriate referrals if a need for legal and financial counsel is expressed.

8. Explore with the family the available resources in the community for volunteers to assist in patient care and companionship. This can help to relieve the emotional intensity of the terminal-care environment for the family and allow the members to get away to pursue other responsibilities or relaxation at regularly scheduled intervals.

9. Observe the health status of the family. Make referrals when appropriate.

10. In the presence of pain, is medication available and provided in such a way that the pain does not have to be experienced and relief requested before it is administered? The anxiety associated with pain can be a detriment to the effectiveness of the medication. Excessive medicating can further isolate the patient and should be avoided.

11. With the slowing-down process of advanced age, the effects of medication, and degenerative disease, attention should be paid to short-term goals and explaining procedures to the patient in a direct, concise, measured, and respectful manner.

12. Does the patient exhibit difficulty in recalling events? Is there a preoccupation with symptoms or ideas? The caregiver can be supportive in these situations by assisting the patient to reconstruct

past events verbally and with the use of notes. This activity will strengthen recall ability and self-esteem. The orderly keeping of notes by a patient is helpful to a sense of security when applied to the reporting of changes in condition to the physician.

13. If the dying person is in an initial stage of shock and disbelief, be patient and willing to talk. Be understanding of anger and accepting. Receptive listening is indicated when the dying person is in a stage of restitution, or sad and depressed, with resolution. Allow privacy and respect the narrowing of interest in interaction with the awareness of death (Kübler-Ross 1975).

14. Remember that the reactions and needs of the dying person, as described above, are also those of the caregivers: family, friends, and staff.

15. Care planning for the terminally ill should include preparation for the bereavement period to follow. Care of the family should be supportive of all needs: emotional, spiritual, physical, and social—toward the goal of satisfactory adjustment to loss. This process requires time and support, which is often not available if it is not part of the care plan from the onset of terminal-care intervention.

References

Aries, P. 1975. "A Moment That Has Lost Its Meaning." *Prism* 3:27–29.

Brickner, P. et al. 1975. "The Homebound Aged: A Medically Unreached Group." *Annals of Internal Medicine* 82:1–6.

Buckingham, R. W. et al. 1976. "Living With the Dying: Use of the Technique of Participant Observation." *Canadian Medical Association Journal* 115:1211–15.

Burnside, I. M. 1973. *Psychosocial Nursing Care of the Aged*. New York: McGraw-Hill.

Dobihal, E. F. 1974. "Talk of Terminal Care." *Connecticut Medicine* 38:364–67.

Erhardt, C. L. and J. B. Berlin. 1974. *Mortality and Morbidity in the United States*. Boston: Harvard University Press.

French, J. and D. R. Schwartz. 1973. "Terminal Care at Home in Two Cultures." *American Journal of Nursing* 73:502–5.

Glaser, B. G. and A. L. Strauss. 1965. *Awareness of Dying*. Chicago: Aldine.

Grollman, E. A. 1974. *Concerning Death: A Practical Guide for the Living*. Boston: Beacon Press.

Keywood, O. 1974. "Care of the Dying in Their Own Homes." *Nursing Times* 70:1516–17.

Kübler-Ross, E. 1975. *Death: The Final Stage of Growth*. Englewood Cliffs, New Jersey: Prentice-Hall.

Kutscher, A. H., S. C. Klagsbrun, R. J. Torpie, R. DeBellis, M. S. Hale, and M. Tallmer, eds. 1983. *Hospice U.S.A.* New York: Columbia University Press.

Rose, M. A. 1976. "Caring for the Cancer Patient at Home." *American Journal of Nursing* 76:416–18.

Shusterman, L. R. 1973. "Death and Dying." *Nursing Outlook* 21:465–71.

Vernon, G. M. 1970. *Sociology of Death: An Analysis of Death-Related Behavior*. New York: Ronald Press Co.

Bibliography

Butler, R. N. and M. I. Butler. 1977. *Aging and Mental Health*. St. Louis: Mosby.

Colen, B. D. 1977. "Death with Dignity—At Home." *The Washington Post*, pp. A-10 and A-11.

Esper, G. 1976. "Hospice Helps Patients to Live Until They Die, Families to Cope." *Bridgeport Sunday Post*.

Fisher Medical Publications Editorial. 1977. "On Dying at Home." *Emergency Medicine* 9:136–38.

Gray, A. 1977. "Dying at Home." *Nursing Times* 73:9–10.

Grof, S. and J. Halifax. 1977. *The Human Encounter with Death*. New York: Dutton.

Hospice Inc. 1977. *Annual Report*. New Haven, Connecticut.

Lack, S. A. 1977. *Philosophy and Organization of a Hospice Program*. New Haven, Connecticut.

Long, M. J., ed. 1972. *Caring for and Caring About Elderly People*. Philadelphia: Lippincott.

Malkin, S. 1976. "Care of the Terminally Ill at Home." *Canadian Medical Association Journal* 115:129–30.

McNulty, B. J. 1971. "St. Christopher's Outpatients." *American Journal of Nursing* 71:2328–30.

Morgan, L. 1976. "A Re-examination of Widowhood and Morale." *Journal of Gerontology* 31:687–95.

Pearson, L., ed. 1969. *Death and Dying: Current Issues in the Treatment of the Dying Person.* Cleveland: Case Western Reserve University Press.

Shneidman, E. S., ed. 1976. *Death: Current Perspectives.* California: Mayfield Publishing Company.

Selvey, C. L. 1970. *Concerns About Death in Relation to Sex, Dependency, Guilt about Hostility and Feelings of Powerlessness.* Unpublished doctoral dissertation, Columbia University.

Steinberg, M. 1976. "Death with Dignity." *Journal of the Connecticut Business and Industry Association* 54:1.

U.S. Department of Commerce. 1975. *Statistical Abstract of the United States 1975.* U.S. National Center for Health Statistics, Vital Statistics of the United States.

U.S. Department of Health, Education and Welfare. 1976. *The Nation's Use of Health Resources.*

Weisman, A. D. 1972. *On Dying and Denying.* New York: Behavioral Publications.

Wessel, M. A. 1975. "To Comfort Always." *Yale Alumni Magazine* (June):17–19.

Will, G. F. 1978. "A Good Death." *Newsweek* (January):72.

21

Relocation Stress and Mortality

RUTH BENNETT

RELOCATION STRESS AND transfer trauma refer to conditions that are thought to result when the elderly are moved from their accustomed environment. Few systematic direct studies of relocation stress in the elderly have been made. Usually, it is inferred either from development of symptoms of serious physical illness or death that occurs in elderly residents soon after institutionalization (Rodstein et al. 1976). However, certainly there is a pervasive clinical awareness of the occurrence of stress upon institutionalization reported by nursing and medical personnel. This is corroborated to some extent by clinical testing using projective techniques in the early work of Lieberman et al. (1969).

I start by summarizing four major reviews of the literature on relocation and its effects on the elderly: Kasl (1972), Kasl and Rosenfield (1980), Carp (1976), and Lawton and Nahemow (1973).

Most of these reviews cite the need for (1) maximum experimental control to establish a causal link between relocation and stress (or mortality)—e.g., random assignment of about to be relocated individuals to a stay or go condition; (2) control over such biasing factors as physical or mental condition, self-selection, and voluntariness or involuntariness of move; (3) measurement of housing condition and neighborhood characteristics of both the environment one is leaving and the environment into which one is moving.

Needless to say, I am in complete agreement with these reviewers and can add very little to what they have written. However, one or two new elements that have either been omitted by these reviewers or mentioned only in passing need elaboration.

The research on relocation stress concentrates chiefly on mortality as an indicator of stress. According to Kasl (1972):

> Relocation and/or institutionalization will have adverse effects on the physical and psychological wellbeing of the elderly if: a) it increases the physical distance to friends, kin, and age peers, as well as to various services and facilities; b) it interferes with their engaging in their usual leisure and social activities; c) it represents a deterioration in the quality of their dwelling unit and their neighborhood along valued dimensions (e.g., independence, privacy, safety, security, convenience, familiarity, and so on). . . . The most convincing evidence of adverse health effects as a consequence of environmental change has come from studies in which institutionalized elderly were relocated to another institution. Almost equally convincing is the evidence that these effects are preventable with careful casework service and psychological support; the elderly need to be fully prepared for the move (cognitively and emotionally) and as much of their former social networks and their familiar physical surroundings and possessions should be maintained as possible. The importance of the more general attributes of the living environment in the new institution (the layout of the buildings, size of rooms, common facilities, etc.) is not at all clear from these studies.

While Kasl's (1972) review is an excellent one as far as it goes, two important omissions seem to be made: (1) He fails to take note of the different findings in the different settings. Thus, while he correctly notes that moving into adequate housing usually has a positive effect—namely, satisfaction with the new housing—he does not note that moving out of a mental hospital also seems to have this effect. (2) He fails to note that the stress reaction has rarely been studied directly. He is correctly critical of Thematic Apperception Test (TAT) studies, which make for much observer-interpretation, but he does not deal as harshly with inferences drawn from death, the major indicator of relocation stress currently in use.

By classifying selected studies of relocation stress according to a combination of variables—including types of patients studied, institution of origin, destination, and whether or not a control or comparison group was used—I have devised a way of categorizing relocation stress studies, which is shown in table 21.1.

There appear to be four major types of studies: institutionalization studies, relocation studies, re-relocation studies, and studies of institutional alternatives. There are also some interesting gaps—for example, no studies of impact of institutionalization on mental patients who are admitted to an institution versus those who are kept on a waiting list (or some other appropriate comparison group). The rea-

TABLE 21.1. Typology of Relocation Stress Studies

Institution of Origin and Destination	Mental Patients		Other Institutional Patients		
	Control Group	No Control Group	Waiting List Control Group	Community Control Group	No Control Group
Community to institution	—	—	Institutionalization studies		—
Institution to other institution	Re-relocation studies	—		—	Relocation studies
Institution to institutional alternatives	—	—		—	Studies of institution alternatives

sons for this are not clear or obvious. Also, thus far there have been no studies of mass relocation with control groups or use of institutional alternatives with control groups. At best, comparison groups are studied.

Once studies are arranged in this manner, it is possible to discern that they yield different types of findings. The following review indicates these differences:

1. Relocation Studies

Relocation studies refer to those conducted on a group of unselected patients or residents who are moved en masse within a single institution or from an old building to a newer one or under conditions of urban renewal. Usually, this process is studied without a control group with which to compare them. However comparison statistics are often gathered—namely, deaths in the moved population in the one to five years prior to the move. These studies usually produce pessimistic results in the institutional group and not in the urban relocation groups. They also yield the most pessimistic findings, as Kasl (1972) noted; he has also encouraged the development of prevention programs, most notably like those of Pastalan (1976).

The pioneering studies of Aldrich and Mendkoff (1963) probably were the first of this kind conducted on the aged. Their findings showed that more elderly patients died upon relocation than had been true in the past as indicated by death-rate statistics. The authors, after checking on the patients' health status in records, attributed relocation deaths to neurotic personality traits such as rigidity and dependency, traits that are typically found in any group of inmates and that seem to render them incapable of adapting to change. Similar studies of what came to be called "relocation stress" were conducted by Blenkner et al. (1967), as well as others, who found other traits to be related to relocation impact; for example, more men than women died on relocation.

By stretching the classification scheme a bit, Tobin's (1972) study may be classified both as a mass relocation study and as an institutionalization study. It is like a mass relocation study when he looks at waiting-list people as if they are institutionalized already in order to contrast them with a community group. Those waiting-list people and institutional inmates show signs of deterioration if they are also passive, dependent types—a finding in line with those of Aldrich referred to earlier. It is my opinion that mass relocation studies—of which there are many and which are reviewed in some detail in Marlowe's (1972) paper, as well as in the reviews cited earlier—tend to lead to pessimism about the relationship between relocation and stress. As had been noted by Lawton and Yaffee (1970), most mass relocations described in research are involuntary, and the voluntary or involuntary nature of relocation may be crucial in determining outcome. Marlowe's (1972) findings seem to support the view that involuntary relocations are highly stressful, especially if they are not viewed as improvements.

Caution should, however, be exercised in drawing generalizations from studies conducted in single institutions on a single cohort of patients at a single point in time. The reasons for an institution's relocating masses of people should be studied, for they may yield evidence of the "goodness" or "badness" of the institution, which may also play a critical role in outcome. If mortality rates are high at a single point in time as compared with earlier times, there is no reason to trace high rates to relocation per se. They may as easily be attributed to overall institutional deterioration, which can result in a policy of mass relocation and in high mortality rates. Both low death rates in the past and lack of policy to mass-relocate inmates may not be signs of institutional "goodness." In early times, institutions may have relocated moribund patients to other types of facilities for what they thought of as more appropriate care and thereby lowered their death rates. Also, more accurate morbidity and mortality figures are probably kept when a study is being conducted, as compared with other times. To summarize this section then, mass-relocation studies conducted thus far do not seem to establish a firm link between relocation and what has come to be termed "relocation stress." They simply establish the need to look at what else is going on in institutions when they mass-relocate people. We cannot continue to neglect the social context within which a set of behaviors is occurring, a point made both by Marlowe (1972) and Slover (1972). Thus, one needs to look at whether networks are disrupted or not, whether diets are changed, and at other social environmental factors. Also, these findings do not seem relevant to community relocations under conditions of urban renewal, to which relocated elderly usually respond positively.

2. Institutionalization Studies

Institutionalization studies seem to go further than mass-relocation studies to try to establish a causal link between relocation and subsequent stress. These studies usually use an available control group— typically waiting-list people—and thereby control for motivation to enter an institution, as well as other related personality and physical health traits. These studies usually yield mixed results: some indicate negative impact, some show positive impact.

Several institutionalization studies by Lieberman et al. (1969)

have documented the adverse effects of institutionalization, indicating that more people have died after admission and within the first few months of admission as compared with those in similar physical condition on the waiting list. Institutionalization has also been found to result in poor adjustment (Lieberman 1969), inactivity (Hadley 1963), and morbidity (Lieberman and Lakin 1963). Several tentative explanations of these findings have been offered by Lieberman and associates (1968), who have conducted most of the research in the area of institutionalization effects. Such explanations range from the maladaptive traits of inmates to insulation (nonpermeability, as Gelfand [1968] calls it) to forced adaptation imposed by the institution. In their early work, Lieberman and associates were more inclined to attribute stress to relocation per se; more recently—perhaps as a result of his joint work with Tobin, Slover, Miller, and others—Lieberman has placed less emphasis on relocation alone. Tobin's (1972) findings indicate that simply by becoming a member of the waiting list, one is a candidate for the deterioration associated with relocation. According to Slover (1972) and Marlowe (1972), the positive or negative quality of the institutions into which discharged patients are relocated have positive or negative impacts on sensitive or responsive persons.

Tobin's (1972) study is unique in terms of design because he observed a community sample that seems comparable to both the waiting-list and institutionalized groups. By doing so, he was able to learn that waiting-list people are more like institutionalized people than like community people. Thus, he calls attention to the possible adverse effects of identifying oneself or being identified as a candidate for institutionalization. Perhaps they suffer from stigmatization.

Some institutionalization studies, as noted earlier, have reported no change or improvement on institutionalization on some measures. For example, Anderson (1964) found that institutionalization had no effect on those admitted to an institution as compared with waiting-list people. An early study by Lieberman et al. (1968) showed some positive, as well as negative, effects on institutionalization. Findings of a study by Weinstock and Bennett (1972) showed higher scores on tests of cognitive performance in all categories of residents as compared with waiting-list people, with waiting-list people showing improvements on tests after admission while former newcomers' and oldtimers' scores tapered off. More recent studies under my sponsorship (Arje 1973, Barron 1976, Haring 1976, and Powell 1978) have also dealt with this.

Effects of quality of institution is an issue raised by the studies included in this class. Institutionalization into a good place may cause improvements; institutionalization into a bad place may cause deterioration. We will have to be able to assess quality of institutions to determine the extent to which it makes a difference upon relocation.

3. Re-relocation or Postdischarge Studies

Related to studies of institutionalization by design—that is, by whether or not there is a control group, usually a group not moved—are re-relocation studies. Re-relocation refers to the transfer of patients to another institution; usually a single patient is moved without the benefit of cohort support as in the case of mass relocation from an old building to a new one. Re-relocation studies are usually of about-to-be-discharged mental hospital inmates, contrasting those detained in an institution with those discharged. In the past this type of study came up with findings that caused us to be optimistic about relocation, as Marlowe (1972) noted in her paper—that is, until she conducted her own study.

Stotsky (1967a, b) was concerned with whether or not the nursing home is an appropriate community resource for discharged mental patients. He compared a group of patients discharged to nursing homes with a group regarded as candidates for placement in nursing homes but who remained in the hospital. He found that for the two groups of patients, short-term changes favored those in the nursing homes. For long-term changes, results were less straightforward.

Slover (1972), like Stotsky, found no short-term deterioration in relocated patients, who remained the same as controls. However, long-term effects of relocation were decidedly negative and nontherapeutic, though nonlethal in Slover's study. Slover carried his study further than Stotsky did. He looked at how quality of the institution into which inmates were placed affected outcome and found that warm, humane, independence-fostering environments are related to positive outcomes. Slover's and Marlowe's lists of environmental dimensions constitute a mandate to conduct large-scale surveys of institutional quality.

Findings similar to those of Slover and Stotsky were obtained by Sainsbury (1969) in England. His findings showed that the mentally ill aged at home were neither better nor worse off than those in hospitals. In fact, an important finding of Sainsbury's study was that elderly mental patients who returned to their homes were not a burden to their families as had been feared. On the other hand, Marlowe's findings are cause for pessimism in that re-relocated Modesto inmates were worse off than the control group and did have a high mortality rate as compared with earlier hospital rates and the control group rate.

Generalizations based on re-relocation studies probably cannot be made to studies of other types. Most re-relocation studies have been conducted on mental hospital inmates who have been relocated at least once before, from the community into the hospital; hence I have coined the term "re-relocation." Conceivably most had been relocated several times before discharge. Those who have survived may be the hardiest of such patients, their weaker counterparts possibly having died upon initial institutionalization. Therefore, Marlowe's findings that this presumably hardy group of re-relocated patients does badly are of particular concern, especially in light of earlier studies (discussed above) in which re-relocated mental patients did no worse than their counterparts in hospitals. However, her findings suggest that before getting too pessimistic, we look into the number of prior relocations experienced by mental patients, as well as the quality of their destinations.

Discussion

One cannot generalize about relocations. Each type described is very different. (Tables 21.2 to 4 are efforts to diagram what seems to be happening in each instance.)

Relocation—that is, mass transfer from an old building to a new one— implies disruption of social networks, as well as confusion generated by new spatial arrangements (table 2).

TABLE 21.2. Stages in the Relocation Process

Time Classification	Duration	Process	Symptoms
Waiting period (in institution)	0–2 years	Some sort of preparation for move.	?
Transfer	One day 0–3 months for a group	With or without cohorts—e.g., friends/roommates.	Confusion/stress/ death
First stage of transition	3–6 months	?	Stress/death
Settling down	6 months–1 year	?	
Newcomer/oldtimer	Irrelevant because these designations are carried over from the former institution.		

What is meant by disruption of networks is that roommates are not necessarily moved from the old building to the new one together. Hence, more anxiety may be generated in the early stages of such a move. Pastalan's work has aimed at reducing confusion resulting from changed spatial arrangements. But no note has been taken of changed roommates, ward mates, staffing patterns, and so on. The move and the aftermath are stressful times.

Institutionalization—that is, moving into an institution for the first time—causes the most dramatic change from community to institution (table 3).

People are moved in one at a time, usually as beds become vacant. There is no freshman class—that is, no group to support one

TABLE 21.3. Stages in the Institutionalization Process

Time Classification	Duration	Process	Symptoms
Waiting period (in community)	0–2 years	Anticipation	Similar but not identical to those in institution
Move into institution	1 week	Orientation	Anxiety/stress
First stage of transition	1 wk–3 months	Becoming a newcomer	Anxiety/stress Death vs.
Second stage of transition	3–6 months		improvement
Settling into newcomer role	6 months–1 year		
Settling into oldtimer role	1 year following		

during the initial adjustment period. Groups awaiting institutionalization report anxiety during the waiting period. Often, families dissociate themselves from persons awaiting institutionalization as if they were already in an institution.

Here we have seen that anxiety and stress occur even while people are on the waiting list. These findings are not explained by health status alone, because when compared to community-residing matched controls, they are more anxious and stressed. The waiting period and the move are stressful times.

Re-relocation—that is, going from one institution to another, conceivably a better one (table 4).

These studies seem to be the most difficult to understand at the moment. So much is going on. Individuals are usually relocated one at a time, to a new setting in which they may either flourish or perish. Much seems to depend on the setting and on whether or not they perceive the move as a "promotion" or a "demotion." Newcomer/oldtimer periods are most stressful.

Each one of these processes may have different consequences attendant upon it. It seems only accidental that these three processes have been associated with different settings. Mass transfers usually occur out of and into homes for the aged (ICFs). Institutionalization

TABLE 21.4. Stages in Re-relocation Process

Class of Time	Duration	Process	Symptoms
Waiting period	0	Unknown	Unknown
Transfer	1 day	"	"
First stage of transition	0–3 months	Becoming a newcomer	Anxiety/stress
		Unknown but patients are moved into others' territory	
Second stage of transition	3–6 months		
Settling into newcomer role	6 months–1 year	Long-stay patients from one institution are newcomers to another	
Settling into oldtimer role	1 year following		

234   *Ruth Bennett*

refers to moving into homes for the aged (ICFs) or nursing homes (SNFs). And re-relocation has usually occurred among mental patients. As for attributing deaths to relocation per se, it is hard to do because so much else is happening.

Needless to say, to determine which type of institution or treatment program is most ameliorative and which is most destructive, random assignment of samples is necessary. However, as we all know, few if any general hospitals or other referral agencies are willing to assign patients on a random basis to long-term treatment programs, though it is easy enough to get patients randomly assigned for drug experiments.

As far as establishing the causal link between stress and death, one needs first to establish which patients are stressed and then follow them up to determine if they are more likely to die earlier in their career as newcomers to an institution than would be predicted on the basis of their health status alone. While Kasl mentions one hypothetical mechanism that could explain the stress/death relationship, namely, increase in cortisol in male mental patients, it is not clear that this occurs in patients outside of mental hospitals.

A word about institutional alternatives as a way of preventing relocation stress: one way to determine this would be to randomly assign candidates for institutionalization to an institution or an institutional alternative. Probably such a study would be easier to do in England, where there are many alternatives, such as geriatric clinics in mental and general hospitals, psychogeriatric hostels, day hospitals, and hospital-run home care programs. According to Kaplan (1972), there are no real alternatives to institutionalization in the United States.

Summary and Conclusions

Three major types of relocation and attendant outcomes seem to occur:

1. Relocation–mass transfer. Without preparation, these may result in death soon after move.
2. Institutionalization. An individual moves alone onto a waiting list or into an institution. Stress and possibly death occurs. Mixed results. Most stressful time may be on waiting list or soon after move.

3. Re-relocation. Mixed results, depending possibly on whether patients see move as promotion or demotion. Most stressful time may be on becoming a newcomer.

Without more control over relocations, it is difficult to attribute deaths to stress caused by relocation. Without prospective, longitudinal studies it is hard to know if the most stressed patients are the ones to die.

To conclude, it is recommended that the study of relocation stress should take the following course:

1. Accurate direct observation of stress before or after relocation that is attributable to the move, leading to ability to designate some patients as more stressed than others.
2. Follow-up of stressed and unstressed patients (1) in a number of contexts such as mental hospitals, nursing homes, housing projects; (2) moved under a variety of conditions—for example, en masse, alone, into a better place, into a worse place, in each of these settings.
3. A prospective longitudinal study should be conducted that tests the hypothesis that the most stressed patients are more likely to die and perhaps die soon after relocation regardless of context.

Needless to say, some of these recommendations are in line with those made by the reviewers cited earlier. The major contribution I have added is the need to observe stress firsthand and not assume that it necessarily precedes death or that all patients who are stressed die sooner than would be predicted on the basis of their health status alone.

References

Aldrich, C. K. 1964. "Personality Factors and Mortality in the Relocation of the Aged." *Gerontologist* 4 (part 1):92–93.
Aldrich, C. K. and E. Mendkoff. 1963. "Relocation of the Aged and Disabled: A

Mortality Study." *Journal of the American Gerontological Society* 11:185–94.

Anderson, N. 1964. "Social Activity, Self-Conception, and Institutionalization of Older People." Paper read at Seventh Annual Meeting of Gerontological Society.

Arje, F. B. 1973. "Project Share: Reactions of Residents of a Home for the Aged to a Selected Remotivation Technique." Unpublished Ed.D. thesis, Columbia University. Abbreviated version appears in Bennett (1980):129–51.

Barron, E. 1976. "Initial Reactions of Newcomers of a Residential Setting for the Aged to a Resocialization Program: An Exploratory Study." Unpublished Ed.D. thesis, Columbia University. Abbreviated version appears in Bennett (1980):152–56.

Bennett, R. ed. 1980. *Aging and Isolation and Resocialization.* New York: Van Nostrand.

Blenkner, M. 1967. "Environmental Change and the Aging Individual." *Gerontologist* 7:101–5.

Carp, F. M. 1976. "Housing and Living Environments of Older People." In R. H. Binstock and E. Shanas, eds. *Handbook of Aging and the Social Sciences,* pp. 224–71. New York: Van Nostrand Reinhold.

Gelfand, D. 1968. "Visiting Patterns and Social Adjustment in an Old Age Home." *Gerontologist* 8(4):272–75.

Hadley, R. G. 1963. *Psychological Changes in Institutional Residents.* Los Angeles: V.A. Center, Mimeograph.

Haring, P. 1976. "Adjustment to a Home for Aged." Unpublished Ed.D. thesis, Columbia University.

Kaplan, J. 1972. "An Editorial: Alternatives to Nursing Home Care: Fact or Fiction." *Gerontologist* 12:114.

Kasl, S. 1972. "Physical and Mental Health Effects of Involuntary Relocation and Institutionalization—A Review." *American Journal of Public Health* 62:379–84.

Kasl, S. and S. Rosenfield. 1980. "The Residential Environment and Its Impact on the Mental Health of the Aged." In J. E. Birren and R. B. Sloane, eds. *Handbook of Mental Health and Aging,* pp. 468–98. Englewood Cliffs, N.J.: Prentice-Hall.

Lawton, M. P. and L. Nahemow. 1973. "Ecology and the Aging Process." In C. Eisdorfer and M. P. Lawton, eds. *The Psychology of Adult Development and Aging,* pp. 619–74. Washington, D.C.: APA.

Lawton, M. P. and S. Yaffe. 1970. "Mortality, Morbidity and Voluntary Change of Residence by Older People." *Journal of American Gerontological Society* 18(10):823–31.

Lieberman, M. 1969. "Institutionalization of the Aged: Effect on Behavior." *Journal of Gerontology* 24(3):330–40.

Lieberman, M. and M. Lakin. 1963. "On Becoming an Institutionalized Aged Person." In C. Tibbetts and W. Donahue, eds. *Processes of Aging,* vol. 1, New York: Atherton Press.

Lieberman, M. A., V. Prock, and S. S. Tobin. 1968. "Psychological Effects of Institutionalization." *Journal of Gerontology* 23(3):343–53.

Marlowe, R. 1972. "Forced Relocation of Geriatric Mental Hospital Patients." Paper presented at Symposium on Studies on Relocating the Elderly, Gerontological Society, San Juan, P.R. December 20.

Pastalan, L. 1976. "Report on Pennsylvania Nursing Homes Relocation Program." Ann Arbor: Institute of Gerontology, University of Michigan. Abbreviated version in Bennett (1980):169–94.

Powell, L. 1978. "Time Limited Counseling as an Adjunct to the Adjustment and Resocialization of Social Isolates Newly Admitted to a Home for the Aged." Unpublished Ed.D. thesis, Columbia University.

Rodstein, M. E., E. Savitsky, and R. Starkman. 1976. "Initial Adjustment to a Long-Term Care Institution: Medical and Behavioral Aspects." *Journal of American Gerontological Society* 24(2):65–71.

Sainsbury, P. 1969. "Principles and Methods in Evaluation of Community Psychiatric Services." Paper read at Eighth International Congress of Gerontology, Washington, D.C.

Slover, D. 1972. "Relocation for Therapeutic Purposes of Aged Mental Hospital Patients." Paper read at Symposium on Studies on Relocating the Elderly, Gerontological Society, San Juan, P.R. December 20.

Stotsky, B. 1967a. "A Systematic Study of Therapeutic Interventions in Nursing Homes." *Genetic Psychology Monographs* 76:257–320.

—— 1967b. "Nursing Home or Mental Hospital: Which Is Better for the Geriatric Mental Patient?" *Journal of Genetic Psychology* 3:113–17.

Tobin, S. 1972. "Studies on Relocating the Elderly from Community to Institutional Living." Paper presented at Symposium on Studies on Relocating the Elderly, Gerontological Society, San Juan, P.R. December 20.

Weinstock, C. and R. Bennett. 1971. "From 'Waiting on the List' to Becoming a 'Newcomer' and an 'Oldtimer' in a Home for the Aged: Two Studies of Socialization and Its Impact Upon Cognitive Functioning." *Journal of Aging and Human Development* 2(1):46–58.

22

Institutionalization—End of Living: Does It Have To Be?

SYMA CRANE, ROSANNA ROOCHNIK,
and DORIS J. BEDELL

*T*HIS PAPER REPRESENTS the joint effort of social work and therapeutic recreation at Beth Abraham Hospital. This hospital, a 504-bed skilled nursing facility for subacutely and chronically ill patients aged sixteen and up, is unique in that its therapeutic recreation services function within the department of social services. Our experience at this institution has convinced us that the best way to meet the psychosocial needs of our patients is to bring together under one umbrella the disciplines of casework, group work, therapeutic recreation, and music therapy.

An institution is a community, albeit skewed by the dependency of its citizens on the service personnel. People live in a community, people die in a community, and the citizens of the community must learn to deal with all its facets. We see as the responsibility, function, and obligation of the professional staff in the social services department the maximization of "living." This paper addresses itself to this aspect of life within our institution.

According to Robinson (1971), "Illness is a state of disturbance in the 'normal' functioning of the total individual, including both the state of the organism as a biological system and of his personal and social adjustments." Such illness connotes special rights such as freedom from obligatory duties and requirements to observe certain rules. Special requirements, too, are imposed on family, friends, and medical (used generically) personnel. Robinson (1971) talks of reciprocal transactions between the symptomatic person and significant others. Illness is characterized as temporary, dependence is legitimized, and the assumption of recovery to a normal functioning is built in. Chronic illness alters this situation. "The symptomatic person will be seen by significant others to have broken the chain of reciprocal transactions, since he will not be able to repay the investment which the relevant significant others would place in the sick, not-sick personal relationship." These relationships must be redefined, for feelings are heightened if such illness leads to institutionalization. The focus of the health care team's treatment of chronically ill and disabled people must relate to caring rather than curing. It is the most disabled, the most functionally impaired, and the sickest whom we care for in the skilled nursing facility and who are the subject of this paper.

The institutionalized person is subject to tremendous losses—loss of health, of community and home, of identity, of dignity, of status, and of self-esteem. These losses often lead to a sense of helplessness and hopelessness. The patients in long-term-care facilities have few opportunities for retaining connections with their former life, for retaining or regaining social skills, and for developing a dynamic and/or challenging life-style.

Given these conditions, how do we help lessen such feelings of hopelessness and helplessness? The trained social worker and therapeutic recreator, as members of a health team, (1) individualize and assess the patient as a person; (2) consider underlying feelings as these relate to the patient's new status within the institution (feelings of rejection, dependency, ambivalence, loss of self-esteem, and so on); and (3) recognize and use the person's current strengths, as well as past coping patterns.

Maslow (1943) developed a theory of human motivation in which he stated that human needs arrange themselves in the following ascending order: physiological needs (food, rest, and so on); safety needs (protection against danger and the like); social needs (need for belonging, for association, for acceptance by his fellows, for giving and receiving love and friendship); ego needs (self-esteem, self-confidence, independence, achievement, competence, status, recognition); and self-fulfillment and self-actualization (needs for realizing one's own potentialities, for continued self-development, for being creative). Recreation and social work deal primarily with the latter three categories—that is, social needs, ego needs, and self-fulfillment and self-actualization.

Our intake social worker (whom the patient already knows from his preadmission contacts) admits the patient and thereby demonstrates our facility's commitment to the concept of personalization and recognition of human needs. On the day of arrival, our recreator brings to the new patient a fresh flower, which serves as a symbol of life—welcome, caring, giving, individualization. A patient representative of the Beth Abraham patient welcoming committee visits the newly admitted patient as a peer. The patient welcomer thereby reinforces the hopeful aspects of institutionalization. The visit says, in effect, "You see, I have made it. Let me help you to do so, too."

Following these initial contacts the roles of the caseworker, group worker, and recreator are clear. The caseworker completes the psychosocial diagnosis and develops a treatment plan to help the individual patient to live to the fullest for the remaining period of life. The recreator serves as a catalyst to help the patient implement expressed and implied desires and interests.

The Case of Miss N

Miss N is an extraordinary example of self-fulfillment and self-actualization. She entered Beth Abraham in a state of depression, following years of being homebound as a result of a crippling accident. After months of concentrated efforts by the caseworker, the group worker, and the recreator, Miss N was able to work through some of the feelings that so often accompany institutionalization (rejection, loss of self-esteem, and so on) and move into an active role, discovering forgotten strengths and assuming true leadership in several patient organizations. For her, institutionalization opened up new avenues of life.

As she lived through new and different experiences and felt

success and accomplishment, she was able to progress to a higher level of living—giving of herself to others. She virtually adopted a gravely handicapped lone patient, fulfilling, in a way, the maternal role that she had never had. She was elected to the chair of Community Voices, a patient social-action organization, which serves as a link between institutionalized patients and the outer community and vice versa, enabling patients to lessen their feelings of abandonment and isolation from the world at large. During Miss N's administration, this organization pioneered in changing the attitudes of the community at large, including those of the political structure. For example, an official election board was established at Beth Abraham so that patients could continue to exercise their basic rights as citizens of the United States, on a regular voting machine. Additionally, at our patients' request to their elected representatives, drop curbs at street crossings were constructed in our neighborhood several years ago. This enabled the wheelchair-bound patients to move more easily and safely on their periodic shopping trips.

Community Voices mobilized itself as any other group might have and joined administration and staff in protest of unjustified Medicaid cutbacks. Hundreds of signatures were collected by patients on petitions to appropriate leaders. As president of Community Voices, Miss N was part of several delegations to the mayor, the governor, and other legislative representatives. Her presence, in her wheelchair, emphasized the needs of the otherwise forgotten institutionalized aged and disabled people. She posed the question "Must institutionalization represent an end of life?"

The Case of Miss S

Miss S, a severely arthritic, completely disabled midlife woman, entered Beth Abraham after years of confinement in another institution. For her, the path of fulfillment was somewhat different.

Her social worker identified the above-average intellectual strengths of this quiet, withdrawn woman and directed her toward becoming part of a small group of patients to be trained as librarians for a patient-operated library within the facility. This library has grown and achieved status comparable to that of a public library. Its patient executive committee, working with a professional group worker or therapeutic recreator, is responsible for determination of policy, managing a budget, and staffing. They are continuously mindful of the changing reading needs of the total patient population and how best to meet them.

Recognizing that fulfillment for Miss S had to be through intellectual pursuits, the group worker enabled her to move into a leadership role on the editorial committee of the patient's quarterly publication, *Beth Abraham Speaks*. This committee selects, edits, and designs the contents. It can and has rejected articles considered inappropriate, including one submitted by the medical director.

Here we can see a patient, individually and as part of a group, resolve her inner conflicts and ambivalence around dependency and begin to achieve a sense of self-worth through varied activities and contributions, reinforcing her ego strengths and living a more normal life. Such a patient can participate in the decision-making process individually and for the group, which the process of institutionalization traditionally removes.

Like the social worker, the professional recreator sees the patient as an individual with a life that has been lived, with memories of a past, with a culture, a style and, a family and set of circumstances unique to that person. The recreational and vocational choices made in the community reflect a life-style and give us clues to the direction the recreator should take to involve the patient. The patient, in collaboration with the recreator, chooses avenues for self-expression available within the institution within new physical limitations.

One patient, Miss B, meets her ego needs and feels fulfilled by being the secretary of many patient committees. She has her own desk and typewriter and has achieved status within the institutional community, despite her severe handicap, including problems of verbal communication. Another patient, severely disabled but verbally creative, has become known as the "poet laureate" of Beth Abraham.

Mr. S, a forty-three-year-old, severely disabled multiple sclerosis patient, had played the trumpet in his premorbid days. Because of his inability to use his hands, he can no longer play the trumpet. However, through a music-poetry workshop it was discovered that he had perfect pitch, and the music therapist is working with him individually and reawakening involvement, through the joy of music.

The Case of Miss K

Miss K, fully oriented, was devastated by her new dependence and angry at the "fates" and herself, as she found herself hopeless and quite alone at the end stage of her life. She had until recently been gainfully employed. She had been involved with her sister's family and had regular social engagements. Her hobbies had included rug-making, embroidery, and needlepoint. Now she was angry, denying her terminal illness and constantly testing those around her.

The social worker was regularly called upon to intervene and interpret her behavior and try to bring what seemed to be an adversary relationship more into consonance. Both the social worker and the recreator clearly recognized the need to help Miss K feel accepted as a thinking, competent person. At her request the recreator wanted to provide Miss K with some handiwork. Aware that Miss K could no longer concentrate on the intricate sophisticated kind of needlepoint that she had formerly done, the recreator chose the following path. To have brought to Miss K only something simple, which she might accomplish but which would have been demeaning, would have reinforced her own sense of current worthlessness. She therefore brought to Miss K one piece of intricate handiwork, as well as several other immediately gratifying crafts, giving to Miss K the opportunity to choose her activity.

Other patients may choose to involve themselves in reproducing living things. A gardening club has attracted far more patients than had been anticipated. They grow flowers, fruits, and vegetables from seed and cuttings and often hold parties to eat their produce. These examples represent only a few of the many programs and activities available to the patients at Beth Abraham through which—with the support of the group work, recreation, and music therapy staff—patients can achieve some sense of fulfillment.

We must state that this presentation has dealt with only one aspect of the social service department's function and role within Beth

Abraham. We must further point out that this paper deals with only one segment of our patient population. Some patients will not participate in what might be "fulfilling" or creative, which we accept as a demonstration of their right to choose. Many others, because of their almost complete physical, mental, and/or emotional inability to make choices, are dealt with in a prescriptive fashion by the professional staff and are not included in this paper.

It is not easy for a staff to be faced with and deal with the helplessness and hopelessness of institutionalized patients on an ongoing, full-time basis. It is emotionally and physically draining; it is frustrating and at times overwhelming. We believe that only the well-trained and experienced human-services professional can cope with such personal stress and professional demands. For caring staff to be able to understand and lend necessary strengths, to give without overwhelming, to empathize without overidentifying, it must have reached a level of personal and professional maturity. Such staff members must be assured of ample opportunity for expressing their feelings and fears through supervision, staff meetings and seminars, in-service training, and the like to achieve job satisfaction and professional growth.

Finally, in addition to the direct services provided to the patient and other members of the caring team, the professional social worker and therapeutic recreator have an equal if not more important role as teacher–trainers. Social-work schools and recreation/leisure studies departments of universities have incorporated into their field placements assignments for students in geriatric institutions, skilled nursing facilities, chronic care facilities, and hospitals for chronically ill patients. The professionals in these settings create the role image for entering students. They are the teachers and the supervisors.

To help a student understand, develop, and grow while working with institutionalized patients is not easy. However, it is essential to train today's students to become tomorrow's practitioners if we truly believe in meeting the needs of our institutionalized aged and disabled people.

Imagine the sense of gratification for a student who hears her patient say, "you didn't know me when I came here right after my stroke a few years ago. I was angry and I wanted to die. Now look at me, I am one of the editors of the patient magazine, a member of the adult-education planning committee, an executive board member of the recreation council and chairman of my floor's social committee. I am living! Don't you agree with me that this warrants a celebration?''

Death is a part of life! In the skilled nursing facility death surrounds us more intensively than it does in society at large. A total commitment to ''life'' is required on the part of all disciplines, augmented by the special knowhow and dedication by the social service and recreation staff to make life worthwhile.

References

Maslow, A. H. 1943. ''A Theory of Human Motivation.'' *Psychological Review* 50:370–96.
Robinson, D. 1971. *The Process of Becoming Ill: Medicine, Illness and Society,* vol. 2. In W. M. Williams, ed. London: Routledge and Kegan Paul.

23

Perspectives on Death
in a Chronic Treatment Setting

DANIEL J. KLENOW, THOMAS P. DUNFEE,
and GARY A. MITCHELL

A wide range of empirical investigations has focused on the social psychological and social organizational dimensions of death in medical settings. These studies have specifically dealt with such topics as death in public and private hospitals (Sudnow 1967), the socialization of physicians to death (Coombs and Powers 1976), death and the chronically or terminally ill (Fitts and Ravdin 1953, Beard 1977, Van den Noort 1977, Reynolds and Kalish 1974), staff coping with death (Waechter 1973, Jaeger and Simmons 1970, Schulz and Aderman 1976), and communicating death news (Glaser and Strauss 1965, Oken 1961, Charmaz 1976). The purpose of the present study is to extend this knowledge base by analyzing the contextual complexities of death in a specialized treatment facility for chronic patients.

The Setting

The data for this study were gathered in a hospital located in a standard metropolitan statistical area of approximately 280,000 in the North Central section of the United States. This hospital is a private,

This research represents part of a larger project funded by a grant from the Kidney Foundation of Indiana.

voluntary, nonprofit, general-medical surgical facility with a 338-bed capacity. In 1976 more than 11,000 patients were admitted, and more than 40,000 were treated on an outpatient basis.

The hemodialysis facilities of this hospital provide the research focus. The unit is under the codirectorship of two physicians who are board-certified in internal medicine and nephrology. The staff includes four registered nurses, four licensed practical nurses, one chief technologist, and six dialysis technicians. The staff is entirely female with the exception of the physicians, one registered nurse, and the chief technologist. The group is relatively young, ten staff members being in the twenty-to-thirty-year age group and seven being in their early thirties. Only one staff member is over forty.

The physicians have been with the unit since its inception. The newest staff member has spent seven months in the unit, one nurse has three and one-half years, and the remaining staff have been with the center for periods ranging from one year to two and one-half years. Turnover has not been a major problem in this facility.

Six of the patients included in the sample are male and seven are female. One patient is under twenty-one, another falls into the twenty-one-to-thirty category, two patients are in their thirties, and three are in their forties. The remaining six patients are over 61. Seven of the patients have had some high school, four are high school graduates, and two have had some college. Six patients have been on dialysis for one to two years, four from two to three years, two from three to four years, and one for more than four years.

The unit became operational in July 1972. From that time it has grown to serve a patient population that includes seventy-four chronic hemodialysis patients. Thirty-two of these patients dialyze in the chronic maintenance unit in a building adjacent to the hospital. Forty-two dialyze under the supervision of a trained partner at home. The patient population varies from time to time as some receive transplants, die, or move to other areas. The general trend is in the direction of a larger patient group.

Methods

The methodological format of this study follows the grounded theory approach advocated by Glaser and Strauss (1964). Therefore, the research methods are most appropriately labeled as the field method (Schatzman and Strauss 1973). This study attempts to generate important social dimensions, theoretical propositions, or hypotheses that are grounded in the data. This is an inductive approach to data analysis known as "the constant comparative method of qualitative analysis" (Glaser and Strauss 1964).

The data-gathering process took place over a fourteen-month span in 1975–76. Methodological strategies included the use of observation and the tracer technique (Schatzman and Strauss 1973), which involves gathering data by following and observing staff members at each echelon (physician, head nurse, registered nurse, licensed practical nurse, and technician) during their work shifts. Intensive semistructured tape-recorded interviews were conducted with all staff members (N = 17) and approximately one-half (N = 13) of the patients in the chronic maintenance unit. The fieldwork was conducted in an openly specified manner—that is, the sociologist was viewed as a student gathering data for a doctoral dissertation.

Analysis

Staff Perspectives

The analysis of this social setting revealed a long-term time frame of chronic treatment. This temporal structure had an important impact on staff and patient interaction patterns. Friendship patterns developed between patients and staff. This is not characteristic in other areas of the general hospital, where patients are primarily seen on a short-term or acute basis. Staff and patients in this unit often described their relationships as a "family." Accordingly, the death of a patient was often greeted by the statement, "It's like losing a member of the family."

The impact of a patient's death on staff members can be understood by focusing on three factors. The first involved ascertaining the type of social relationship that existed between the staff member and the deceased patient. If the staff person barely knew the patient, then, of course, the impact was minimal. The death of a patient-friend, on the other hand, was very upsetting. The development of a protective attitude of "detached concern" (Lief and Fox 1963) was used by some staff in an effort to cope with these potentially upsetting deaths. As one staff member pointed out, "One needs to protect oneself from becoming real personal friends because often very tragic things happen to patients."

Staff reactions to the death of a patient could also be understood by focusing on the characteristics of the patient. If the patient had engaged in behavior that could be viewed as intentional noncompliance—for example, skipping treatments or drinking too much—then feelings of sadness and loss were mitigated, because primary responsibility was attributed to the patient. A final factor in understanding staff reactions to a patient's death required an analysis of the medical status of the patient prior to death. If the patient was sick over a long period of time, then the death was often viewed in less negative terms, since the patient was now through with the misery and pain.

The death of a patient also presented problems for staff members because of the difficulty they had in breaking this news to the other dialysis patients. They generally did not want to be the ones to break such news and were unsure of how much information to give about the details of the death. Staff frequently believed that this news had a negative impact on the patients. It was this view that led staff members to avoid communicating the death news to other patients. However, even when the death was communicated, an attempt was often made to associate the death "with something other than the dialysis." The problem in communicating death news was increased by at least two factors. The first factor dealt with the physical structure and ecology of the dialysis unit. Patients received their treatment in one large room and were able to take note of the presence or absence of others on their shift. This created a pressure on staff members to communicate the death news, since the absence of a patient could not be successfully ignored. At the same time, another factor operated as a communication inhibitor. All these patients shared the same general medical status: end-stage renal failure. This common denominator formed a strong basis for interpersonal identification and social comparison. According to many staff members, this was the factor that made the news of the death of another patient so potentially depressing. Many staff assumed that patients held the following orientation:

"Will what happened to this patient also happen to me?" Experience with and belief in this patient orientation operated as an inhibitor to the communication of death news.

Patient Perspectives

The impact of the death of a dialysis patient was also ascertained from the sample of patients. They were asked the following question toward the end of an intensive semistructured interview: "How do you view the death of a fellow patient?" The responses were given quite openly, and the question did not seem to be distressing to these patients.

The death of a dialysis patient is not an infrequent occurrence. The mortality rate of dialysis patients in this unit was 7 percent yearly, making the possibility of death in a fellow patient quite real. Death was most often related to nonrenal disease such as complications of arteriosclerosis—that is, heart attacks and strokes. Dialysis-related deaths also occurred, however, if less frequently than non-dialysis-related deaths. In this group of patients, patient compliance was a major factor. While direct dialysis-related accidents are possible, such an event did not occur in this unit.

The patient data can be understood by isolating the dominant perspective or "loss rationale" expressed in the interview. The term *loss rationale* was elaborated by Glaser and Strauss (1964) and refers to the development of a perspective on a death that reduces the emotional upset generated by the event. Examples of such loss rationales include: "It's their own fault." "It was a blessing he passed on, he was in such pain." "She had a full life." Four distinct loss rationales were presented by the hemodialysis patients in this study.

The first loss rationale involves comparing the medical status of the deceased to the medical status of the patient developing the loss rationale. This perspective focuses on supporting the conclusion that the deceased was in some way different from the living. Five patients employed this type of loss rationale. This self-protective strategy involves determining the cause of the patient's death; therefore information seeking is of great import. Patients very often realized or were told by staff members that many of these deceased patients were also burdened with heart problems, diabetes, or some other complicating condition. In attempting to develop a loss rationale, one patient went as far as calling the spouse of a deceased patient (she had never met the spouse) in an effort to ascertain the cause of the death. This patient stated, "I wasn't afraid, but I was kind of leery. I wanted to know if these things [points to her fistula] was the cause of that." This patient's concern was satisfied when the spouse indicated that the death was due to dietary indiscretions rather than blood access (fistula) problems. The process of social comparison used in the development of this loss rationale is further indicated by the following statement:

> I know that they were in bad shape, had heart trouble or something like that, see. Sure, it makes you feel bad when somebody you've been with all the time like that while you're on the machine dies. But most generally they have heart trouble, or are diabetic, or something like that, which I never have been.

This patient clearly exemplified the comparisons that take place between the self and the deceased.

The second loss rationale, expressed by three patients, is a variation of the first. Again, the medical status of the deceased patient is the focal point. However, in this perspective the deceased is not compared with the patient forming the perspective but rather is compared with the living patient's own condition at the point of death. As one patient indicated:

> The way I feel about it is he's better off. Because if he was sick enough to die he is much better off. Now they're out of their pain and misery and that's it.

This theme was echoed in the response of another patient who said, "Perhaps I feel a mixture of relief that they don't have to put up with some of the symptoms."

The third loss rationale is typified by the use of social comparison to differentiate the noncompliant patients who have died. These patients were viewed as different from other deceased patients because the responsibility for their death could be attributed to the patient. Two patients using this loss rationale related the following:

And I feel like sometimes a patient that dies or something, sometimes it depends upon them. They don't stick to their diet. They don't do what they are supposed to do.

Unless they have gained too much weight or their potassium is too high and that's their fault.

Staff members also use this attribution process as a loss rationale in gaining perspective on this type of death.

Two patients exhibited fatalistic perspectives on the death of other patients. One simply stated, "It's your way to go." The other espoused a religiously grounded fatalism. This patient stated:

I feel that when a patient pass away, really Jehovah knows what's best. There is nothing that could be did about it, you know. You feel sorry for them but, you know, only one person knows best and that's Jehovah.

As this patient indicated, any of these types of loss rationales develop with feelings of sadness. Indeed, as Glaser and Strauss (1964) indicate, these loss rationales "serve to balance off the effects of social loss on nurses." We may extend this to include the personal loss that patients also experience.

Discussion

The data indicate that the staff and patients in this hemodialysis unit employ a variety of loss rationales when viewing the death of another patient. These loss rationales were not clearly linked or patterned toward any particular variable—for example, age, sex, or occupational status. However, further research employing a larger sample may uncover such patterns. Existing research (Glaser and Strauss 1964, Christopherson and Lunde 1977) suggests that these types of loss rationales are used in settings dealing with other medical conditions. For example, Christopherson and Lunde (1977) studied the psychosocial adjustment of a group of cardiac-transplant recipients and discovered that these patients developed special strategies for dealing with the death of a fellow transplant patient. These researchers stated:

Each surviving patient typically protects himself emotionally by developing, after a few days, theories about the death which make him different from the deceased. "He smoked (or drank) a lot." "He didn't exercise enough, but I do." "He died of something not related to the transplant." Each of the reasons expressed has an element of truth, but each also serves an obvious protective function for the patient who remains.

Again, we see the development of similar types of loss rationales with the cardiac-transplant patients.

These data also bring out an element of divergence in terms of general staff and patient reactions to death. Staff frequently tried to avoid communicating death news, because they felt that it had a negative impact on patients. This attitude may have developed from experiences that supported such an evaluation. Another factor may have involved the age differentials between staff and patients. The staff were generally quite young, early twenties and thirties, and were far from death as a personal reality. Since the thought of their death may have been highly disruptive at this early stage in their lives, they may have assumed and/or projected the same feelings onto the patients. Kastenbaum (1969) has suggested essentially this same interpretation to account for the assumptions that the young have about the death perspectives of older people.

The patients in this setting did not appear overtroubled by the issue of death. This may indicate that the various loss rationales effectively protected the patients from emotional upset. Their lack of any great concern with death may also have been due to the research design of the study. Patients and staff were not interviewed after an actual death had occurred. These patients may also have been desensitized to death because of the fact that they had been living with a serious chronic condition for many years. In addition, the majority of the patients in the study were older. Research (Jeffers et al. 1961, Swenson 1961, Bengtson et al. 1977) has indicated that, in general, elderly people are not extremely fearful of death. These and possibly other factors account for the issue of divergent perspectives on the part of staff and patients.

References

Beard, B. H. 1977. "Hope and Fear with Hemodialysis." In E. M. Pattison, ed. *The Experience of Dying,* pp. 268–75. Englewood Cliffs, N.J.: Prentice-Hall.

Bengtson, V. L., J. B. Cuellar, and P. K. Ragan. 1977. "Stratum Contrasts and Similarities in Attitudes Toward Death." *Journal of Gerontology* 32:76–88.

Charmaz, K. 1976. "The Coroner's Strategies for Announcing Death." In L. H. Lofland, ed. *Toward a Sociology of Death and Dying,* pp. 61–82. Beverly Hills, Calif.: Sage Publications.

Christopherson, L. K. and D. T. Lunde. 1977. "Selection of Cardiac Transplant Recipients and Their Subsequent Psychosocial Adjustment." In R. H. Moos, ed. *Coping with Physical Illness,* pp. 352–66. New York: Plenum.

Coombs, R. H. and P. S. Powers. 1976. "Socialization for Death: The Physician's Role." In L. H. Lofland, ed. *Toward a Sociology of Death and Dying,* pp. 15–36. Beverly Hills, Calif.: Sage Publications.

Fitts, W. T. and I. S. Ravdin. 1953. "What Philadelphia Physicians Tell Patients With Cancer." *Journal of the American Medical Association* 153:901–4.

Glaser, B. and A. L. Strauss. 1964. "The Social Loss of Dying Patients." *American Journal of Nursing* 64:119–21.

—— 1965. *Awareness of Dying.* Chicago: Aldine.

—— 1967. *The Study of Grounded Theory.* Chicago: Aldine.

Jaeger, D. and L. W. Simmons. 1970. *The Aged Ill: Coping With Problems in Geriatric Care.* New York: Appleton-Century-Crofts.

Jeffers, E. C., C. R. Nicholas, and C. Eisdorfer. 1961. "Attitudes of Older Persons Toward Death: A Preliminary Survey." *Journal of Gerontology* 16:53–56.

Kastenbaum, R. 1969. "Death and Bereavement in Later Life." In A. H. Kutscher, ed. *Death and Bereavement,* pp. 28–54. Springfield, Ill.: Charles C Thomas.

Lief, H. I. and R. C. Fox. 1963. "Training for 'Detached Concern' in Medical Students." In H. I. Leif and N. R. Lief, eds. *The Psychological Basis of Medical Practice.* New York: Harper and Row.

Oken, D. 1961. "What To Tell Cancer Patients." *Journal of the American Medical Association* 175:86–94.

Reynolds, D. K. and R. A. Kalish. 1974. "The Social Ecology of Dying: Observations of Wards for the Terminally Ill." *Hospital and Community Psychiatry* 25:147–52.

Schatzman, L. and A. Strauss. 1973. *Field Research: Strategies for a Natural Sociology.* Englewood Cliffs, N.J.: Prentice-Hall.

Schulz, R. and D. Aderman. 1976. "How the Medical Staff Copes With Dying Patients: A Critical Review." *Omega* 7:11–21.

Sudnow, D. 1967. *Passing On.* Englewood Cliffs, N.J.: Prentice-Hall.

Swenson, W. M. 1961. "Attitudes Toward Death in an Aged Population." *Journal of Gerontology* 16:53–56.

Van den Noort, S. 1977. "Life, Limbo, and Death with Multiple Sclerosis." In

E. M. Pattison, ed. *The Experience of Dying,* pp. 268–75. Englewood Cliffs, N.J.: Prentice-Hall.

Waechter, E. H. 1973. "Nursing and the Dying Patient." In R. H. Davis, ed. *Dealing with Death,* pp. 47–60. Los Angeles: Ethel Percy Andrus Gerontology Center.

24

Introducing a Hospice Program to a Long-Term Care Facility

FLORENCE SAFFORD

*T*HE GRAPHIC TERM *long-term care facility,* which came into usage along with Medicare and Medicaid, is really a pseudonym for an old-age home or home for the aged. And an old-age home, according to public opinion, is a place where old folks go to die.

To counteract this negative image, most good facilities try to provide an optimistic and cheerful environment. Services and activities are designed to encourage the aged residents to live as fully as their individual capacities and desires dictate. The goals of good institutional care include treating the loneliness and depression that often accompany old age. The ideal milieu of such a facility is therapeutic.

Where, then, does the concept of a hospice program, which offers specialized care for the dying, fit into a therapeutic milieu? The average age of the residents at the Isabella Geriatric Center (New York City), as in similar facilities, is 84 years. Statistically and realistically, each resident can be viewed as being in a terminal stage of life. Every week there is a reminder of terminality, as two or three residents die. Although the deaths are noted and regretted, there is an unspoken agreement not to dwell on morbidity. For every resident who dies, a new resident needing care is admitted. Death is accepted by most older people as a natural event in very old age. However, in order to be able to enjoy the unknown span of life ahead, most tend to deny ubiquitous death and instead plan ahead for the next pleasant event.

The staff also uses the mechanism of denial to support and encourage a frequently fragile population. At times, in the process of fostering positive attitudes, the staff may not tune in to those residents who may be nearing death and who may need to talk out their feelings about dying. A hospice program sensitizes staff to their own attitudes about death and the process of dying and seeks to help members of the staff be more open to the cues of dying residents in need of specialized attention.

At the Isabella Geriatric Center, the hospice program was introduced by our former medical director, who was also affiliated with St. Luke's Hospital in New York City, which pioneered the hospice concept as part of an acute-care hospital program. St. Luke's, in turn, modeled its program after St. Christopher's in London, a small, free-standing facility dedicated to humane treatment of the terminally ill. There are now several models of hospice programs: free-standing facilities, units within acute-care hospitals, and models linking home care and institutional services. The basic principle common to all models of hospice care is that the terminally ill and their families need compassionate treatment by members of a care team that is sensitive to their special needs.

Even with 100 percent commitment of the staff in principle, however, it is not a simple matter to put the plan into practice. This is particularly true when the project is not separately funded or staffed but is conceived as an additional program in an institution that is constantly struggling to meet its goals with limited staff and budgets.

Many planning sessions were held, beginning in the fall of 1975, by a multidisciplinary committee, comprising administration, nursing, medical, dietary, and social service, before the acute-care model could be transposed to the organizational structure of a long-term-care facility. The committee developed the principle of a hospice team, consisting of the direct caregivers closest to the residents in the institution: the doctor, nurse, aide, and social worker. Other members of the staff are involved in the individual plan for each hospice patient, as needed, such as the director of volunteer services, the clergy, the resident care coordinator, and the director of housekeeping. The social worker is designated as coordinator of the team and has the responsibility of arranging team conferences once a week, or more often if needed, as long as the hospice patient and/or his family require special services.

The following stated philosophy and objectives are modeled after those of St. Luke's hospice:

Philosophy

The Isabella Geriatric Center's hospice committee is concerned with meeting the total medical, psychological, social, and spiritual needs of the critically ill and dying patient. Staff endeavors are directed toward creating an atmosphere of understanding, comfort, and support to enable the patient to die with dignity.

Objectives of Project

1. To assist patients to a state where they experience relief from distressing symptoms, pain, and fear of pain.
2. To achieve objective signs in patients indicating feelings of peace and security.
3. To review patients weekly, or as often as indicated, in team conferences to determine if goals of hospice care are appropriate.
4. To ensure that patients experience increased contact with staff and volunteers as death approaches, if the patients want and need it.
5. To give patients and family the opportunity to draw closer together as death approaches.
6. To support families in the bereavement process.
7. To educate and assist the staff in developing an awareness of their own response to death.
8. To offer the staff the support of the hospice team and hospice committee as they work with the dying.
9. To provide staff who can support the patient and family through the grief and bereavement process.

Procedures have been made as simple as possible, since hospice tasks are, in practice, an addition to the normal job responsibilities. Any member of the hospice team can refer patients to the hospice program when it is felt that they are terminal within three or four months, when they or the family are aware of the condition, and when there is a need for special services.

The following policies were developed for our institution.

Policies

1. The director of medical services, in conjunction with the attending physician, will review medications with the primary goal of relieving uncomfortable and unpleasant symptoms.
2. Visitors will be permitted to visit the patient at all times.
3. Meals for visitors will be available in the house dining room.
4. Dietary service will provide coffee for relatives in the patient's room.
5. Parking will be provided to relatives at all hours.
6. The chaplain will be available at the patient's request.
7. Dietary service will comply as far as possible with patient's wishes regarding choice of food.
8. Patient will be allowed alcohol as approved by the attending physician.
9. If the terminal resident has special needs that cannot be met by the family, the resident care coordinator and specially selected volunteers will be notified by the social worker of the team to help provide for special needs.
10. Contact between staff and resident will be increased if appropriate.

In order to start the program, a series of staff meetings was conducted by the director of social service with the medical staff, nurses, aides, and social workers. During these sessions, based on the work of Kübler-Ross, the staff was encouraged to examine their personal attitudes toward death and dying, as objectified in their own behavior toward the terminal patient. There was general acknowledgment that it is a difficult task to be supportive to the patient who needs to talk about his anxieties concerning death, and avoidance is a common practice. Having the support of others in the hospice team can make it easier to overcome the fears that lead to denial and avoidance.

Because of the lack of time and special budget to implement this program, it has taken a long time to follow through with thorough case finding. Unclear guidelines during the first year concerning criteria for referral to the program led to many referrals of patients who were on the critical list and who were no longer capable of benefiting from services. Although support was offered to their families, this was not different from the normal services provided by the staff.

Only twelve patients were treated actively as hospice patients during the past year. They had all been active and independent, despite advanced old age and chronic conditions, until the last three or four months of their lives. The hospice program definitely made the staff more sensitive to their needs. They were provided with a range of services such as special foods (smoked goose, Chinese food brought in, homemade rice pudding, etc.), increased contacts with families and distant friends and relatives, extensive room service, and private rooms in the nursing home if possible.

It is not a large percentage of our population that seems to need a hospice program. Most older people have come to accept the inevitability of death, having experienced many losses of loved ones during their lifetime. The vast majority of our residents are realistic, expressing a wish to have a quick and easy death. Their greatest fear is senility or a prolonged period of infirmity. Many who are debilitated and weary welcome death and wish for it as a release.

But some residents, facing death, react differently. They may become angry, hostile, manipulative, withdrawn. They may reject the staff they need for assistance and support. From the perspective of a developmental life-cycle approach, the staff must assist them in working through their life-cycle task of accepting death. The staff must learn to identify when the approach of death revives unresolved conflicts that can be worked through, easing the passage toward death.

The philosophy of Isabella Home has always been highly individualized care and a consistent concern for the quality of life of each resident. However, as an institution, it is subject to budgeting considerations and rules and regulations for efficient management, which sometimes conflict with the desires of an individual resident and the family. The advantage of hospice, according to our medical director, is that "it allows us to break our own rules."

By breaking our own rules and by forcing ourselves to examine and change our behavior toward some of our terminal patients, we were able to provide these patients with a comfortable and meaningful terminal stage and a death with true dignity. In providing these services, the staff derived great satisfaction and is gaining in the capacity to reach out and identify those terminal patients in need of hospice.

Part
Four

Educational Issues
for Patients and Caregivers

25

Death Education
for the Elderly:
Facing the Inevitable

SANDRA E. TARS

*D*EATH EDUCATION IN the United States has come a long way during the last decade. Whereas academic coursework in the area of death and dying was almost unknown before the publication of Kübler-Ross's pioneering research caught the public imagination in 1969, it is now commonplace. Most colleges, universities, and medical schools have at least one, and usually several, courses in which the cosideration of issues related to death and dying is a major focus. Feifel (1977) notes that "surface consideration of death these days has become lively—almost chic." Yet, Feifel points out, "despite these wellsprings of contact, Americans still approach dying and death warily and gingerly." Nowhere is this more evident than in the consideration of death issues related to the elderly.

As one surveys the burgeoning literature on death and dying, it becomes increasingly evident that the aged, although statistically the group most likely to die, is the group least likely to be discussed in theory or research or focused on in education. College students take courses, professionals attend seminars, paraprofessionals receive training, patients dying of cancer or other "glamour" diseases of the moment receive counseling, but little mention is made of educative efforts directed toward the aged in the community as they approach their last days and years.

Gerontologists frequently emphasize the many death-related stresses prevalent in the later years of life. Theories of primary prevention in mental health indicate the importance of identifying such common stresses and of finding ways to help individuals who would otherwise fail to master them. Much emphasis has been placed on educative techniques in dealing with identified stresses at earlier points in the life cycle. Educational materials have been developed not only for community providers but also for the general public. One rationale behind this aproach is that by increasing knowledge of a range of alternative behaviors and choices, one increases the ability of the individual to find an appropriate solution to a given problem situation. This paper focuses on a number of areas in which such educative efforts directed toward elders and significant others in the community might pay dividends.

There has been no scientific assessment of the need for death-related educational activities experienced by the elderly or by persons living or working closely with them. A number of areas of concern do emerge from consideration of personal professional experience in both clinical and research endeavors with community-dwelling elderly individuals and their families.

One issue frequently raised by elders is the difficulty they experience in attempting to discuss their own death with family members or close friends. The following comments are typical of those raised in a number of discussions with groups of elders: "If only young people could understand that there are many things worse than death. I'm not afraid of dying. But there are some things I want to talk about with my children before I go." "I don't want to dwell on death. But every time I bring it up they say, 'Oh Dad, you're not going to die tomorrow. Let's not worry about it.' Well, I'm 78 and I'm not going to live forever. I wish they weren't so afraid to talk about my death." Individuals in these groups have gone on to help each other work out some potential strategies for broaching this subject to their children. Mutual support has also been given through sharing difficulties commonly experienced.

Such comments also indicate the need for attention to increasing the awareness of younger family members of their elders' potential need to discuss death-related topics. Middle-aged offspring need to be aware that such open discussion is appropriate and not indicative of "morbid thinking." They may also need support in dealing with their own need to deny the inevitable death of their parents. Kastenbaum (1977) has discussed a number of the difficulties involved for middle-aged persons facing parental bereavement in terms of their own life-span development vis-à-vis death.

Another major area of concern is related to the particular cultural experience of death of persons in the current cohort of elderly. Persons born in the last years of the nineteenth century and early decades of the twentieth century typically had many more close, personal encounters with death than those born later in this century. Before the decline in infant and maternal mortality, the advent of public-health sanitation measures, and the development of antibiotics, death struck persons throughout the life span, rather than predominantly those in their older years. Today's elders consequently saw people of all ages die and generally experienced death of a significant other by their early twenties, if not before. This is in marked contrast to the personal experience of death of later cohorts.

Several aspects of this greater personal contact with the death experience are of note. The first is related to the context of death in the early years of this century as compared with the present. Previously, terminal care was often given in the home, by family and friends. The dying individual was in many ways the center of attention. Today's elders may contrast this, perhaps in an idealized recollection, with the anonymous, impersonal experience of death for those dying in hospitals and nursing homes, often with family and friends prevented from being at their bedside by inflexible regulations. Many of today's elders would prefer to receive the same sort of treatment they participated in when giving terminal care to family or friends in earlier years. The fear of dying alone, in a strange place, is often expressed. The educative issues raised by this concern include: (1) the opportunity for the elderly to discuss their wish to die at home, cared for by loved ones; (2) discussion of the real or perceived reluctance of children or family to accept such a responsibility; (3) the need to resolve ambivalence over this desire versus the contrasting wish not to be a burden. Discussion with others faced by this same issue might help many elders to look at the alternatives available to them and to make an informed decision about how to proceed within the context of their own individual situation.

A less desirable legacy of the elderly person's previous experience with death may come in the fear of death as a painful event. Many elders describe agonizing deaths suffered by members of their families, before the current spectrum of treatments and pain killers was available. Misconceptions and fears about the ordinary process of dying need to be dealt with.

Another educative approach further addresses the issue of dying in the institution. Many elders are poorly informed about their civil rights as community residents and patients. What right do they have to: (1) refuse removal to a hospital or nursing home; (2) refuse medical treatments that may prolong life; (3) choose the place and manner of their own death? When elders have access to such information, they are better equipped to insist on the treatment most appropriate to their own needs at the time of crisis.

Increased knowledge of civil rights may heighten awareness of areas where rights of individuals to make their own choices are denied. "Senior power" may well be wielded to promote social change through legal efforts and pressure on institutions to change to meet the needs expressed by this cohort. Hospitals have made drastic changes in their policies, practices, and facilities in the wake of widespread childbirth education. Death education might likewise have impact in increasing the ability of us all to die in the place and manner of our own choosing.

A final area that may be addressed is related to the developmental tasks ascribed by a variety of theorists to the later years. Erikson (1950) describes the final life crisis to be that of ego integrity versus despair. He describes the attributes of this stage as follows: "It is the acceptance of one's one and only life cycle and of the people who have become significant to it as something that had to be . . . and an acceptance of the fact that one's life is one's own responsibility" (1968). "The lack or loss of this accrued ego integration is signified by a fear of death. . . . Despair expresses the feeling that the time is now short, too short for the attempt to start another life and to try out alternate roads to integrity" (1950). Butler (1963) has similarly indicated the importance of reminiscence in the later years of life to help the individual attain a revised or expanded meaning of the past. This reorganization of the past may give new perspective and meaning to one's life and allow one to face death without fear. Open-ended growth groups, which allow elders to exchange thoughts and experiences, may help to promote this function in a positive way.

The preceding suggestions for productive educational initiatives are based on a conception of elders as persons who are open to new information and who will actively use information gained to promote both personal and social change. Perhaps it is a comment on the agism prevalent in the professional community that so little appears in the literature addressing the needs of the group of aged that do not yet need to be "taken care of." A few words from author/poet May Sarton (1978) may serve as a provocative conclusion to us all in examining our own attitudes toward educative efforts that may promote growth in the large community of intellectually alive elders:

> Lately we have had a great infusion of information about the old. . . . They are a problem. We must show concern. They are suddenly at 65 called "senior citizens" though no one has ever heard of a junior citizen and citizenship is hardly a category since it is almost universal. I mind being stuffed into a pigeonhole, "taken care of" as though I had ceased to exist as a growing person. . . . It is not, perhaps, that the old are a problem, but that the best things about old age are so outside our ethos that we cannot, some of us, even imagine a state of growth that might have to do with contemplation, pure joy, and above all the elimination of the nonessential. . . . The old have more right to self-interest, in the sense of self-exploration. . . . At 65 and after I think we have earned the right to make our souls in peace, and the making of a soul in peace depends on time, time for reflection, time that may look empty from the outside. . . . Old age is not an illness, it is a timeless ascent. As power diminishes, we grow toward more light.

References

Butler, R. N. 1963. "The Life Review: An Interpretation of Reminiscence in the Aged." *Psychiatry* 26:65–76.

Erikson, E. 1950. *Childhood and Society.* New York: Norton.

Erikson, E. 1968. *Identity: Youth and Crisis.* New York: Norton.

Feifel, H. 1977. "Death in Contemporary America." In H. Feifel, ed. *New Meanings of Death.* New York: McGraw-Hill.

Kastenbaum, R. 1977. "Death and Development Through the Life Span." In H. Feifel, ed., *New Meanings of Death,* New York: McGraw-Hill.

Kübler-Ross, E. 1969. *On Death and Dying.* New York: Macmillan.

Sarton, M. 1978. "More Light." *New York Times,* Jan. 30, p. 21, col. 1.

26

Recreation As a Survival Strategy:
A Biophilosophy of Life Over Death

ARLENE SEGUINE

A MERICANS ENTERING THE last quarter of the twentieth century have become heirs to a new legacy in the course of human evolution. The current biomedical revolution has bequeathed to them ever-expanding parameters of their own longevity. As beneficiaries of this extended life endowment, they automatically become trustees of new survival skills.

Gerontologists are now challenged by a new role, that of biophilosopher. As physicians and surgeons in the domain of geriatric medicine, and recreation specialists and physical educators in the realm of gerontologically oriented academia, they must be more than medical practitioners and exercise geriatricians. In short, their professional commitment extends to embracing a wider humanistic perspective: concern for guiding the new breed of older Americans toward the survival strategy necessary for coping with the sociocultural demands created by their prolonged maturity.

In its narrow meaning, biophilosophy is the interfacing between the science of life and the system of inquiry. But in its broader contemporary context it is the symbiosis between genetics and ethics as they relate to the changing dynamics of aging in counterpoise with our expanding perceptions of dying. Moreover:

New definitions of death have been sought, and tentatively reached, and these imply new definitions of life. A multitude of new capacities has given rise to a multitude of new questions that reverberate with overtones that are ethical, moral, legal, religious, social, political—in a word philosophic, that is, biophilosophic (Rosenfeld 1975).

To steer the course of future evolution suggests a kind of prophetic wisdom—lighting the path of futuristic mankind as they step forward onto new "landscapes of learning" (Greene 1978:2) discovered in the added seasons of life. In essence the biophilosopher serves as a fount of knowledge by providing "Educare for the mind in concert with furnishing Medicare for the body" (Beverley 1976). Thus, biophilosophy provides the conceptual framework for unprecedented expansions of dynamic living.

In their article entitled "Suppose We Died Young, Late in Life?" physicians Ernst L. Wynder and Marvin M. Kristein (1977) of the American Health Foundation remind us:

> By the year 2,000 the U.S. population over 65 years will have grown by 40% and the 45–64 year-old population will rise 50%. . . . Epidemiologic evidence shows that we can prevent a substantial proportion of chronic diseases by improved lifestyle and preventive medicine. Healthy older persons can continue physically and intellectually productive and active into their 80's.

In addition, Robert N. Butler (1975), then director of the National Institute on Aging, lends his perception of this demographic metamorphosis, which opens new windows of investigation for the biophilosopher:

> The old are people caught in a cultural time lag—suddenly there are large numbers of them and no one knows quite what to do. In each succeeding decade the proportion of elderly to young in the population increases. Anticipated breakthroughs in major killers like cancer and heart disease may swell the ranks of the old even more.

While the advances of gerontology usher mankind toward a new dawning of senescence, it befits the biophilosopher to orient us regarding the quintessence of survival. At last, science has collaborated with nature's order of priority: "In no other species in a natural state do we find elderly post-mature individuals. . . . It must have some species-sustaining purpose, or the forces of natural selection could not have preserved it'' (Jonas and Frai 1977). Implicit in this hallmark achievement is the biophilosophic problem identified by the renowned gerontologist Alexander Comfort (1976:11):

> But the things which make oldness insupportable in human societies don't at all commonly arise from consequences of this biological aging process. They arise from ''sociogenic aging.'' This means, quite simply, the role which society imposes on people as they reach a certain chronological age.

In other words, while science extends life expectancy, society must simultaneously strive to literally ''come of age''—perceiving positive images of aging by anticipating the new lexicon of sociocultural challenges yet to be encountered in our dynamically changing biosphere. Clearly, this implies episodic changes in our future lifestyles and new perspectives relating to death education. This, in turn, calls for a critical reevaluation of what social gerontologists call the disengagement theory, which suggests that advancing age influences people to become socially withdrawn from society. In actuality, though, it is the impact of both physical and social stress. ''The real difficulty lies in the fact that it is the correlates of old age, i.e., failing health, loss of peers, death of relatives, and the general shrinking of the social world due to factors related to aging that produce [this undesirable human condition]'' (Tallmer and Kutner 1969).

The recent extension of the mandatory retirement age already presages new life stages and positive changes in America's attitude toward our older population.

> The three stages of adulthood—socialization, training, work, parenting and retirement, and leisure—no longer follow precise chronological age. . . . Education, leisure, family-building, and socialization are now occurring in repetitive sequences throughout adult life. Individuals may have several careers, matriculations, more than one family, several sabbaticals and even several status situations as their chronological time clocks run their courses (Wheeler 1978).

In addition, the effect on subsequent survival of terminating one's work productivity at age 65 or 70 has not been thoroughly explored. Much research remains to be done in terms of the so-called disenchantment phase, or postretirement transition period, often characterized by feelings of depression, nihilism, or resentment. In fact, several investigators, including the American Medical Association Committee on Aging, indicate that normal retirement may initiate or accentuate medical problems (Haynes et al. 1978).

The consciousness raising evidenced by the aging awareness movement sweeping the country has multiple implications for medical practitioners and recreation specialists who are both involved in helping older persons retain their facility for optimal mobility. We can no longer remain apart in our traditionally separate professional niches but must become officially allied in the same gerisphere of humanistic pursuit. In short, our professional commitment extends to anticipating the fresh psychosocial aspirations generated by the newly created rites of passage along life's unfolding continuum.

With the numbers of older adults growing legion, and the human life span becoming even more protracted, recreation offers new vistas of survival strategy within a biophilosophical context. It provides the time cushions, or psychophysical buffers, against the impact of accelerative technological change. Moreover, leisure enrichment creates the ethological framework for preserving life's continuity in an emerging culture of transience intensified by a stress-filled environment.

> Not only to *live,* but to live *fully* may be the test of our civilization. To have years added to our lives without adequate provision or education for zestful living in those years can spell tragedy for a growing segment of our population. . . . We need to start now to educate attitudes toward retirement years and to encourage skills and appreciations which can carry over into meaningful leisure consumption in later maturity (MacLean 1963).

In other words,

> Old age may not be a virtue, but it is the chance to plan our leisure so skillfully that the world will continue to widen for us. . . . It is the capacity of an individual, through the power and resources of his mind, to lift himself above the cares and trivia of ordinary life, so that he inhabits a realm of culture and inspiration, drawing upon the accumulated wisdom of the past (Bogan 1975).

Survival has always been the keystone of man's existence. But the incredible advances in gerontology demand an almost revolutionary survival savvy unparalleled in the annals of mankind. Paradoxically, this may even mean finding new life in the subject of death. For example, tomorrow's mankind can hope to embody two, possibly three, lifetimes in one—live twice or three times longer than their antecedents of only a few generations ago. Instead of traditionally approaching sixty-five to eighty with apprehensions of death, they can now aspire to planning for a "third age"—previously, yet unwittingly, tagged "retirement." Indeed, today's mankind stand at the threshold of a future world beckoning them into a lifelong theater of experiences totally undreamed of.

In view of this, contemporary mankind has reached a most remarkable crossroad. This requires what the educational philosopher Maxine Greene (1978:5) calls "emancipatory education." Taken in a gerontological context, this means disavowing the negative connotations embraced by the concept of agism and supplanting them with positive strategies for attaining the acme of maturity. It means transcending passivity by discovering new horizons of selfhood—or more appropriately, elderhood.

Recreation encompasses the biophilosophical framework for exploring new facets of human capacity. Since its roots are found in the relatively new science of ethology (Browne 1968), the precise study of animal behavior, it provides the natural context for modern mankind to stay in touch with their inherited rituals of life while simultaneously defining new vistas of a futuristic mileiu. Such a goal includes "pursuing our question, our uncertainties [so that] we may find a kind of freedom . . . the freedom that accompanies fresh perceptions and the touch of possibility" (Greene 1965:8).

The question posed is: "How can recreation as a survival strategy be perceived as a biophilosophy of life over death?" Perhaps the answer lies in recognizing that the link between the present and the future is ethological. Furthermore, this ethological concept can be the cross-professional bridge between geriatric medicine and recreation education, since both are biologically oriented. With both fields embracing this common ethological approach, the unfulfilled "American Dream" (Hochschild 1973:17) can be finally realized—that is, by turning it around, so that the older person no longer symbolizes the exact opposite, or flip side, of this classic youth-oriented ideal but instead emerges as a self-fulfilled individual motivated by the wisdom of experience and by the courage for embracing new dimensions of self-discovery within the life-death cycle.

Familarity with ethologic principles can open unexplored channels of communication and thus engender the critical awareness that is prerequisite to maintaining a sense of personal continuity within a cultural kaleidoscope marked by such shifting scenes as job bumping, knowledge explosions, electronic media, drug trips, suicidal increases, alcoholic copouts, to mention but a few facets. In addition, the rapidity of change imposed by our technological innovation has heightened the feelings of temporariness and unpredictability in today's life-styles. And this is compounded by the paradox that within our so-called kinetic society in America, we impose a mandatory retirement age that abruptly condemns citizens to a state of exile by putting them outside the mainstream of life—a quasi-deathlike existence.

Recreation, on the other hand, provides the open-sesame for enabling people to preserve or recapture their sense of self by engaging in group dynamics predicated on three primary laws of nature—territoriality, the pecking order, and weaponry (Browne 1968). It also allows individuals, both singly and collectively, to remain in touch with themselves while simultaneously maintaining the perspective that life is a series of reintegrations. The very theme of "territorial rites" pervades virtually almost every aspect of the life-death cycle. Within the rubric of gerontology, medical science has responded strongly to the law of territoriality by successfully extending the property of life. And within the context of bioethics, medical practice is earnestly exploring this new lease on life by carefully reassessing the domain of death. The greatest acknowledgment of this territorial imperative, however, is the *"Zeitgeist"* attitude personsified by the Gray Liberation Movement, which advocates guaranteed lifelong sociocultural benefits coupled with politicoeconomic rights. All of these territorial claims, of course, come under the mantle of biophilosophy with its "right-to-life" guises.

Taken in its broadest scope, the concept of territoriality is currently being revamped in terms of its impact on new trends in human development and the inherent future patterns of living. Viewed holistically: "The importance of attending to the second half of adult life is not simply that we need maps for that portion of the journey too. It is that no part of the life cycle makes complete sense without the whole cycle being meaningful'' (Bridges 1977).

Implicit in this observation is the need to reexamine our traditional trends of lifetime distribution of education, work, retirement, and leisure. This suggests the possibility of American society's embracing a new philosophy in the future, which may end the work-leisure dichotomy and result in a more integrated and fulfilling life-adjustment cycle. Instead of the linear life pattern based on the sequential education-work-retirement plan, with leisure as an extraneous footnote to a formerly productive life, we would have the cyclical life pattern (Best and Stern 1976:9). This innovative plan will remove the customarily fixed barriers between the educational, occupational, and retiremental phases of life. Viewed from this perspective, territoriality is defined in terms of how to portion mankind's entire life span while achieving a balance between work and nonwork spheres, with recreation spaced intermittently throughout life's timetable. Such a conceptualization of recreation offers the older adult an unhampered range of life-styles, locations, and opportunities for engaging in a vocation/vocational pursuits on a rotating basis, which opens up an entirely new range of potentialities, including recognition, self-worth, mastery, exhilaration, joy, and fulfillment. In other words, leisure is no longer relegated to the status of "spare time," providing little human growth for a retired individual suddenly enveloped by endless free time. "Perhaps the central difference between old people now and old people fifty years from now will be in the meaning of work, and in the distinction between being useful and feeling worthwhile" (Hochschild 1973:20). This newly evolving interpretation of leisure behavior purports that "leisure in the holistic orientation is seen as a complex of multiple relationships involving certain choices which indicate both societal and individual aspirations as well as life styles" (Hendricks and Burdge 1972). Wilkins and Ragatz (1972) state: "This new venture is based on the hypothesis that leisure and education have become the most critical determinants of the potential quality of man's life in postindustrial societies."

Replacing the traditional linear life-style with the cyclic blend of education, career, and recreation patterns presages evolutionary definitions relevant to the "territoriality of life." This, in turn, motivates new perspectives about the second principle of ethology—the pecking order—which is closely bound to the territorial concept. While territoriality implies a sense of ownership, the pecking order refers to the establishment of a hierarchy of rank from the lowest member to the proud leader. In essence, it is nature's way of maintaining order and discipline and, as a result, the survival of the group as a whole. This kind of rank ordering provides the competitive basis for survival both in the animal world and in human society. It is the social process that enables individuals to compete continually for a place in the group structure/organization and thereby have a renewed reason for living and being a person. Paradoxically, mandatory retirement violates the natural laws of territoriality and the pecking order by removing man from the struggle of the competitive job market without offering equally challenging alternatives. Fortunately, though, the cyclic lifetime plan is designed to eliminate the sense of emptiness and social dislocation heretofore engendered by the linear prototype.

Closely articulated with these theories of territoriality and status is the third law of weaponry. This suggests that mankind have the instinct to be a weapon maker in order to eliminate their adversaries and give their group a measure of security by gaining control of the territority and establishing rank order. With their domain secured, this manipulative tendency continues to function in obedience to the law of self-defense of personal property. When mankind are forced to retire so early in today's society, their retirement income too often symbolizes a truncated weapon of financial survival in an increasingly inflated economy.

But now the cyclic alternative life span offers a fresh direction through which American society can envision new logistics of living within the conceptual framework of ethology—by obeying the laws of territoriality, the pecking order, and weaponry. Similarly, this ethological approach can serve as a cross-professional bridge between the two disciplines, or territories, of recreational education and geriatric medicine in our quest for touching new frontiers of lifelong learning—a continuing education demanding all "life-support" systems in balanced concert. As professionals concurrently involved with the pecking order of life over death, we must attend to reassessing the priorities for living a harmoniously orchestrated life congruous with the scenario of centenarian mankind. Viewing life expectancy in terms of one-hundred-year expanses is not only revolutionary from an evolutionary point of view but also urgent with regard to optimal survival strategy. This professional alliance can foster a reciprocal relationship wherein the knowledge of aging quite naturally criss-crosses between the psychomotor dynamics of gerontological recreation and the sociophysiological phenomena of geriatric medicine.

With the rapid advent of lifetimes' being measured along century-wide yardsticks and punctuated by rotating intervals of intermittent education, multiple careers, varied status situations, several families, and intergenerational relationships, now is the opportune time for the mutual designing of curricula reflecting the specialized body of knowledge commensurate with the maturational development of the elderhood years. This would naturally embody an interfacing between both gerontology and geriatrics, the two sides of the aging process as they occur along a transgenerational spectrum of life. Since both professions are involved with attending to the functional, or movement-oriented, aspects of human performance, this provides the common foundation for intersecting with the cognitive and affective domains of learning. And practically speaking, the current trend in higher education is toward a transprofessional approach, as evidenced by the increasing number of university-hospital affiliations. In essence, what subject could be more interdisciplinary than the topic of aging itself—a more and more universally recognized dominion stemming from our intergenerational awakening?

It is ironic that the study of aging in America is a concept whose time has finally come! All of a sudden, it seems, the calibrations of life can be marked off by a slide rule that adds new measures of viability. But the question is of what quality is this newly bestowed gift? The answer lies in our shared accountability as professionals in medical education and recreation education for girding future generations with the wisdom for pursuing a dignified and purposeful life. Having reached a new expansion in life, we must now give definition to a new forum for learning and individual expression: "a gymnasium for my mind," as one 88-year-old individual described it, "where I can exercise my brain and thoughts" (Coleman 1978). By endowing contemporary mankind with new life stages, we have automatically sanctioned their rite of passage into an unmapped province—their very own gerisphere. Implicit in this achievement is our shared responsibility for furnishing future mankind with the appropriate coping mechanisms predicated on the three principles of ethology: territoriality, the pecking order, and weaponry, in relation to the provocative world of humanity as couched in the context of leisure education.

Moreover, this cognizance has equal applicability to our approach to death, the final rite of passage: "To offset the general denial of the reality of dying, some physicians have turned their attention to the dying process" (Black 1976).

"William Carlos Williams, the noted physician and poet, understood the paradox inherent in trying to sustain a sense of purpose and future in our lives as we speculate on death or stand before our graves" (Coleman 1978). Yet Kübler-Ross (1969) found new life in the subject of death by providing insight into transcending the "conspiracy of silence" surrounding the dying person. She also identified five stages of the dying process—denial, anger, bargaining, depression, and acceptance—which are intended as rough guideposts for following dying persons' relationship with the people around them. And between the interfacing of life and death is the continual procession of survival, punctuated by the landmarks of nature in the form of the ever-transforming laws of territoriality, the pecking order, and weaponry.

This paper has identified and investigated the impending necessity for defining a survival wisdom commensurate with the extending parameters of longevity created by the advances of gerontology. As Americans approach the threshold of a new legacy in human evolution, the proportion of elderly to the young is rapidly increasing. This necessitates new definitions of life, which in turn imply new interpretations of death. Consequently, life takes on a futuristic dimension unparalleled in the annals of mankind.

The time has come for a professional articulation between geriatric medicine and gerontological recreation. Our shared humanistic mutuality can be effectively expressed in reciprocal learning settings that generate life-saving and life-giving experiences. This calls for innovative gerontological courses in medical education interposed with the recreation curriculum. We must build a cross-professional bridge along which tomorrow's generations can *grow* old, not just *get* old. In this way, we can maintain a grasp for shaping the choreography of life. Who knows, as members of this universal brotherhood, the lives we save may be our own!

References

Best, F. and B. Stern. 1976. *Lifetime Distribution of Education, Work, and Leisure: Research, Speculations and Policy Implications of Changing Life Patterns.* Washington, D.C.: Institute for Education, Leadership, George Washington University (December).

Beverley, E. V. 1976. "Lifelong Learning: A Concept Whose Time has Come." *Geriatrics* (August) 31:114–26.

Black, P. McL. 1976. "Focusing on Some of the Ethical Problems Associated With Death and Dying." *Geriatrics* (January) 31:138–41.

Bogan, S. D. 1975. "In Praise of Leisure." *Modern Maturity* (August–September) 18:68.

Bridges, W. 1977. "The Discovery of Middle Age." *Human Behavior* (May) 6:68.

Browne, E. 1968. "An Ethological Theory of Play." *Journal of Health, Physical Education and Recreation* (September) 47:36–39.

Butler, R. N. 1975. *Why Survive? Being Old in America.* New York: Harper & Row.

Coleman, C. A., Jr. 1978. "Gymnasium for the Mind." *Geriatrics* (April) 33:97–100.

Comfort, A. 1976. *A Good Age.* New York: Crown.

Greene, M. 1965. *The Public School and the Private Vision.* New York: Random House.

—— 1978. *Landscapes of Learning.* New York: Columbia University, Teachers College Press.

Haynes, S. G., A. J. McMichael, and H. A. Tyroler. 1978. "Survival After Early Retirement." *Journal of Gerontology* (March) 33:269–78.

Hendricks, J. and R. J. Burdge. 1972. "The Nature of Leisure Research: A Reflection and Comment." *Journal of Leisure Research* 4:216.

Hochschild, A. R. 1973. *The Unexpected Community.* Englewood Cliffs, N.J.: Prentice-Hall.

Jonas, A. D. and D. F. J. Frai. 1977. "Why People Get Old: The Purposes of Postmaturity." *Modern Medicine* (April) 45:63–68.

Kübler-Ross, E. 1969. *On Death and Dying.* New York: Macmillan.

MacLean, J. R. 1963. "The Challenge of Leisure in Old Age." *Recreation* (May) 56.

Rosenfeld, A. 1975. "A New Philosophy Must Guide Our Survival Strategy." *Modern Medicine* (March) 43:39–43.

Tallmer, M., and B. Kutner. 1969. "Disengagement and the Stresses of Aging." *Journal of Gerontology* (January) 24:70–74.

Wheeler, H. 1978. "Aging: The New Look." *Modern Maturity* (August–September) 21:16–18.

Wilkins, M. H., and R. L. Ragatz. 1972. "Cultural Change and Leisure Time." *Journal of Health, Physical Education and Recreation* (March) 43:34–37.

Wynder, E. L., and M. M. Kristein. 1977. "Suppose We Died Young, Late in Life . . . ?" *Journal of the American Medical Association* (October) 238:1507.

27

Issues for Residency Training in Internal Medicine

MICHAEL M. STEWART

Categories of Older Patients

*I*n the course of an average week's work, a resident in internal medicine at any of this country's major urban medical centers is likely to be directly involved in the care of dozens of elderly patients. There are clinical problems to be diagnosed and treated, families to meet, social service consultations and dispositions to be arranged, and, not infrequently, dying patients for whom decisions must be made regarding terminal care and the difficult issues of prolonging life through further use of expensive technology and heroic life-support measures. In many teaching hospitals, fully half of the patients on the inpatient medical service are older than 60, and this group may account for 60 to 70 percent of total medical inpatient bed days. The elderly are truly a dominant feature of hospital life, and the hospital is, in fact, where most of them die.

As a rough generalization, older patients cared for on medical inpatient services can be grouped into one of four categories from the perspective of the resident in training: dramatic cures, heroic rescues, diagnostic puzzles, and chronic cripples.

1. *Dramatic cures.* These patients are often the delight of the teaching service. They arrive critically ill and confused, but their diseases turn out to be surprisingly treatable and reversible, such as bromide overdose, pernicious anemia, or occult pneumonia, and they leave the hospital remarkably improved, their recovery an apparent tribute to curative medicine.

2. *Heroic rescues.* These are elderly patients whose obviously severe metabolic and physiologic decompensation on admission reflects the complex interplay of multiple chronic diseases, such as concurrent hypertension, congestive heart failure, diabetes, and renal insufficiency. The challenge is to balance the complicated metabolic equation, in order to restore adequate function in several diseased organ systems by a period of delicate readjustment. Discharge of such patients from the hospital is a gratifying experience, however temporary this outcome may prove to be.

3. *Diagnostic puzzles.* Some older patients, usually persons not previously known to the medical service, present with signs and symptoms of unusual diseases or clinical syndromes, such as obscure cardiomyopathies, fevers of unknown origin, or complex neuromuscular problems. Such clinical problems stimulate the investigative curiosity of the resident, who suspects and attempts to document a specific diagnosis.

4. *Chronic cripples.* There are many older patients with obvious debilitating problems already diagnosed (strokes, chronic lung disease, renal failure, complications of diabetes, incontinence, organic brain syndrome) for whom there appears to be little hope of major functional improvement. Such patients may oscillate between nursing home and hospital but are never expected to be fully self-sufficient again. Many of them are totally dependent on the medical care system for their ongoing management and survival. The major therapeutic objective of a hospital stay is often to restore the patient's ability to return to a nursing home or some other form of custodial care.

In the minds of many medical residents, these four admittedly oversimplified stereotypes exemplify the field of clinical geriatrics as actually encountered during residency training in the large urban teaching hospital. There may be limited additional opportunities for learning to manage the problems of older patients in ambulatory settings (usually a once-a-week clinic), as well as short rotations to a neurology service and perhaps to psychiatry, where diagnostic skills in clinical geriatrics may be emphasized. But it seems fair to say that although medical problems of the elderly constitute a major time commitment for the majority of medical house officers, these problems are usually approached from the viewpoint of acute medical care intervention, rather than as problems of elderly persons' requiring periodic medical care in the context of their total life situations. Moreover, geriatric medical problems are often viewed as burdensome in terms of time and effort, clinically frustrating, psychologically stressful, and of marginal value as learning experiences.

Is there anything wrong with this situation? Is not this the reality of modern medical care, where that 11 percent of the U.S. population who are over age sixty-five account for some 30 to 40 percent of national medical care expenditures and some 50 percent of total physician patient-care time? Can we really expect medical residents to view clinical geriatrics differently?

Some major concerns with the situation as presented include the following:

1. Medical problems specific to the elderly usually receive insufficient attention in clinical training programs in internal medicine.
2. Effective management of medical problems of the elderly cannot be learned without concern for the overall life situations of persons in the geriatric age group, specifically including attention to issues such as economic status, social support networks, value and belief systems, and alternatives to institutionalization. It is rare, however, for training programs in internal medicine to focus on these specific issues.
3. Medical care for older patients should not be viewed solely from the hospital perspective, given the availability of nursing homes, home care services, hospices, geriatric day care centers, senior citizen centers, and other forms of organized out-of-hospital care. Unfortunately, few medical residents have any firsthand experiential knowledge of how these services work or how well.

The clinical field of geriatric medicine has not yet achieved a clearly identifiable academic locus. There are only a few chairs of geriatric medicine in American medical schools and few programs or divisions of clinical geriatrics within departments of medicine. Thus, although problems of the aging and the broad field of gerontology have received mounting attention in the past several years (Butler 1975, Kart and Manard 1976, Rostow 1977, Binstock and Shanas

1976, Moss and Halamandaris 1977, Busse and Pfeiffer 1977), there has not yet been a consistent response on the part of academic medical centers. A policy statement by the Association of Professors of Medicine regarding the importance of including geriatrics within the educational purview of academic internal medicine is a significant step, and it follows other recent exhortatory pronouncements in widely read internal medicine publications (Leaf 1978, Moser 1978). Moreover, the literature in clinical geriatrics has been enriched by a number of recent books of varying length, breadth, and depth aimed specifically at those who manage the general medical problems of elderly patients (Adams 1977, Brocklehurst and Hanley 1976, Steinberg 1976, Reichel 1978a,b). However, the topics of aging, the elderly, and geriatrics have received scant attention in recent editions of major textbooks of medicine, and neither the undergraduate curriculum in most medical schools nor the formal educational content of medical residency training programs include geriatrics as a clearly bounded learning area for physicians in training. It would be of interest, for example, to know how many medical residents had bought, had read, or were even aware of any of those five texts on clinical geriatrics noted above.

Therefore, it is hardly surprising that specific concern for the thanatologic aspects of geriatric care has not been developed as an explicit facet of internal medicine training. Indeed, some of the important preliminary questions we should be asking are the following. Is detailed concern for dying and death among elderly patients an appropriate issue for specific attention in the training of the internist? Should the dying elderly patient be approached differently from any other patient with a terminal illness or any other elderly patient? Do we understand the various subjective and objective aspects of the process of dying sufficiently well to translate them into effective learning experiences and practice guidelines for medical residents? Do we even have an adequate number of clinical teachers who can assume responsibility for these sensitive educational tasks?

Geriatric Care: Clinical Considerations

There are certain aspects of clinical care for elderly patients that should be underscored. These are primarily technical considerations that, by current standards, are entirely within the professional domain of the practicing internist but that rarely receive systematic attention during residency training. The major considerations here are the following: comorbidity, polypharmacy, alterations of mental status, dependency needs, and medical care planning.

For most patients over age 60, *comorbidity,* or the concurrent existence of more than one significant disease (usually chronic diseases), is a fact of life. A complete "active problem list" for the typical octogenarian may include six or eight major diagnoses, since senescence is usually multisystemic and different organ systems may decompensate at the same time. There have been few rigorous studies of the efficacy of therapeutic interventions for specific comorbid states among the elderly. Therefore, for many (perhaps most) combinations of disease states among older patients, we simply do not have good objective evidence regarding therapeutic efficacy and the relative risk of alternative therapeutic approaches.

Comorbidity in the elderly frequently dictates the need for *polypharmacy,* that is, the simultaneous use of several medications. Polypharmacy itself entails new and additional risks. Since no medication is risk free, since drugs may interact with each other, and since the metabolic and therapeutic response of the elderly patient to any medication may be altered to the patient's detriment, polypharmacy for the elderly patient must be viewed as an issue requiring constant monitoring and readjustment. The risk of iatrogenic complications is increased under these circumstances, although practical systems for monitoring adverse drug reactions are not yet widely used.

Altered mental status is a difficult issue on which to generalize. Physiology, pathology, psychology, and pharmacology may all play major roles. Of particular importance is the distinction between altered mental status that may have a reversible or at least a treatable psychiatric or emotional basis (especially depression in its various forms) and altered mental status due to systemic disease, medications, or various forms of senility. Skills in assessment of mental status and thorough neuropsychiatric evaluation of elderly patients are critical elements in medical training but two of the most underemphasized. Diagnoses of the cognitive disorders of later life ("dementia," "organic brain syndrome," "senility") are frequently used in a manner inconsistent with the usual scientific criteria of reliability, reproducibility, and validity (Eisdorfer and Friedel 1977).

Dependency needs of the elderly include those of any sick patient, that is, the need for sensitive and empathic professional consultation and management during the treatment and recovery period, as well as those needs derived from the inherent dependency of being old (retired, impaired, alone, bereaved) and those that may be created by specific constraints of the day-to-day life setting. The expected patient-physician dependency relationship is therefore unusually complicated for elderly patients by the existence of an additional degree of social dependency that the physician must take into account. In the abstract, it hardly seems necessary to remind ourselves that illness and social dependency can be mutually reinforcing. In the busy atmosphere of a hospital ward or clinic, however, this fundamental fact is all too frequently overlooked.

Finally, with regard to *medical care planning,* it is obvious that the participants in the development of an effective medical care plan for any patient, over whatever time period, may need to include not only the physician and the patient but also family members and other persons, agencies, or institutions on whom the patient depends. For elderly patients, this may involve social workers, home health aides, physical therapists, and a variety of other professionals. However, hospital discharge planning is often conducted in a perfunctory "sign-out" fashion. Moreover, the related concept of a periodic ambulatory health and medical care planning conference for the older patient is just now beginning to be seriously discussed as an important aspect of ongoing geriatric care.

Geriatric Care: Some Desirable System Characteristics

It would be unfair to conclude that the prevalent lack of systematic attention to the broad range of issues involved in caring effectively for elderly patients is somehow the fault of medical residents or their clinical mentors. While it is true that certain improvements in geriatric care and teaching are both desirable and feasible within the existing system, learning to provide geriatric care during a period of medical residency training in a major academic medical center seems analogous to trying to learn meteorology by analyzing the weather reports on television; the subject matter may be relevant to the learning objective, but the learning context is inappropriate, the information is skewed, and the process of induction can carry the serious student only so far. Respect for our students and the conditions in which they need to learn geriatrics should give us pause.

What is needed, both for the geriatric patient and for serious students of clinical geriatrics, is a multidisciplinary, multilevel, multisite system of care, involving both acute and convalescent inpatient facilities, long-term care both in institutions and at home, a variety of ambulatory settings, and ready access to special services that are in particularly high demand by elderly patients (podiatry, optometry, physical and rehabilitation medicine, social service, psychogeriatric care, etc.).

An instructive description of a hospital-centered system of acute and chronic care services has been provided by Libow (1976) in his discussion of an integrated network of geriatric services at City Hospital Center at Elmhurst. The major subunits included an inpatient acute care medical service; an in-hospital skilled nursing facility to which geriatric patients could be readily transferred from the medical service; a comprehensive geriatric follow-up clinic in the outpatient department (OPD); a hospital-organized and managed home care program; close working relationships with several nursing homes in the community; a formal hospital contract with the local visiting nurse service; and, at least for a brief period, a grant-supported psychogeriatric service with inpatient, OPD, and home visit capabilities. This integrated geriatric care system involved attending physicians, residents, social workers, staff nurses, nurse-practitioners, public health nurses, physiatrists, respiratory therapists, and others. It reflected an unusual degree of commitment to a broad-gauged geriatric care program, with a geriatric residency program woven into all its various activities and levels of service.

In such a program, a medical resident in training can learn, through direct involvement in the management of individual patients, the subtleties, complexities, possibilities, controversies and constraints involved in ongoing overall care of the elderly. It is real training for the real world. For example, if residents' involvement in planning the discharge of a 75-year-old patient from the medical service requires a presentation to a multidisciplinary home care conference in the same hospital, or a future appointment to the hospital's geriatric clinic, or an explanatory visit to a nursing home to which the patient is to be sent, both an appreciation of the system's capabilities and a new sense of their own responsibilities as physicians are most likely to occur. In short, geriatric medicine will be better learned where the geriatric care system requires the learner to discriminate between, and to participate in, realistic options for posthospital patient management.

Geriatrics and General Internal Medicine

In recent years, and particularly since the creation of family practice as a formal specialty in 1969, clinical training of physicians and physician extenders in primary care has emerged as a major national priority, both in terms of health manpower development and distribution and in terms of the citizenry's mounting concern for access, quality, and cost of care. The robust new specialty of family practice is undoubtedly here to stay, but there has also been a corresponding and vigorous effort within the specialties of internal medicine and pediatrics to develop their own new cadres of primary care physicians. Thus, there have developed within the past few years many new academic divisions of general internal medicine, designed to train physicians to provide primary medical care characterized by ease of access, temporal continuity of the relationship between doctor and patient, a commitment to whole-person care, an assumption of responsibility for coordinating and integrating specialty consultations and referrals, and a specific interest in disease prevention, health maintenance, and reduction of specific risk factors.

Two of the currently most debated questions in departments of medicine and their new divisions of general medicine are the following. What precisely should be included in the "clinical curriculum" in general internal medicine, as differentiated from the content of existing residency programs? What implications (if any) does this desired clinical curriculum have for modifying or extending the education of medical students prior to becoming primary care medical residents? To many persons involved in academic program development, there appear to be at least four major learning areas in which the education of medical students and the clinical training of medical residents need to be redefined and strengthened if we are to make any substantial progress in producing a new generation of competent general internists. These areas are as follows: (1) epidemiology, biostatistics, and quantitative analysis; (2) humanism, communications, and interpersonal relationships; (3) knowledge and understanding of the health care system, its subsystems, and its determinants; (4) mastery of additional specific clinical skills and techniques not previously regarded as inherent to internal medicine.

Among the extraordinary range of knowledge, attitudes, and skills that have thus been proposed as appropriate educational goals for inclusion in residency training for primary care, clinical geriatrics has been a recurrent consideration. Moreover, since The American Geriatrics Society has adopted the posture that geriatrics should not become a formal clinical subspecialty, and since the Association of Professors of Medicine, representing the professional discipline of internal medicine, has declared its intent that clinical geriatrics shall be an integral component of internal medicine, there is every reason to believe that the new divisions of general medicine will become ever more heavily involved in clinical geriatric training.

There are, however, very few readily identifiable teachers of clinical geriatrics within existing departments of medicine, and it will likely be some time before there is a clear academic agenda for education, research, and newly organized forms of geriatric care. Where does this leave those of us who are responsible for developing training programs in general internal medicine? Is geriatrics really "in"? If in, how should we proceed, both conceptually and practically, to respond to this important challenge?

My own personal view is that there is no reason to doubt either the educational relevance of a specific focus on clinical geriatrics or the propriety of the general internist's taking a major interest in the care of the elderly. Training of the medical resident in clinical geriatrics will be enhanced by the following steps, all of which are feasible today:

1. Systematic efforts to use grand rounds, mortality conferences, journal clubs, and other teaching conferences to discuss the life context of patients, the appropriateness and adequacy of data included in the medical record from a geriatric viewpoint, and the identification of possible alternative interventions that might have been employed.

2. Registration by medical residents of all patients followed in the OPD, for the purpose of selecting specific cases for conferences on problems in the medical management of the geriatric outpatient
3. Analysis by each medical resident of the total care provided to one or more patients over age 65, including a statement of therapeutic treatment goals, assessment of goal achievement, and analysis of costs incurred, as well as efficacy
4. Implementation of the requirement for a formal minimum data base to be recorded on all geriatric outpatients and inpatients, for purposes of later epidemiologic, therapeutic, cost-analytic, and educational purposes

Given the commitment of a division of general medicine to promoting clinical geriatrics as a specific area of interest, these four measures could be implemented with only a modest increase in cost. It is also highly likely that these efforts will identify a number of remediable hospital system problems in clinical care of the elderly.

Concluding Personal Comments

It is more than a decade since Kübler-Ross first proposed the paradigm of five stages of reaction to dying (denial, anger, bargaining, depression, and acceptance), and there has been considerable debate over the semantics, epistemology, and clinical relevance of terms such as aging, senescence, dying, death, and being dead. Ethics in medicine is now a lively, fertile, and controversial field, and we are besieged with books, articles, and new journals. Geriatrics is also, at least for the moment, a fundable and well-funded special area, and interdisciplinary studies are growing in number. Thus, the stage appears set and the moment timely to introduce the subject of geriatrics, with all of the related issues I have mentioned, as a formal and demarcated component of clinical training in general medicine.

As a clinician, however, I also view the events of the past ten years as a general encouragement to keep doing what I feel I have been trained to do. I first met a dying elderly patient as an intern on the medical service at the Massachusetts General Hospital. She was "my" patient. I had a responsibility that I resented but dimly perceived, struggled to fulfill, and only gradually understood. As is true in many patient-physician relationships, there were periods of pain, hard work, self-realization, and enormous doubt. I believe we would be doing a great disservice to our colleagues and our residents in internal medicine if we should suggest that anyone knows how best to manage the exquisitely personal encounter between the dying elderly patient and the caring physician. As a scientist, I certainly agree that we must continue to analyze, quantify, and evaluate the nature of this transaction. As a humanist, I also agree that we should aim to preserve the patient's dignity, opportunity for personal choice, and right to participate in discussions regarding the conditions of treatment and management.

There seems to me no better way to deal with thanatologic aspects of the care of the elderly than by identifying clinical geriatrics as an appropriate and high-priority area in the training of the general internist. From the clinician's perspective, dying and death are facts that can best be approached within the framework of the physician's overall responsibility for caring for patients in a sensitive and humane fashion.

References

Adams, G. 1977. *Essentials of Geriatric Medicine*. New York: Oxford University Press.

Binstock, R. H. and E. Shanas. 1976. *Handbook of Aging and the Social Sciences*. New York: Van Nostrand Reinhold.

Brocklehurst, J. C. and T. Hanley. 1976. *Geriatric Medicine for Students*. Edinburgh: Churchill Livingstone.

Busse, E. W. and E. Pfeiffer. 1977. *Behavior and Adaptation in Late Life* (2nd edition). Boston: Little Brown.

Butler, R. N. 1975. *Why Survive? Being Old in America*. New York: Harper and Row.

Eisdorfer, C. and R. O. Friedel. 1977. *Cognitive and Emotional Disturbance in the Elderly*. Chicago: Year Book Medical Publishers.

Kart, C. S. and B. B. Manard. 1976. *Aging in America: Readings in Social Gerontology.* Port Washington, N.Y.: Alfred Publishing Co.

Leaf, A. 1978. "Medicine and the Aged." *New England Journal of Medicine* 297: 887–90.

Libow, L. S. 1976. "A Geriatric Medical Residency Program: A Four Year Experience." *Annals of Internal Medicine* 85:641–47.

Moser, R. 1978. "Health Care of Elderly Must Be Improved." *Forum on Medicine* 1:39.

Moss, F. E. and V. J. Halamandaris. 1977. *Too Old, Too Sick, Too Bad: Nursing Homes in America.* Germantown, Md.: Aspen.

Reichel, W. 1978a. *Clinical Aspects of Aging.* Baltimore: Williams and Wilkins.

——, ed. 1978b. *The Geriatric Patient.* New York: H. P. Publishing Co.

Rostow, I. 1977. *Socialization to Old Age.* Berkeley: University of California Press.

Steinberg, F. U. 1976. *Cowdry's the Care of the Geriatric Patient* (5th edition). St. Louis: Mosby.

28

Inservice Thanatologic Training for Long-Term-Care Facility Staff

SHURA SAUL

*L*ife in a long-term-care facility is a vertiable collage of experiences for the residents/patients, their families, and the staff. The public generally stereotypes the institution as a static place where sickness, age, and handicap are confined and removed from the sight and mind of the "outside world." The human condition, however, defies stereotype, and wherever there are people, a range of circumstances will differentiate each person, just as the common denominator describes the group. The individual experiences of residents in this facility lie along a volatile spectrum of physical and psychosocial circumstances ranging from return to health to death itself. A multitude of life happenings occur: holidays, birthdays, family joys, and problems comingle with the struggles of living through each day, coping with illness, and fears of tomorrow. Altogether, these constitute the quality of life as it is lived and shared within the communal setting. Services to meet patient needs echo these circumstances and involve skilled nursing, restorative and rehabilitative care, psychosocial attention, and supportive assistance in all activities of daily living.

In the midst of and alongside this varied activity is the continuous presence of death and its requirement for ongoing compassionate assistance before, during, and after the fact. Since most possibilities for privacy, as generally practiced, are eradicated in this setting, almost all aspects of life are shared. Death—like life—is a communal reality for all who live in, work in, and visit the institution.

The long-term-care facility is an open system serving groups of people with a diversity of needs. The staff as a whole is a key component. Patient care is offered through many people. An individualized plan of care for each patient involves the expertise, input, and cooperation of several disciplines and departments. The plan must flow from a unified philosophic stance, which helps shape staff attitudes and affects staff performance. If care for the dying patient (and the family) is to be supportive and compassionate, a training program must teach the relevant philosophy and skills and must also recognize the uniqueness of dying and death in this communal living situation.

Shaping such a program requires an in-depth understanding of staff needs in this area and immediately raises the curtain on a complex pattern. The staff in an institution is an admixture of people: a small world of different cultures, ages, and levels of experience, knowledge, and skill. Different staff members perform different functions at different distances to the patient.

There is the staff that is closest to the patient in terms of frequency and intimacy of contact—for example, touching, daily or almost daily interaction. This category includes:

1. *Members of nursing staff:* aide or orderly, charge nurse, and other nurses in direct patient care.

2. *Housekeeping and dietary staff:* especially those who make beds, clean patient rooms, handle personal laundry and serve food.

3. *Activity and social-service staff:* especially those who work on the nursing unit in direct daily interaction with patients; also those who may appear less often but whose discipline's offerings may have a profound effect on the patient's (and family's) life and thoughts.

4. *Rehabilitation staff:* the physical therapist and occupational therapist (and their aides), who may be treating the patient as often as four or five times weekly.

5. *Transportation staff:* whose interaction with patients in daily routines may be important and yet overlooked

The staff at the next level of distance—in time and space—from the patient include:

1. *Administrative and professional staff:* administrators, department heads, supervisors, consultants.

2. *Medical staff:* physicians, psychiatrists, medical consultants, pharmacists, dentists; also, auxillary staff such as lab technicians.

3. *Bookkeeping and office staff:* important to include here people dealing with family around finances; also, receptionists and switchboard operators so crucial in communication.

Paradoxically, although some of these people interact less frequently with patients and their families, the importance of their services, their level of expertise, and their power within the system contribute heavily to the quality of patient care—both directly through their own roles and indirectly through other staff. All levels of staff share and contribute uniquely in the training program.

Administration sets the tone of the entire institution as a caring place where individual needs are met with dignity and concern, develops the range and quality of programs, and coordinates service teams. In developing the in-service program, administrative investment is vital, for the administrator must endorse the program's purposes and methodology, must accept the time needed to teach and reinforce learning, and must support the role of the educational director as different from that of the task supervisor (Saul 1972). Supervisory and administrative staff have the responsibility for sharing in the teaching program—as teachers themselves and as consultants and evaluators. Through their roles with the staff on the unit they reinforce learning and evaluate the effectiveness of the teaching program in terms of improved or altered job performance and new learning needs. Such staff communication with and feedback to the in-service director are mandatory. A training program in death and dying begins with the participation of administrative and supervisory staff, which must itself understand and experience the flow of learning to be launched throughout the institution. Administrators and supervisors are both teachers and learners in this program.

The medical staff offers leadership and expertise in diagnosing and treating the whole person through a unified, scientific understanding of physical and mental health needs. The attitude and relationship of the medical staff to patients, families, and other staff are critically important in all aspects of care—but especially in the care of the dying patient. Medical intervention in symptom and pain control and in treatment of the patient's physical and emotional condition is primary in this patient-care program. This staff must be involved in planning and teaching the thanatologic training program. Through their own work with patients, they demonstrate philosophy and methods of care to be explained to other staff members. This aspect of their role is an important dimension of the training program.

Three other categories of people interacting with the patients on a close and frequent basis are family members, friendly visitors (volunteers), and other patients. This paper focuses, however, on staff, recognizing that programs for these groups would flow essentially from the staff program.

Just as the staff scene is varied, so too is the actual dying process of patients. Some patients die suddenly. Others—long-term residents—become terminally ill at some point, very much as they would if they had been living in their own homes. Some die within the facility itself; others must be sent to the hospital for their final hours. Still others—sent to the hospital for other reasons—die there unexpectedly. Some patients are admitted to and die in a long-term-care facility after all possible medical attention to their acute care needs has been given in the hospital.

The staff must cope with long-term dying, short-term dying, unexpected death, and emergency transfers—as these affect patients, both the dying and the living, and themselves.

Each task performed by a staff member and the way it is performed flows from that person's perception of and preparation for her role. The in-service program shapes itself around the needs of patients but also relates to the concerns of the staff in meeting these needs within the system. It must relate to staff feelings, as well as to its varied skills. The staff is required to deal concurrently with patients in various stages of illness and health. The in-service program must recognize the common denominator of human caring that ties staff, patients, and families into the interactional patterns of the institution and reinforce staff's key role in expressing this dimension through performance and participation in the complexities of the human relationships within the system. When all the people care about one another, then some of the people (staff) are able to care for others (patients).

It is within this matrix of mutuality and diversity, scientific knowledge, and disciplinary skills that the program of training for care of the dying patient is developed. Because learning suggests change and may be threatening to staff, the entire educational program should be nonthreatening and supportive. Because the subject of death is so threatening to most people, this is doubly true in in-service about death and dying.

What To Teach and How To Teach It

Most of us are neither motivated nor trained to recognize our feelings, to deal openly with them, or to be aware of their effect on our behavior. All the staff need help in this area. Untrained workers in the institution are thrust into a range of emotional experiences with little preparation. These persons deal with death and dying in the institution as they have dealt with it in their own lives, depending on their sociocultural and/or religious training.

Like the untrained worker, the trained worker may turn away from the threat and pain of caring for the dying patient, despite the need for expertise. A patient's death may be viewed as one's failure, or as evidence of the futility of one's efforts (Shulz and Aderman 1976). Doctor, nurse, and others may "give up" on the patient, who then remains abandoned during this crucial, frightening time of life (Fleming 1976). Stereotypes about the aging person may also impede needed professional intervention. Since it is considered "natural" for an old person to die, the consequent stereotyped expectation may be that the dying older person needs minimal, if any, comfort or support. The disoriented, or mentally ill, dying person may be seen as being "out of it" and thereby denied appropriate care. Without an individualized approach to maximize the comfort and dignity of the dying person, such patients may be neglected, even abandoned. The in-service program, therefore, must help professionals, as well as nonprofessionals, to become aware of their own feelings toward these patients, of their own stereotypes and expectations, to see the patient as a person and thus to free them to use their discipline skills (Cassell 1973). Like the administrator, the trained worker who demonstrates an active helping role in the care of the dying patient provides "leadership by example," which is itself a teaching method.

Intellectual discussions about death have limited value because of the powerful emotions evoked by the subject. Instead, the in-service program should provide experiential and "rap" sessions to encourage the sharing of feelings and experiences related to death in personal and professional life (Saul and Berlin 1977). Such interchange leads to new insights about oneself and, in turn, frees the worker to make needed adjustments.

> After attending several "rap" sessions, a nurse who had participated only minimally to this point told the group: "My father died when I was 4 years old. My mother lifted me up to kiss his face. I'll never forget the feeling of touching his lips which were stone cold. The memory has remained with me through all these years. I think it has affected the way I deal with death today."

When staff members begin to learn about each other's experiences, they are less apt to judge and more likely to compensate for each other's inadequacies. This is how a true caring team develops.

> One of the nurses began to tell about the death of her daughter in childbirth, and the death of her son in Viet Nam. The staff began to comfort her as she wept quietly and openly. They began to realize how we often separate our feelings about our patients from others in our lives; how we may develop a "shell" which gives others a false message.

The stereotyped notion of a "hardened professional stance" becomes softened, and the worker learns that the true professional stance is the human response coupled with professional helping skills. Such peer discussions are also useful, for they allow recognition and legitimization of both positive and negative feelings, as well as the chance to share some techniques in care—for example, the difficulties of bathing a comatose patient or dealing with a hostile or unresponsive one. Peer sharing leads to a high level of support among staff, a support that extends to the dying patient. It takes time to develop such openness. The training program should plan several consecutive sessions for the same group in order to develop a trusting atmosphere in which staff will be able to risk such emotional exposure.

Through such sessions, workers also gain insight into their own defenses. The greater the sensitivity to the dying person, the greater the worker's emotional response and, therefore, the need to develop constructive coping mechanisms. Workers can learn to differentiate between functional defenses, which enable them to work with compassion and skill, and dysfunctional defenses, which result in tasks performed with bitterness, impatience, hostility, and guilt.

Such experiential sessions are usually interdisciplinary, involving people working together on the unit. At times, it is also helpful to schedule such sessions for the staff of each department. The in-service program should provide for both. Formal classes may be augmented by other types of experiences to encourage learning and fruitful communication—for example, spontaneous, on-the-spot conferences (especially when an emotional situation has occurred); joint sessions for staff and patients on the nursing unit; individual conferences with staff members as needed; the use of stories, poems, films, music, flowers, touching, weeping, smiling—verbal and nonverbal media to develop the humanistic environment in which staff members and patients perceive one another as helpers through difficult times. All these are part of a training program that uses all experiences as a basis for learning.

In the long-term-care facility, workers serve patients and families who are in direct confrontation with the dying process, as well as those who—like the staff—are in painful proximity to it. In both cases, the staff must be trained for supportive intervention.

Mrs. R. told the social worker about her fear of dying alone. Except for specific tasks, the staff tended to avoid entering her room. The death and dying team met with all those caring for Mrs. R. to discuss her fears and needs. The care plan was reviewed and each team member asked to add some way to increase the patient's comfort. In addition to others, the aides offered to spend extra moments with her whenever possible and to chat with her while they were attending her. The social worker brought her paper work into Mrs. R.'s room to alleviate her loneliness.

Patients, like the staff, need help in dealing with their feelings about the death of a fellow patient—both as loss in their lives and as threat of their own death.

When Mrs. E. died, her friends and neighbors on the nursing unit talked about their loss and consoled one another at a community floor meeting. The staff joined them to share their memories of her fine personal qualities. Her soft, easy death was seen as a consolation, and several patients shared openly their wish for a similar passing. People were pleased to express their feelings and, at the end of the meeting, thanked the group leader for the opportunity.

This communal aspect of the death-and-dying experience suggests the need for all staff to understand the use of the group as an interventive modality in patient care and to learn some skills in group leadership. Training in this area should include didactic and experiential sessions to teach group work, and opportunities for coleadership with a trained worker followed by interpretive sessions to analyze the group process. The staff of all disciplines should participate in this training, for in addition to teaching skills, it offers increased understanding of group services and improves communication within the system.

Patients' reactions vary. The staff needs insight into their range of responses to death, to learn to connect various behaviors of the patients to the death-and-dying experience, fears, fantasies, and concepts. The in-service program should train the staff to view behavior as a form of communication and to identify and understand the range of behavioral responses (for example, confusion, anger, disorientation, aggressiveness, fearfulness) as they are encountered in frightened, sick, old patients.

Dying persons must be perceived as living persons whose needs and wants, in all areas, should be ministered to and met: they are not to be "written off" as "nonexistent" or "untreatable," because the illness is terminal (Saunders 1973). This approach suggests that the doctor may find it necessary to treat medical conditions other than the fatal one; that the patient might have concerns to share with the social worker other than dying; that a recreationist or a nutritionist may be able to enhance the life experience at this point; that a rehabilitation specialist might make the patient more comfortable. All these services contribute to enhanced comfort and dignity. From such a stance flows all possible creative effort by the staff of each department in serving this patient and the family.

The educational program, then, begins with comprehensive training related to the human emotional responses to death and offers a generic body of information about physical, mental, and emotional health and illness of elderly patients and how their care needs may be met in the institution. In these aspects of training, workers are involved in both disciplinary and interdisciplinary learning experiences.

In addition, each discipline must teach specific methods of care for the dying patient. Again, some concern individual departments, others involve more than one. For example, methods of administering medications, the timing for cleaning a room, offering a recreational activity, the content and conduct of a social-service interview, method of preparing and offering food—these are disciplinary skills to be taught within each department. They may also involve more than one department. Symptom control—an important dimension in caring for the dying patient—is both departmental and interdisciplinary. Each department offers its expertise in alleviating a specific symptom—for example, pain, hunger, loneliness. All staff must be aware of one another's offerings to ensure integration of treatment.

In dealing with the family, too, stereotypes must be eradicated (Butler and Lewis 1973)—for example, the myth of family abandonment and noncaring; the "good" and the "bad" children. Sessions must be held on the entire subject of working with families so that understanding of the contemporary family circumstance is deepened. The staff needs the opportunity to clarify and adjust perceptions and correct some deep-seated prejudices to free them to deal supportively with the family. A primary piece of learning—for all the departments—is acceptance of the dual role of staff toward family: as "partners" in care of the dying patient but also as supporters to the family during this difficult period of stress. The nursing staff is particularly close to the family, in time, space, and task performance, and needs help in learning how to work with family members.

Mr. G. a very sick, comatose patient, returned from the hospital for the fifth time. He had been expected to die each time he was transferred. Mrs. G.—exhausted by her devotion through his four years of illness in this facility—had also prepared herself, each time, for his death. She stood in his room, weeping quietly. Upset and guilty about their own feelings, the staff on the nursing unit became "very busy" with other patients and avoided Mr. G. The nursing supervisor came to the unit and quietly discussed with them how Mrs. G. must be feeling just now and asked them to help her by attending to Mr. G.

The staff felt awkward and angry. Projecting their feelings onto Mrs. G., they asked, "Why is she crying?"

Experiential workshops are useful in helping the staff to explore such feelings about the family, to gain new insights into family needs at this point, and to help the staff develop professional helping relationships with the family.

The staff can learn, also, to share some parts of patient care with available family members. Emotional reassurance is reinforced by offering a constructive role so that the family member who can becomes part of the caring team. The staff can teach family members to assist with management of bed and bedclothes; turn and lift the patient; get the patient to the lavatory; feed and give drinks; help with cleanliness of body, hair, and teeth; relieve or prevent constipation; maintain freshness and cheerfulness in the room; and keep up the patient's interests and spirits (in keeping with physical limitations) (Scott, n.d.). The staff must learn the capacities and limitations of such cooperation with the family so that expectations may be realistic and frustrations minimized. Case conferences, with and without family members, become a dimension of staff training. The death-and-dying team should also hold meetings with individual families to share with them the total care plan. The staff needs training for participation in such meetings and for developing their roles within them. Role plays are an excellent modality for teaching these skills.

Follow-up services to families after the death of a patient also require some learning by the staff (Pincus 1974). In this phase of service, all staff assume new roles and tasks growing out of their relationship with the patient and family during the dying process. Classes should review the specifics of these both on a departmental and interdisciplinary level.

The unique demands of the institutional system, its interdisciplinary services, and the need for careful coordination suggest an additional dimension for in-service training: how, when, where, and by whom which service is best offered needs discussion and team planning. The educational program must address this phenomenon of institutional work and offer training in communication, coordination, and team participation. Experiential workshops that include exercises in open communication, cooperation, offering and receiving criticism and feedback, suggesting adaptations in behavior, and task performance are all needed (Jones 1968).

The welding of a caring team includes, also, a knowledge of one another's roles and offerings and the ability to use one another as resources in the mutual helping effort toward the dying patient and his family.

Throughout all such ongoing education—which is interwoven with the services themselves—the death and dying team within the facility plays a key role in planning and implementing the program. This team should include at least one administrator, the medical director, in-service trainer(s), director of nursing services, department heads, and at least one other nurse and nurse's aide. A family member and a representative of the resident council may participate, although not necessarily from the inception of the program. The team should have the opportunity to share learning with others in the field, to attend conferences and workshops, and to invite knowledgeable people to teach in the facility.

Finally, a reading program should involve all the staff. Such a program makes available books and periodicals on the subject, as well as selected readings. A useful method of teaching and helping the staff to understand its own development, is to reproduce bits of the record of work within the facility, responses from staff, patients, and families to the efforts of the death-and-dying team, and so on. In this way, the staff is helped to reflect on its own offering, to evaluate its services, and to learn from one another.

Working with illness, old age, and death can be painful and difficult. It is important that the entire facility support and accept the efforts of the death-and-dying team, for these support the life and health of the total patient population, as well as the individual dying patient. The staff in the long-term-care facility is in intimate and long-time contact with one another and with their patients. They themselves need help, encouragement, and support from their colleagues and the total facility if they are to deliver service with compassion and dignity. In this total effort, the educational thrust within the facility plays a positive and creative role.

References

Butler, R. and M. I. Lewis. 1973. "People and Their Families." Chapter 7 in *Aging and Mental Health*. St. Louis: Mosby.

Cassell, E. 1973. "Learning to Die." Health Conference on Meeting the Problems of Older People. New York Academy of Medicine.

Fleming, S. 1976. "Can We Humanize Dying in the General Hospital?" Conference sponsored by the department of psychology, York University, Ontario, Canada.

Jones, M. 1968. *Beyond the Therapeutic Community*. New Haven, Conn.: Yale University Press.

Pincus, L. 1974. *Death in the Family*. New York: Pantheon.

Saul, S. 1972. "Training the Health Care Team in an Extended Care Facility." *Mental Hygiene* 56:96–101.

Saul, S. and M. Berlin. 1977. "Helping Staff Deal With Death in the Institution." *Nursing Homes* (Nov/Dec).

Saunders, C. 1973. "Care for the Dying." *Patient Care* (June) 3:6.

Scott, P., n.d. "Some Information for Those Caring for Patients." Mimeographed. London: St. Christopher's Hospice.

Shulz, R. and D. Aderman. 1976. "How the Medical Staff Cope with Dying Patients." *Omega* 76.

Public Policy
on Dying and Death

29

Public Policy Questions
Related to Death With Dignity

WILLIAM E. ORIOL

CONGRESS HAS A well-founded modesty in dealing with issues related to death and dying. Even before the Karen Quinlan case polarized positions—or perhaps made it even more difficult to have fixed positions—national legislators looked to state law, the courts, church, and family to make the hard individual decisions. These judgments are required more and more often, it seems, as questions of life and death surface with increasing frequency and occasional notoriety. But death, like aging, is universal, and legislators—along with everyone else who wishes the final phase of life to be worthy of all that preceded it—must ask themselves from time to time whether public policy is exercising positive or negative influence on the conditions surrounding death in our nation.

This paper deals with the recognition given to this questioning of public policy a few years ago, when the Senate Committee on Aging first dealt with "Death With Dignity: An Inquiry Into Related Public Issues" (U.S. Senate 1972). It also traces more recent challenges to the "institutional bias" so often blamed for contributing both to the unsympathetic treatment of the dying patient and to callous treatment of the very ill older patient. It also confronts the mounting interest within the Congress and elsewhere in the hospice and other movements now at work to make "the last days of life worth living."

The 1972 Hearings

The 1972 Senate Committee hearings focused only partially on public policy issues related to the right to prolong life by extraordinary means when all hope for recovery—or in some cases, even for consciousness or lucidity—has vanished.

As committee chairman Frank Church explained, the committee had no preconceived conclusions or proposals for government action. The senators realized that there was a long way to go before anyone could even begin to think about changes in public policy, if indeed such changes should prove to be desirable. The committee emphasized that they wanted "to take no action that will in any way suggest that we regard any person as expendable, whether that person is one year old or 100 years old." It was recognized, however, that "the 'right to die' issue has its greatest impact upon the elderly population. Chronic illness and terminal illness will increase as our population of older, and very old, Americans continues to increase. Today's unresolved questions related to our subject are likely to intensify unless, finally, they are faced squarely" (U.S. Senate 1972).

Dr. Elisabeth Kübler-Ross, one of the witnesses at the hearing, had already written in her classic *On Death and Dying* a protest against the machinery of the modern medical institution, saying that a patient's dignity may be crushed even while the institution works to save his life:

> He may cry for rest, peace, and dignity, but he will get transfusions, a heart machine, or tracheotomy, if necessary. He may want one single person to stop for one single moment so that he can ask one single question, but he will get a dozen people around the clock, all busily preoccupied with his heart rate, pulse, electrocardiogram, or pulmonary functions, his secretions or excretions, but not with him as a human being.

Similar complaints were made at the hearings, which soon shifted from individual right-to-die issues to the adequacy of present care arrangements for the terminally ill patient and the family. There appears to be undue emphasis on institutionalization, which increases public and private costs of treatment and contributes to anxiety or helpless apathy among patients. The wish to die at home was repeatedly emphasized by the witnesses, who also stated that the opposite trend had become entrenched in the national health system. At least 80 percent of the population, the senators were told, die in institutions—facilities such as hospitals and nursing homes. Furthermore, it was found that the number of home health programs had actually been declining since the peak year of 1969.

The trends anticipated at the 1972 hearings have since emerged more clearly. The decline in home health care and other in-home services may have been arrested,[1] but the Congress and the administration now see more clearly than ever before that the future demands for humane and sympathetic care of the long-term chronically ill and, finally, dying patient will require a far greater effort than was foreseen even at the White House Conference on Aging in 1971.[2]

The Prevalence of "Frailty": The Numbers and Their Meaning

Talk about policy planning for tomorrow's aged is haunted by a set of numbers that comes up regularly, whether the subject is housing, health care, social services, the four-generation family, or declarations in general about the "graying" of America. Typically, the statistics declare that:

1. The number of significantly disabled, including noninstitutionalized, older individuals, is already great and will become markedly greater within the next few decades, with the most dramatic gains occurring in the fastest-growing group, those seventy-five and over.
2. Our present methods of dealing with widespread disability among the elderly depends heavily, and often needlessly, on expensive institutional care when we should be concentrating to make the most of family help where it exists and to utilize friends and others when possible.

The Numbers

For some years it has been customary to refer to persons of 65 and over as "Every Tenth American." However, Herman Brotman, consultant to the Senate Committee on Aging, has reported that now one in every nine Americans is aged 65 or above. He has also drawn a few comparisons. In 1776, about 50,000 persons in our new nation were 65 plus, or 2 percent, or every fiftieth American in a population of 2.5 million. By 1900, it was 4 percent, or every twenty-fifth American. Projections for the future say that by the year 2035 nearly one-fifth of the population—more than 55 million people—will be sixty-five and over.

How much of this elderly population will need help to live on their own terms, outside of institutions, taking care of their daily existence? The U.S. Commissioner of Aging, Robert Benedict, analyzed this situation for the Subcommittee on Aging (U.S. Senate 1978). Benedict reported that the proportion of the elderly who are over 75 now is about 38 percent. By the year 2030, that total may be nearly one-half of the elderly population.

Furthermore, a large percentage of those now 75 and over fall into the category of what the Federal Council on Aging (1977) has called "the frail elderly," or those individuals whose ability to function in the ordinary business of daily living has become limited because of the increased infirmities of later life. Those frail elderly number from 3½ to 4½ million people.

Commissioner Benedict testified:

> We can expect that the continuing increase of the very old population will mean a greater incidence of disability and isolation over the years. The population 65+ will increase by about 500,000 persons each year over the next half century. It is estimated that between 80,000 and 100,000 of those persons will need assistance to remain in the community.

And he added:

> These facts portend increasing pressures on the family, special living arrangements, community service programs, and nursing homes and other institutions.

Congress has already begun to react in a number of ways to parts of the challenge outlined by Commissioner Benedict. But we are not starting with a clean slate. To deal with the future, we have to correct mistakes or unfortunate tendencies of the past.

Health Issues

For more than a decade, the Senate Special Committee on Aging has criticized the sharp rise in institutional care and the slow pace in developing noninstitutional alternatives in long-term care (U.S. Senate 1974). The 1971 White House Conference on Aging reported the following:

> Despite the demonstrated need, it is estimated that there are only 30,000 homemaker–home health aides in the entire United States, serving all categories of social and health needs: the ill, aged, disabled, children, and others with social and/or health problems. At a minimum, homemaker–home health aide agencies should have available 300,000 homemaker–home health aides or one homemaker–home health aide per every 1,000 persons in our total population. For older persons, the ratio should be approximately one per 100 as a minimum. (White House Conference 1971).

Soon after this conference, the Senate Committee on Aging released two reports on home health widely regarded as authoritative and challenging (Senate 1972, 1973). Legislation challenging the rigid Medicare requirements for the provision of such care was introduced but got nowhere. The chairman, Senator Church, was more successful in winning approval of a modest program to start up home health agencies where none existed.[3] In 1976, a report *Adult Day Care Facilities for Treatment, Health Care, and Related Services,* was issued by the committee. As the title suggests, a summary was offered of what was happening in what are often called day-care centers, which provide health care and other services for several hours each day to persons who return home each night. Brahna Trager was impressed by what was being accomplished, but she also stated:

> The present challenge is one which places, upon planners and organizers of facilities and services, and upon public and private funding

sources, the necessity to provide for community based ambulatory treatment, rehabilitative and compensatory supports by means of a multifaceted, community-based approach in order to assure to disabled members of the population an equitable share of that societal concern which is the basis of all civilized cultures.

And she added:

Isolated examples of resources and services geared to the long-term needs of high-risk members of the population have been demonstrated in the United States; the needed comprehensive network of services has not, either in fact or as public policy, yet been developed.

In the absence of that community base, we must, of course, rely on institutional care for large numbers of people. As stated in our annual report:

An estimated 1.6 million people of all ages were institutionalized in chronic hospitals and facilities for deaf, blind, and disabled, in nursing homes, and in personal or domiciliary care facilities in 1976. This institutional population will increase to 2.1 million in 1980 and 3 million by 1985. Between 80 percent and 90 percent of this institutionalized population is elderly.

Public money spent on nursing home care alone now comes to about $5.8 billion a year. We have some idea of the high cost of needless placement in acute-care hospitals. In making his case for the administration's hospital-cost containment bill, then HEW Secretary Joseph Califano (1977) said that 100,000 of the 700,000 persons now in such institutions do not have to be there. He estimated that $2.6 billion a year, or $7 million a day, in excess charges were being generated because alternative care was not available.

This kind of high-level concern is welcome, but in order to correct past mistakes to prepare for foreseeable future demands, look at what must be done in this area alone:

— The ingrained bias toward institutional care must be further recognized, challenged, and corrected.
— A few specific changes in Medicare reimbursement practices are needed. These changes are difficult to enact.
— The community base, talked about with increasing fervor, must become the subject of varying strategies for development and implementation.

Housing: The Congregate Struggle

Another part of the struggle to build a community base is related to housing. A few specifics related to legislative effort point out the difficulties inherent in broadening that community base.

The Senate Committee on Aging turned its attention in November 1975 to congregate housing for older adults—or as it was called in a report, "Assisted Residential Living Combining Shelter and Services" (U.S. Senate 1975). The preface to that report referred to an estimate that approximately 3 million older persons in the United States could be considered to need assisted housing.

Assisted, or congregate housing, involves more than group meals. It means, in the case of public housing, dealing with a specific problem:

> Many tenants now in public housing have "aged" in their present quarters as have those in private housing in the community. As could be anticipated, an increasing number of public housing agencies are faced with the fact that either they must evict the more frail and impaired who cannot sustain the shopping, cooking, or heavy housekeeping chores designed for the hale and hearty, or they must develop—on a crash and perhaps ill-founded basis—some semblance of the services those aging occupants need to maintain at least semi-independence in a residential setting.

Even though the authority for providing services to people in public housing had been made part of a 1970 act and even though that authority had been reinforced with additional statutory language in 1973, nothing had happened by the time of the report and nothing has happened yet, even though an estimated 45,000 persons now in such quarters need a congregate housing environment. On March 8, 1978—after long months of drafting, redrafting and mobilizing support, sometimes over heavy opposition—Senator Harrison Williams was able to introduce the Congregate Housing Services Act of 1978 (S. 2691), which gives local housing authorities the funds needed to purchase or develop services for appropriate tenants, working with local areas on aging. It has been a struggle, and the struggle has resulted in partial success. A $10 million appropriation was authorized in September 1978 to begin this program.

The Attitude Factor

One witness at the 1972 hearing told about the last months of her terminally ill husband. She and he had worked out their own personal equilibrium, their own dual recognition of trial and death by cancer. But they nevertheless had a problem. Their own physician would not acknowledge that he was treating a dying patient. The husband and wife found it necessary to join his pretense, and the doctor maintained that pretense to and even beyond the death of his patient, who also happened to be a personal friend (U.S. Senate 1972).

What may seem to be a tender rejection of harsh fate to someone close may actually have its roots in the curricula and professorial attitudes in many, perhaps most, of the nation's schools of medicine. Time and time again, the Senate Special Committee on Aging has asked why the physicians of the future receive so little training in geriatric medicine, including care and concern for the dying older person, in their formal university training. This was the theme expressed by Senator Charles Percy at a hearing conducted in conjunction with the Gerontological Society a few years ago. He said: "In our investigations we actually found, through testimony given to us, that doctors and physicians avoid dealing with the elderly, especially nursing home patients. . . . They testified before our subcommittee that they really elected and preferred to take care of younger people who can return to society. As one of them said: 'We have a feeling that we can return them to society as productive members'' (U.S. Senate 1976:5).

Dr. Robert Butler, director of the National Institute on Aging, was even more emphatic:

> The real question is not whether geriatric medicine should be a specialty, certified or otherwise. . . . Rather, the question is how can we expose every physician to the procedures of primary care which are necessary to deal with older patients just as we have exposed other primary care physicians. . . . The body of knowledge required to care for old people is not just disease-categorical; it is broad in perspective and in keeping with the complex character of human experience— including the multiple physical, personal, and social processes that occur with age (U.S. Senate 1976:11).

If physicians individually require more understanding of illnesses and disability and death among older American, do directors of institutional facilities also need more understanding? Here again the Senate Committee on Aging has complained about the poor treatment given in some nursing homes to very ill patients, just as it has celebrated those facilities that determinedly do the opposite, sometimes in spite of governmental requirements.

Additional light is thrown on the subject of institutional care of the dying by a small study that may have wide implications (Koff 1975). A questionnaire was mailed to 85 nursing homes in 1975, requesting information on several subjects, including practices related to death and dying. Most reported that deaths during the prior year averaged one-fourth of their stated bed capacities, and this indicated the commonness of mortality and the need for its skilled handling.

However, as indicated in this excerpt, it would appear that an almost furtive embarrassment, rather than skill and sensitivity, prevailed:

An important part of the questionnaire asked the nursing home administrator or the director of nursing how residents of their institution were informed of the death of another resident. In 62 of 77 responses to this question, residents were told of another resident's death only if they asked about the deceased; they otherwise were informed only through the "grapevine" of the institution. In one response, residents were told that the deceased resident had been transferred to the hospital rather than removed to the mortuary because he died. In 10 homes, close friends and roommates were informed of the death by the nurse in charge. In one home a friend of the deceased was asked to tell the other residents. In only six homes were residents informed of a death at a residents' council meeting, prayer meeting, or other group event. In response to a question regarding the procedure used by the institution in removing the deceased from the home, the majority of those responding suggested that the dead patient is screened, removed from the room, or placed in a holding room or storage room away from the residential area. The majority of the respondents replied that doors to other patients' rooms are closed when the body is moved down the hall. In contrast, one respondent stated that "no residents are kept from seeing the deceased being removed. It may be their last opportunity to pay tribute to a friend."

The author concluded:

> In spite of the large numbers of persons who are currently dying in
> nursing homes and our expectation that this figure will continue to
> increase, it appears that the practices of nursing homes related to death
> and dying are not yet supportive of the needs of the people who con-
> tinue to live in those institutions.

As the nation becomes more and more aware of the high costs
and frequent shortcomings of institutional care, the trickle of research
related to the quality of care given in nursing homes will, it is to be
hoped, be broadened and related to efforts at attitudinal change.

Hospices and the Federal Government

Hospices figured in the 1972 hearings, but only in a tentative and
prospective fashion. Reverend Edward F. Dobihal, Yale University
Divinity School, described plans then nearing completion:

> Hospice . . . plans to work in close collaboration with a major
> university center, an excellent community hospital and a VA hospital,
> extended care facilities, two health maintenance organizations, the
> VNA, homemaker associations, et cetera. But in our preliminary plan-
> ning all of these organizations agreed that terminal care was not now
> adequately being provided and that it could best be provided through
> an independent program, affiliated with others for specific service,
> teaching, and research.
> Those plans have been realized and now Hospice of New Haven
> is one of the few full-fledged hospice programs in the United States
> (U.S. Senate 1972:133).

Since then, the hospice movement has become much more
familiar and formidable to the Congress and to the executive branch.

A good summary of administration concerns was given by
Faye G. Abdellah, assistant surgeon general and chief nurse officer
of the U.S. Public Health Service. She emphasized the relationship
between hospices and home-care programs, saying that the New Haven
home-health-care-based hospice found that 70 percent of its patients
died in their own homes. She added:

The development of hospice programs and the role which home health agencies will play in their development and operation is going to entail some legislative changes. Training programs will have to be developed for home health agency personnel. Major third-party reimbursements including Medicare and Medicaid will have to be amended to incorporate the payment of care under a hospice program (1978:35)

Secretary Califano established a task force to examine activities within and outside HEW to make recommendations about the appropriate federal role.

In Congress, a movement to mobilize facts and legislative options was activated. Senator Robert Dole, in May 1978, told the Senate that he, Senator Kennedy, and Senator Ribicoff were joining forces to secure up-to-date information on the status of the hospice movement in this country. He also speculated on the possible broadening of current pilot projects: "The National Cancer Institute has a limited demonstration project ongoing at this time. However, there is no doubt that much more information is necessary before we begin to address the issues of reimbursement, standards, licensure requirements, staffing, and health planning for Hospice facilities and programs" (*Congressional Record*, p. S7689).

He added a further caveat, together with a challenge:

Our experience with the Medicaid mills and other unscrupulous health care operation has taught us that we must move with the utmost caution in the development of these programs. But move we must—the growth of the hospice movement is a long-range goal—an effort to ameliorate some of the existing conditions for the terminally ill in hospitals is something that must begin today. We must also push our health manpower education system to more fully prepare health professionals to deal with the problems of the terminally ill and of their families.

Conclusion

If this nation will engage in serious debate about a national health program for all age groups, the concerns related to long-term care of the chronically ill and final care of the terminally ill should not be submerged, minimized, or left solely to "social services." The growing desire to provide a "community base" for a comprehensive array of institutional and noninstitutional care is heartening, but it will remain so only if governmental policymakers recognize the dangers of building a "separate but equal" long-term care system rather than incorporate health and social services for the chronically or terminally ill into a more humane, less institutionalized, and much more flexible system, which, in meeting the growing needs of the elderly, is likely to serve other age groups as well to their greater satisfaction than is now the case.

The magnitude of the task was summed up very vividly by Secretary Califano before the Committee on Aging:

> We must build a rational, comprehensive, efficient, and humane system for delivering health services.
> Such a system would include:
> - Adequate, supervised residential facilities for those who lack families but want to live in their communities,
> - A range of alternatives between the hospital and the nursing home, including a system of home health care,
> - Innovative and compassionate ways of caring for the terminally ill outside the traditional hospital or nursing home.

And he added: *"Such a system is easy to describe. But it is nowhere to be found.* We have, instead, a confusing and expensive patchwork of financing systems that spawn an even more inadequate delivery system" (Califano 1978; emphasis added).

The Secretary may have overstated the case somewhat; there are very encouraging prototypes of the "spectrum of care" for older persons in advanced stages of development in a few cities in this nation. But he is nevertheless overwhelmingly correct in the assessment of the challenge to the entire nation in the future as the "graying" of our population intensifies. A national policy directing us toward development of more universally available systems of the kind described above is badly needed.

Notes

1. A program to provide startup funding for new in-home service agencies, first proposed by Senator Church in 1973, was under consideration in 1978 for another renewal.

2. A section on physical and mental health declared: "A comprehensive system of appropriate health care requires that a full spectrum of presently known services be readily accessible. These must be of high quality and be delivered in the appropriate setting and at the appropriate time, with concern for the dignity and choice of the individual, and within a framework which guarantees coordination among the various levels of care, continuity of care over time, and the efficiency and effectiveness which will assure supportable costs."

3. Enacted in July 1975, the home health grant demonstration program was so belated in beginning operations that Senator Church asked for an extension in 1976. This extension was incorporated into the Health Maintenance Organization Act of 1976, Public Law 94-640. It authorized $10 million to finance the initial costs of establishing and operating home health agencies and to expand services of existing agencies, along with $5 million for training professional and paraprofessional personnel for home health agencies. On September 17, 1976, HEW announced fifty-six awards totaling $3 million under the initial grant program.

References

Abdellah, F. G. 1978. "Long-Term Care Policy Issues: Alternatives to Institutional Care." *Annals of the American Academy of Political and Social Science* (July).

Califano, J. 1977. Testimony Before House Subcommittee on Health and Environment, May 11, and Senate Finance Committee, June 7, 95th Congress, 1st session.

Califano, J. 1978. Testimony Before Senate Special Committee on Aging, "Retirement, Work, and Lifelong Learning," 95th Congress, 2d session, July 17.

Koff, T. H. 1975. "Social Rehearsal for Death and Dying." Paper given at First North American Symposium on Long-Term Care Administration, Toronto, Canada, July 28.

U.S. Senate. 1972. Special Committee on Aging. 92d Congress, 2 session, August 7, 8, and 9.

U.S. Senate. 1973, 1974. Special Committee on Aging, *Home Health Sevices in the*

United States, 92d Congress, 2d session, April; *Home Health Services in the United States: A Working Paper on Current Status,* 93d Congress, 1st session, July.

U.S. Senate. 1974. Committee on Aging, Subcommittee on Long-Term Care, *Nursing Home Care in the United States: Failure in Public Policy,* 93d Congress, 2d session, November.

U.S. Senate. 1975. Committee on Aging, *Congregate Housing for Older Adults,* Report No. 94-478, 94th Congress, 1st session, November.

U.S. Senate. 1976. Special Committee on Aging, "Medicine and Aging: An Assessment of Opportunities and Neglect," New York City, October 16.

White House Conference. 1971. "The Session Report: Homemaker-Home Health Aide Services." *1971 White House Conference on Aging: Toward a National Policy on Aging, Final Report,* vol. 2. Washington, D.C.: U.S. Government Printing Office.

Commentary

Elizabeth R. Prichard

In 1982, Congress passed legislation to provide Medicare payments for Hospice services, to become effective in November 1983. Although recognition was finally given to the care of the terminally ill, it is significant to note that this was the only new federal health care measure passed by Congress in 1982. In Mr. Oriol's presentation, we are provided with the substance of the deliberations of Congressional committees over a period of several years; the informed investigative process; the testimony of knowledgeable persons; the concerns of Senators Dole, Kennedy, and Ribicoff; and the well-planned steps to ensure a program of quality. To these we must add the mounting concerns and pressures from the public and the recommendations made by professional organizations. The response of Congressional leaders and the support given their proposed action augured well for the outcome.

However, the Hospice Bill which has emerged is at variance with the original aims and intent of its proponents. The Bill has a rigidity in terms of home health care services, hospitalization, and managerial authority that can be attributed to ambivalence in recognition of care of the dying and their families and/or lack of understanding of the care to be provided for the terminally ill within the total health care system. The basic health care concept (especially important in the care of the terminally ill), that of the interdisciplinary team, is not fully recognized. It is to be hoped that many, if not all, of these deficiencies will be corrected in the final Regulations yet to appear.

This Hospice Bill is the first to give some recognition to a long-established need, and further steps to assure both cost effective and quality care—the issues now at stake—are dependent upon our educational resolves. Mr. Oriol cites two statements which are relevant to this point. One is in the remarks of Senator Dole: "We must also push our health manpower education system to more fully prepare health professionals to deal with the problems of the terminally ill and their families." The second statement was made by Joseph Califano, then Secretary of the former Department of Health, Education and Welfare, when he appeared before the Committee on Aging: "We must build a rational, comprehensive, efficient and humane system for delivering health services." To achieve these goals much more understanding is needed about basic human needs and their relation to health care needs. There must be a constant pursuit of knowledge that will be integrated into sound and effective health care delivery systems that will benefit all age groups of our society.

30

Limiting Life-Sustaining Medical Care for the Terminally Ill

LOU GLASSE and DAVID R. MURRAY

*T*he purpose of this paper is to initiate discussions in New York State and elsewhere on a public policy issue of importance to terminally ill persons, their families, and the medical profession, that is, the right of dying persons to refuse or limit life-sustaining medical care. There is hardly an aspect of life and living untouched by the workings of government. The same can be said of death and dying, for public policies determine much of what must and must not be done before, during, and after death.

We in the field of aging are, or should be, particularly sensitive to issues associated with death and dying. Aging is characterized by many losses: most obvious are the losses from the deaths of friends, neighbors, relatives, and spouses. Although this reality is inescapable, death seems to have been a "semi-taboo" subject for books about aging and the aged. For example, a 1977 survey of 48 such books found that very few contained any more than a passing reference to death (Wass and Scott 1977). We are not sure of the reasons for this absence of discussion of death and dying; perhaps it is a result of the very multitude of problems that face older persons. However, we are sure that there is a critical need to discuss a wide range of interests and learn more by bringing together those in the field of aging and those in the field of thanatology.

Brief Overview of Selected State Public Policy Issues

Before discussing the main topic of this presentation, it is appropriate to list briefly several state-level policy areas of relevance to death and dying. Such policies, although wide ranging, are a legitimate concern of those in the field of thanatology. For a moment, consider the scope of issues related to both government and thanatology. Several are the direct result of advances in medical technology; others are more traditional.

Some of these many concerns include the following:

— A statutory definition of death itself—the controversy over the "usual and customary" definition (cessation of respiratory and circulatory functions) or a "brain death" definition (total and irreversible cessation of brain functions). The ability to forestall otherwise imminent death by mechanically prolonging respiratory and circulatory functions has raised both this issue of definition and the question of the right of a terminally ill person to refuse treatment.

— Public policy also determines how we care for the dying and their families and whether that care is provided at home or in an institution. For example, the hospice concept of compassionate care and support for the dying and their families is now receiving the serious attention it deserves. We wonder whether hospice-type care now exists de facto in nursing homes or similar facilities. We also wonder as we begin to develop hospice care if some nursing home services could be reoriented to meet the needs of the terminally ill and their families.

— Regulation of the funeral industry can be raised as an area of relevance, particularly in relaton to consumer protection issues, such as the need for full disclosure of which services are required, which are at the choice of the buyer, and what are the costs of such services. It appears that this issue will be resolved after a decade of controversy when a new FTC rule becomes effective in 1984.

— Other issues that can be raised include wills and estates, pensions,

death certificates, the regulation of life insurance, and the coverage of health insurance, especially in relation to home care for the terminally ill.
— Mention should also be made of the Uniform Anatomical Gift Act, which has been enacted in every state. Adoption of that uniform act makes it public policy to encourage anatomical gifts.

Limiting Life-Sustaining Medical Care For the Terminally Ill

The Issue

These issues illustrate the wide scope of government actions that relate to death and dying. This discussion is, however, about only one such issue: the need for state legislation to establish a clear, legal option for those who choose to refuse or limit life-sustaining medical care. Only in the last few years has this become the subject of public discussion and governmental action.

Increased public awareness of this issue, owing to personal experience and media coverage of specific cases, has resulted in increasing public concern. Most people now feel that extreme efforts result in a loss of dignity for the terminally ill patient, an unwanted delay to the conclusion of a life, and unnecessary suffering, as well as an unnecessary financial burden, for the family. Most people also believe that they have a right to refuse "heroic" efforts on their behalf if their own religious or philosophical beliefs permit such a refusal.

Many are also concerned about the great potential that currently exists for foul play and unethical practices. No adequate legal safeguards or guidelines are now available for the terminally ill patient, the immediate family, the physician, or the medical facility to protect them from abuse or liability resulting from either action or inaction on anyone's part. In addition, court cases have failed to establish clear or consistent guidelines in these matters.

Currently, only a few states have a statute that permits persons to provide written instructions for withholding or withdrawing medical care if they should become terminally ill or mortally injured.

Background

Two main questions are discussed in this presentation: "Does a person have the right to refuse medical treatment even though that refusal might hasten that person's death?" and "What safeguards are necessary to protect all parties intimately involved in the dying process?" Public attitudes and opinions are examined and current legal problems and a suggested approach are discussed.

A person's right to what has been called "death with dignity"—choosing the manner of death when inevitable—has been debated for centuries. It has received increasing attention since the turn of the century and, thanks to the strides of medical science, has become the topic of more intensive and urgent debate during the last few years.

During the last fifty years, efforts to eradicate infectious and parasitic diseases have enabled greater numbers of people to live to an advanced age. Improved treatment methods, such as the use of antibiotics and the "miracle drugs," have helped to virtually eliminate these diseases or bring them under control. However, public health measures, such as vaccination and inoculation, played the major role. Other efforts, such as improved sanitation, were also major components of disease prevention programs.

The old, in particular, now live to become the victims of degenerative diseases that progressively impair their health; they usually die, not from a single condition or disorder, but from the effects of a constellation of associated illnesses often brought on by their debilitated condition. Swift deaths from heart attacks, accidents, and violence will continue. However, most of us will develop lingering, chronic conditions ending with death from a cancer, a heart or major cardiovascular disease, or a cerebrovascular disease. Furthermore, it is not uncommon for the death of an older person to be preceded by a period of coma, paralysis, incontinence, and/or mental abnormality (Brocklehurst and Hanley 1976:239, 242). This is our likely future, and we should consider, when we are healthy and best able, just what such circumstances will mean to us and how we want them dealt with.

We know that medical science has continued its efforts to improve treatment. Also, medical science has developed the capacity to maintain the signs of biological life without consciousness or the distinctly human qualities of life. These elusive "qualities of life," and the fact that individuals disagree on what they are, cause problems in both accepting and understanding the so-called "right to die." Because these qualities of life are personal, it should be the personal responsibility of each individual to struggle with the questions that must be asked. Each person should be able to demand either a cessation of efforts to prolong dying or a continuation of efforts to forestall dying. We have that right morally; we should have that right legally.

The absence of a legal choice regarding the cessation of life-sustaining medical care unnecessarily complicates the dying process for many terminally ill persons. The 1971 White House Conference on Aging dealt with this issue in its section on spiritual well-being and recommended that: "Religious bodies and government should affirm the right to, and reverence for, life and recognize the individual's right to die with dignity." This affirmation of both the reverence for life and the right to die is needed today and reflects the growth of public opinion in support of the right-to-die concept.

Changes in Public Opinion

Over the years, many polls and surveys that relate to death with dignity have been reported. Although few have included any reference to legal protections for the dying person, one common element is clear: the person is incurably, hopelessly, or painfully ill. These polls or surveys indicate both increasing support for the right to die and an improved understanding of the concept (Russell 1975:102, 198, 200).

In 1947, a Gallup poll was conducted on the question: "When a person has a disease that cannot be cured, do you think doctors should be allowed by law to end the patient's life by some painless means if the patient and his family request it?" Of those responding, 37 percent said "yes"; the majority, 54 percent, said "no"; and 9 percent had "no opinion."

In 1973, Gallup asked the same question and found that public approval had greatly increased in 26 years. A majority (53 percent) now agreed with that same statement. Interestingly, this question as phrased would allow the physician actively to end the patient's life, rather than simply withhold or withdraw treatment.

A Harris survey, also taken in 1973, reported that 62 percent of Americans believe that ''a patient with a terminal disease ought to be able to tell his doctor to let him die rather than to extend his life when no cure is in sight.'' Only 23 percent disagreed with this statement, which put the physician in a passive rather than active role.

In early 1977, a comparison of a sample of magazine readers with a sample of persons aged 65 and older was reported (Wass 1977). Among its findings was that 73 percent of both groups agree that ''after reasonable care has been given, a person ought to be permitted to die a natural death.'' None of the elderly surveyed believed in ''prolonging life at all cost.'' This feeling of older persons is related to several of their other attitudes about death, dying, and dependency.

Older Persons' Attitudes

In our society, an aura of mystery, fear, and apprehension surrounds death. In spite of this, most individuals—the aged and the dying especially—are willing to discuss death openly. In addition, discussions of death and dying are not necessarily upsetting to elderly persons.

Most older persons accept the fact that people become ill, that they become old, and that they die. This acceptance is coupled with the view held by most older persons that death is a new beginning. Studies of the elderly in nursing homes found that approaching death is usually accepted without fear or regret. Most are able to speak openly about death.

This acceptance of the inevitable death does not mean that grief and suffering are accepted similarly. In fact, suffering and dependency are viewed with great anxiety. In addition, older persons generally fear their own pain in dying, regret the emotional and financial burden they may become to others, and consider with distaste the grief their death would cause loved ones. Most stressful, however, is the older person's fear of dependency. These fears of pain and dependency are very real in the lives of older persons. Written instructions for treatment of a terminal condition would help relieve this anxiety and give peace of mind to many older people.

Currently, the right to refuse treatment when terminally ill is legally recognized in only a handful of states. Individuals seeking to express their wishes in a death-delaying situation must rely on an expression of intent, whether oral or written, which has no legal standing. As a result, there is no assurance that those wishes will be honored.

The Dilemma of the Medical Profession

Of major concern to any public policy on this issue are the needs and problems of the medical profession, which itself has recognized the necessity of guidelines and protections—both legal and medical—in those cases when patients request that life-sustaining measures be withdrawn or withheld. Under present law in most states, no one has either the authority or responsibility legally to comply with such a request.

In order to discuss the moral and legal problems confronting the medical profession, and physicians in particular, it is necessary to provide a brief glimpse into the situations encountered—the personal agonies experienced by patients, families, and physicians; the conflicting professional, moral, and legal doctrines; and the consequences of both action and inaction.

For many who have witnessed death and the attempts in institutions to forestall death, the dying person can no longer be seen as a victim of death itself, but rather as the victim of a system that seriously fails to care for and about the individual. The system of "care" has been described by many as one that ignores the needs and values of the dying person. All too often, patients become objects with no right to assert their beliefs or express their feelings. This is the tragedy of care of the dying.

Without consultation, with assumed permission, the health care system often attaches a wild array of alien gadgets to the dying person's debilitated "life support system" in order to maintain the biological signs of life for at least a few more moments. One physician has observed that: "The terminal patient may desperately want rest, peace, and dignity; yet he may receive only infusions, transfusions, a heart machine, and a team of experts all busily occupied with his heart rate, his pulmonary functions and his secretions, but not with him as a person" (Reich 1972:71). We must ask: To what decent or justifiable end is this directed?

In spite of the legal risks, some physicians, in order to relieve needless suffering, do allow patients to die, although few will admit it publicly. However, there is great pressure within the medical profession itself to hold off death. Another physician has characterized the peer pressure in this way:

> Passive withdrawal of life-supporting systems such as tubes and intravenous feedings simply to allow a person to die unencumbered by technical artifices is subject to authoritative scrutiny. What a supervisor or colleague might say is frequently given considerable weight in the decision-making process of a medical staff member. A professional must account for his action, especially in an institution, and a patient's private wishes often become secondary to institutional policy (Krant 1974:70–71).

Even with informed and written consent from patients and families, physicians who comply with requests to limit life-sustaining measures would be jeopardizing their careers and inviting censure, lawsuits, or murder charges. It is easy to understand why the medical profession is searching for ethical and legal guidelines.

Although the physician and family alike may be sympathetic to the dying person's wishes, the law makes no allowance for the individual patient's decision. Initially, any person has the right to accept or refuse medical treatment. Unfortunately, when that same patient is dying, there is no clear legal recognition of this right of refusal, leaving the physician to face conflicts and dilemmas that should not exist. The Hippocratic Oath, the positions of medical societies, personal philosophy, conflicting court cases, and the vagueness of law all contribute to the physician's problem.

The ambiguities of law, however, pose particular problems. Although some physicians claim that legislation is not needed to terminate useless treatment, others disagree. Legal experts, for example, counsel physicians and facilities that all possible steps, even if unreasonable in the eyes of the patient, must be taken to prolong life. Failure to do so could result in charges of criminal negligence or manslaughter.

On the other hand, compounding the issue still further, is a directly opposing legal principle. Courts have consistently upheld and expanded the right of adults to give informed consent to the medical care they are to receive. As a result, if a physician treats a patient without the patient's informed consent, the physician may be committing assault and battery. Since court cases have been inconsistent and confusing, the physician's dilemma is thus intensified in a "damned if you do, and damned if you don't" situation.

Because of increasing concern, medical associations have issued guidelines, which, although helpful, provide no legal protection. In 1973, the American Hospital Association issued a new Bill of Rights. Among the rights were these:

— Patients have the right to receive from their physician information necessary to give informed consent prior to the start of any procedure and/or treatment.
— Patients have the right to refuse treatment to the extent permitted by law and to be informed of the medical consequences of their actions.

Obviously, the key phrases in these two rights are: "consent prior to the start" (implying no withdrawal of consent after the beginning of treatment) and "to the extent permitted by law" (thus in effect denying refusal if no appropriate law exists).

Also in 1973, the New York Medical Society adopted the following statement, which was prepared by its committee on ethics:

The right to die with dignity, or the cessation of the employment of extraordinary means to prolong the life of the body when there is irrefutable evidence that biological death is inevitable, is the decision of the patient and/or the immediate family, with the approval of the family physician.

Although the medical society statement considers the rights of the dying, the physician may override the decision by disapproving it.

A legal solution to the physicians' and facilities' problems must be enacted. In the case of persons with terminal conditions, we cannot say, "Let nature take its course," for we have already intervened in the natural process of dying by forestalling death. We must let each individual, within that person's own moral framework, decide for himself or herself whether or not to delay death.

The Living Will

The so-called "living will" is a declaration that states the wishes of a person concerning the medical care to be administered for a terminal condition. It is not a legal document and there is no guarantee that the wishes will be followed, especially in view of the uncertain legal consequences. As a result, the living will is categorically inadequate as anything other than a simple expression of wishes. The existence of a living will can also be very unfair to a physician, causing conflicts between the patient's desires and the physician's need for legal protection. Over the years, the living will has been refined and improved. But it remains a nonlegal document in spite of its inclusion in references of modern legal forms.

This discussion does not use the term "living will" in order that we avoid confusion with the nonlegal and relatively ambiguous statement that has developed over the years. Instead, the word *directive* is used for the specific written instructions and declaration of an individual's wishes for treatment of a terminal condition.

Suggested Legislative Approach

New York State, and each state, should enact legislation that: (1) validates the right of a terminally ill adult to refuse further medical treatment and experience a less prolonged death and (2) establishes specific safeguards to protect this right, the patient, the family, and the medical profession. This would establish a clear, legal option for people to choose the type of care they are to receive if terminally ill.

Brief Legislative History in New York State

Since shortly after the turn of the century, several "right to die" proposals have been advanced in New York State. It was not until years later, however, that relatively serious consideration was given to this issue.

In 1946, clergymen, physicians, and others became active in supporting a right-to-die bill for New York State. A bill was developed that included, among its several detailed provisions, that an adult, suffering from a painful and fatal disease verified by the physician to be incurable, could petition the court to permit death. The bill was offered to the legislature in 1947, but there was much resistance and it was never introduced. Other efforts ensued, but by the end of 1952, it was evident that no bill would be introduced in the state legislature.

It appears that little further legislative attention was given to this issue until 1976, when a bill similar to the 1947 proposal was introduced. The bill would have permitted a terminally sick or injured person to petition the Supreme Court for removal of artificial life-sustaining devices.

Also in 1976, the Assembly Subcommittee on Health Care held hearings that included the "living will" as a topic. Testimony on this subject included both support and opposition. Of special interest was the statement in support made by a representative of the Medical Society of the State of New York. The statement read in part:

> A legal procedure should be available for any adult of sound mind to draw up a prearranged "Living Will" which will determine the disposition of his or her life when the quality of that life is no longer viable. We interpret the quality of life as a measure of health, excluding pain and suffering, which has no end point except death. It is our opinion that to prolong life merely for continued existence where there is no hope of health or happiness, is in a sense to subject a human being to cruel and unusual punishment. If the natural course of events would bring death regardless of intervention, then "heroic procedures" should be under the control of the terminally ill person and he or she should have the prior right to decide when he or she wished all futile efforts to be discontinued.

In 1977, five bills on this issue were introduced in the New York State Legislature. Three were patterned generally after California's Natural Death Act, which permits a person to sign a directive. Two would prohibit any cessation of "extraordinary treatment for the sole purpose of accelerating the death of an incompetent, comatose, or unconscious patient" if the treatment is of reasonable benefit to the patient. The intent of the latter two bills is to protect patients who are incompetent and hopeless, without interfering with the rights of competent patients to refuse treatment.

In 1978, each of these bills was automatically reintroduced, and three additional bills on this issue were introduced. From 1979 on, only a very few bills on this issue have been introduced. Unfortunately, those bills that provide for a directive are not as specific as needed and, therefore, do not offer adequate protections.

As is so often the case when dealing with public policy, especially in a state as diverse and complex as New York, we must seek a balance of protections and assurances both for the individual and for society itself. We are sensitive to the many concerns that surround this issue and are certain that the suggestions we make will not be met with unanimous agreement. If, however, we are to contribute to discussions of this issue in New York State, we must be ready to accept open debate.

In addition, we must be ever mindful of the basic realities of the lawmaking process. For example, California's Natural Death Act suffered nine separate amendments before being enacted. Accepting these realities, taking them into account, and setting our sights on the achievable are essential. There is a pressing need for legislation. However, in light of the complexity and seriousness of this issue, as well as the range of opinions to be considered, we must take adequate time for full discussion.

Essential Elements of Legislation

Adequate legislation will ensure that a patient's right to die is confirmed and that the patient and others are protected. Following is a summary description of some of the provisions necessary for legislation.

General Provisions
   The overriding principles of any legislation must recognize the wide scope, the limitations, and the potential of medical technology. At the same time, individual rights and specific protections must be included:

1. Mercy killing by any person must be expressly prohibited.

2. Any affirmative act to end a life, other than to permit the natural process of dying, must be prohibited. In addition, the law must allow the patient to request medications necessary to relieve pain, ameliorate symptoms, or promote comfort, even though these may hasten death.

3. It must be clear that life-sustaining procedures can be withheld or withdrawn only when they would serve to artificially prolong the moment of death when death is imminent.

4. Definitions as set forth in law should be carefully drawn and very specific. Any legislation would be seriously flawed if terms such as *terminal condition* and *life-sustaining procedure* were vaguely defined. This, unfortunately, is frequently the case in proposed legislation. The California law is, however, explicit and provides the following definitions:

— "Terminal condition" means an incurable condition caused by injury, disease, or illness, which, regardless of the application of life-sustaining procedures, would, within reasonable medical judgment, produce death, and where the application of life-sustaining procedures serve only to postpone the moment of the patient's death.

— "Life-sustaining procedure" means any medical procedure or intervention that uses mechanical or other artificial means to sustain, restore, or supplant a vital function, which, when applied to a qualified patient, would serve only to artificially prolong the moment of death and where, in the judgment of the attending physician, death is imminent whether or not such procedures are used.

Written Instructions

The major safeguard for all concerned and the core of any adequate legislation would be a written document, the directive, which specifically states the patient's wish that life-sustaining procedures be withheld or withdrawn if the patient has a terminal condition.

1. Only a mentally competent adult may execute a directive.

2. The directive must follow a specific form in accordance with law.

3. The directive must be in writing and must be signed and dated.

4. The directive must be effective and legally binding immediately upon signing and may be reexecuted or revoked at any time. Unfortunately, several of the existing laws make this document advisory rather than legally binding. In those cases, one has absolutely no assurance that one's wishes will be followed. Like a last will and testament, this document should be legally binding and effective immediately. Obviously, adequate provisions for revoking this document must also be available.

5. The directive should be effective until revoked. Some be-

lieve that this document should be effective only for a limited period, at which time it must be reexecuted to remain effective. A will has no such limitation, and setting an arbitrary period of effectiveness does not seem reasonable. Granted, many are uncomfortable about a matter of such seriousness. However, with adequate provisions for revocation, there is no compelling reason to set a limit on duration.

6. The directive must be signed by two witnesses not entitled to the estate of the person and not rendering medical care at the time of signing. Many of the existing right-to-die laws exclude any person related by blood or marriage and all medical personnel, in addition to those entitled to the estate of the person at the time of signing. Such wide restrictions are unnecessary, and we suggest that each state parallel its existing safeguards for a last will and testament—that is, those with a direct pecuniary interest should be excluded. Because this interest could include medical personnel, such persons should also be excluded if rendering care at the time of signing. In addition, we must recognize that some nursing home patients are vulnerable to exploitation or are simply unable to make decisions. Although a document would be applicable only if signed by a competent adult, we believe that how best to protect some nursing home residents is an unresolved issue in need of further consideration.

7. The directive should designate a person to act on behalf of the patient, if incapacitated. This reflects the need for interpreting the patient's wishes and making decisions if the patient is unable to communicate. The written document should allow for designation of any patient-selected individual to serve in this capacity. No state has such a provision, and we suggest that the spouse and blood relatives not be excluded.

Additional Protections for the Individual

In addition to the directive itself, there are several other suggested provisions that, while of value to others, are intended primarily to protect the patient:

1. The directive may be revoked by a patient at any time, regardless of mental state or competency, by signing a written revocation or orally stating that the directive is revoked or by destroying

the directive. The directive may be destroyed by another person at the patient's direction and in the patient's presence.

2. Any person may orally communicate a revocation to the physician.

3. At least two physicians, one of whom must be the attending physician, must have personally examined the patient and certified the condition of the patient as being terminal as defined in law.

4. In emergency situations where the physician must make a life-or-death decision, the physician must be required to follow commonly accepted practice. The intention is that in emergency circumstances, such as a heart attack or when an accident victim is treated in a hospital emergency room, the physician make all reasonable efforts to preserve life. This is to further clarify item (3) in the "General Provisions" section above.

5. Health insurance, life insurance, and health care providers must be prohibited from making benefits or services conditional in any way on the existence or absence of a directive.

6. The death of a patient pursuant to a directive must not constitute suicide.

7. It must be a criminal offense with severe penalties for any person to falsify, forge, conceal, destroy, or tamper with a directive with the intent to create any false impression of the wishes of a patient.

Additional Protections for the Family

Two suggested provisions are of special interest to the patient's family:

1. The execution of a directive must not restrict, inhibit, or impair the issuance of life insurance policies and must not change or cancel the provisions of an existing life insurance policy.

2. A major problem faced by families is what to do if, when treatment is refused, the medical facility attempts to discharge the terminally ill patient. No law considers this problem, and we believe that this has not received adequate attention. We suggest that a patient must not be discharged from a medical facility, without the patient's or the family's consent, simply because life-sustaining treatment is refused. If continuing care, usually provided by a medical

facility, is needed owing to the terminal condition or to provide patient comfort, or if adequate care is unavailable at home, the patient must not be discharged. This should not, however, restrict the reasonable transfer of a patient to a facility or setting with a more appropriate level of care for the patient. We must recognize the potential for hardship to the family if the terminally ill patient were discharged. This problem clearly shows the need for hospice care.

Additional Protections for the Medical Profession

It was noted earlier that the physician urgently needs legal protection. The following provisions are intended to protect the physician:

1. No physician should be required to comply with a directive if it is against that physician's moral or ethical beliefs. If a directive has been executed and the physician disagrees, the physician must make this known to the patient.

2. It must be clear that permitting a patient to die a natural death, when a directive has been executed, would not make a physician, other medical personnel, or a facility guilty of any criminal offense or professional misconduct, unless reasonable professional care or judgment was not exercised.

The general provisions and additional protections listed above would serve to protect all those intimately involved in the dying process.

A word of caution is in order, however. In spite of the details in this paper, it was not practical to include complex legal language. Any serious attempt to draft legislation on this issue must proceed with caution and not rely on this summary as a single source of information.

In addition, when developing legislation, it is essential to keep in mind the words of a 94-year-old person who said, "Legislation bearing upon the right to live should be as effective in protecting life, where circumstances indicate that course desirable, as in providing for the ending of life where that conclusion is called for" (Morgan 1972:5). This principle must be upheld and supported by any law addressing this issue.

Conclusion

Within the context of this discussion, "dignity" is the acceptance of life as having a beginning, a middle, and an inevitable end. The final affront to dignity is in the denial of a conclusion of life, especially when that denial is imposed by someone other than the individual personally facing death.

Each person must ask: "If given the choice, how would I choose to live those last days? Which would be the greater tragedy— an artificially extended existence or a natural passing away?" Each person must find his or her own answer and be afforded the honor that it will be carried out.

References

Brocklehurst, J. C. and T. Hanley. 1976. *Geriatric Medicine for Students*. Edinburgh, London, and New York: Churchill Livingstone.

Krant, M. J. 1974. *Dying and Dignity: The Meaning and Control of a Personal Death*. Springfield, Ill: Charles C Thomas.

Morgan, A. E. 1972. Testimony Before U.S. Congress, Senate, Special Committee on Aging, *Death with Dignity—An Inquiry Into Related Public Issues, Part 2*, Washington, D.C.: U.S. Government Printing Office.

Reich, W. T. 1972. Testimony Before U.S. Congress, Senate, Special Committee on Aging, *Death with Dignity—An Inquiry into Related Public Issues, Part 2*, Washington, D.C.: U.S. Government Printing Office.

Russell, O. R. 1975. *Freedom to Die: Moral and Legal Aspects of Euthanasia*. New York: Human Sciences Press.

Wass, H. 1977. "Views and Opinions of Elderly Persons Concerning Death." *Educational Gerontology: An International Quarterly* (January-March) 2: 21–22.

Wass, H. and M. Scott. 1977. "Aging Without Death?" *Gerontologist* (August) 17:377–80.

White House Conference on Aging. 1971. *Toward a National Policy on Aging, Final Report*, volume 2, Washington, D.C.: U.S. Government Printing Office, p. 59.

Index

Abandonment: fear of, 33
Acceptance, 126, 131, 138, 208
Acceptance (stage), 212, 221, 280, 291
Accidents, 210
Accommodation, 27
Activity staff, 295
Activity theory, 28
Adaptation, 14, 195, 196-99, 203, 206; to aging, 25-26; denial as, 136; diphasic nature of, 9, 14; to fact of death, 16; forced, 229; ongoing, to partial loss, 31-39
Administrative staff, 296
Adolescence, 9, 14
Adult Day Care Facilities for Treatment, Health Care, and Related Services, 313-14
Adulthood: stages of, 273
Aesculapian authority, 101
Aesthetics: in care of aged dying, 107-8
Age: and chronic illness, 118; and death perspectives, 253; and negative attitudes, 55, 56; and risk of dying during bereavement, 175, 176, 177-78, 181
Aged: behavioral deficiencies of, 26; status of, 21; views of, 20; see also Dying aged (the); Elderly (the); Old age
Aggression, 35; fear of, 34
Aging, 41, 199-200; attitudes toward, 82; biological change in, 194; biophilosophical approach to, 271-81; as developmental phase, 22, 41, 42, 268-69 (*see also* Adaptation); generalized trends in, 33; loss in, 324; meaning of, 18-30; nonadaptive re-

sponses to, 34; as ongoing adaptation to partial loss, 31-39; optimal, 27; as part of life cycle, 49-50; professional interest in, 190; psychodynamics of, 41, 44; social factors in, 273; study of, 279, 280; successful, 23, 26, 28; systems approach to, 41, 48-51; theoretical concepts of, 22, 24-25T
Aging awareness, 274
Agism, 87, 269
Agitation, 10, 11
Alarm reaction, 10
Alcohol consumption, 182
Alcoholism, 180
Aleutian Islands, 20
Alienation, 26, 182
Ambulatory settings, 283, 288
American Cancer Society, 165
American Geriatrics Society, 290
American Hospital Association:Bill of Rights, 332
American Medical Association, 274
Anal phase, 13
Anaplastic carcinoma, 157
Anatomic integrity, 48
Anger (stage), 212, 221, 280, 291
Anticipatory process, 12-13
Anxiety, 37, 43, 198, 213; in cancer patient, 167, 170, 171; defense against, 197; in doctor, 138-40; guilt as source of, 136; infantile, 12, 15; at institutionalization, 233; need to discuss feelings of, 214; re pain, 220; in relocation, 232; in sleep, 12; re suf-

Columbia University Press Geriatrics Text

Contributors

Margot Tallmer, Ph.D., Professor, Hunter College of the City University of New York

Austin H. Kutscher, D.D.S., President, The Foundation of Thanatology; Professor of Dentistry (in Psychiatry), Department of Psychiatry, College of Physicians and Surgeons, Columbia University; Professor of Dentistry (in Psychiatry), School of Dental and Oral Surgery, Columbia University

Elizabeth R. Prichard, C.S.W., Director of Social Work Services (retired), The Presbyterian Hospital in the City of New York

Robert DeBellis, M.D., Assistant Professor of Clinical Medicine (Oncology), College of Physicians and Surgeons, Columbia University

Mahlon S. Hale, M.D., Associate Professor and Director of Psychiatric Consultation Services, Health Sciences Center, University of Connecticut, Farmington, Connecticut

Ivan K. Goldberg, M.D., Associate in Clinical Psychiatry, Department of Psychiatry, College of Physicians and Surgeons, Columbia University

Virginia W. Barrett, R.N., M. Ed., Community Health Nursing Consultant, Columbia University Center for Geriatrics and Gerontology, New York, New York

Martin Albert, M.D., Ph.D., Professor of Neurology and Director, Behavioral Neuroscience and Geriatric Neurology, Department of Neurology, Boston University Medical School, Boston, Massachusetts

Doris J. Bedell, M.A., M.T.R.S., Assistant Director, Department of Social Services in Charge of Therapeutic Recreation, Beth Abraham Hospital, Bronx, New York

Ruth Bennett, Ph.D., Deputy Director, Columbia University Center for Geriatrics and Gerontology, New York, New York; Associate Professor of Clinical Psychiatry, joint with School of Public Health, Columbia University

Darryl C. Carter, M.D., Professor of Pathology and Chief of Surgical Pathology, Yale University School of Medicine, New Haven, Connecticut

Syma Crane, M.S.W., C.S.W., A.C.S.W., formerly, Director, Department of Social Services, Beth Abraham Hospital, Bronx, New York

Thomas P. Dunfee, M.D., Hemodialysis Units and Department of Medical Education, St. Joseph's Hospital, South Bend, Indiana

Edward B. Elkowitz, D.O., Clinical Associate Professor, Downstate Medical Center, Brooklyn, New York; Adjunct Clinical Associate, New York College of Osteopathic Medicine, Old Westbury, New York

Dennis A. Frate, Ph.D., Research Associate Professor, Research Institute of Pharmaceutical Sciences, The University of Mississippi, University, Mississippi

Carel B. Germain, D.S.W., Professor, Graduate School of Social Work, University of Connecticut, West Hartford, Connecticut

Lou Glasse, M.S.W., formerly, Commissioner, New York State Office for the Aging, Albany, New York

Irwin M. Greenberg, M.D., D.M.Sc., Director of Psychiatric Services, Waterbury Hospital Health Center, Waterbury, Connecticut; Associate Clinical Professor of Psychiatry, Yale University School of Medicine, New Haven, Connecticut

Barry J. Gurland, M.D., Clinical Professor of Psychiatry, College of Physicians and Surgeons, Columbia University; Center for Geriatrics and Gerontology and Long Term Gerontology Center, Columbia University Faculty of Medicine and New York State Office of Mental Health

Dennis Haffron, M.S., Executive Director, Alliance for Labor Community Services, Rockford, Illinois; formerly, Executive Director, Winnebago County Council on Aging, Rockford, Illinois

Paul Hardy, M.D., Veterans Administration Medical Center, Boston, Massachusetts

Peter Q. Harris, M.D., Ph.D., Assistant Professor of Psychiatry, Dartmouth Medical School, Hanover, New Hampshire

David B. Kassoff, M.D., Clinical Assistant Professor in Psychiatry, University of Medicine and Dentistry of New Jersey, Rutgers Medical School, New Brunswick, New Jersey

Daniel J. Klenow, Ph.D., Associate Professor of Sociology/Anthropology, North Dakota State University, Fargo, North Dakota

Aaron Lipman, Ph.D., Professor of Sociology, University of Miami, Coral Gables, Florida; Fellow, Gerontological Society of America

Jacob Loke, M.D., Assistant Professor of Medicine, Pulmonary Section, Yale University School of Medicine, New Haven, Connecticut

Pauline Loveless, Ph.D., Assistant Dean, College of Criminal Justice, Sam Houston State University, Huntsville, Texas

Dwight N. McNeill, M.P.H., Director of Clinical and Facility Support, Edgehill Newport, Newport, Rhode Island

Donald A. Mahler, M.D., Assistant Professor of Medicine; Director of Pulmonary Function Laboratory, Pulmonary Section, Department of Medicine, Dartmouth Hitchcock Medical Center, Hanover, New Hampshire

Richard A. Matthay, M.D., Associate Professor of Medicine, Yale University School of Medicine; Associate Director of Pulmonary Section, Department of Internal Medicine, Yale University School of Medicine, New Haven, Connecticut

L. Herbert Maurer, M.D., Associate Professor of Medicine, Section of Hematology/Oncology, Dartmouth Hitchcock Medical Center, Hanover, New Hampshire

Gary A. Mitchell, M.D., Hemodialysis Units and Department of Medical Education, St. Joseph's Hospital, South Bend, Indiana

H.R. Moody, Ph.D., Deputy Director, Brookdale Center on Aging, Hunter College of the City University of New York, New York, New York

David R. Murray, State Program Director, National Long Term Care Channeling Demonstration Program, New York State Office for the Aging, Albany, New York

William A. Nelson, Ph.D., Associate Professor of Clinical Psychiatry, Dartmouth Medical School, Hanover, New Hampshire; Chief, Chaplain Service, Veterans Administration Medical and Regional Office Center, White River Junction, Vermont

William E. Oriol, formerly, Staff Director, United States Senate Special Committee on Aging; Fellow, Gerontological Society of America

Lawrence W. Raymond, M.D., formerly, Yale University School of Medicine, New Haven, Connecticut

Frank Y. Reynolds, M.D., Professor of Medicine and Head of Pulmonary Section, Yale University School of Medicine, New Haven, Connecticut

Bernard Rollin, Ph.D., Professor of Philosophy, Colorado State University, Fort Collins, Colorado

Rosanna Roochnik, M.S.W., A.C.S.W., formerly, Assistant Director of Social Services, Beth Abraham Hospital, Bronx, New York

Florence Safford, D.S.W., formerly, Department of Social Work Services, Isabella Geriatric Center, New York, New York

Shura Saul, Ed.D., A.C.S.W., Educational Coordinator, Kingsbridge Heights Nursing Home, Bronx, New York; Adjunct Professor, Brookdale Program for Aging, Wurzweiler School of Social Work, Yeshiva University, New York, New York; President, Board of Directors, Bronx-Northern Manhattan Coalition for the Elderly in Long Term Care

Arlene Seguine, Ed.D., Associate Professor of Gerontology and Thanatology, Hunter College of the City University of New York; President, Health Council of the New York State Association for Health, Physical Education and Recreation

Irene L. Sell, R.N., Ed.D., Professor of Nursing, Richard L. Conally College, Long Island University, Brooklyn, New York

Stanley E. Slivkin, M.D., Assistant Professor of Psychiatry in Residence, University of California at Los Angeles, School of Medicine; Staff Psychiatrist, Los Angeles Veterans Administration Medical Center, Brentwood Division, Los Angeles, California

Max M. Stern, M.D., Clinical Associate Professor Emeritus, State University of New York, Downstate Medical Center, Brooklyn, New York; Professor Emeritus, Lecturer and Training Analyst, Division of Psychoanalytic Education, State University of New York (now, The Psychoanalytic Institute at New York University Medical Center, New York, New York)

Michael M. Stewart, M.D., Vice President, The Rockefeller Foundation; Associate Professor of Clinical Medicine, College of Physicians and Surgeons, Columbia University

Sandra E. Tars, Ph.D., Chief Psychologist, Hutchings Psychiatric Center, Syracuse, New York; Assistant Professor of Psychiatry, State University of New York Upstate Medical Center, Syracuse, New York

Glenn M. Vernon, Ph.D., Professor of Sociology, University of Utah, Salt Lake City, Utah

Marcella Bakur Weiner, E.D., Adjunct Professor, City University of New York; Executive Director, Geriatric Problem-Solving, Inc., New York, New York

COLUMBIA UNIVERSITY PRESS/
FOUNDATION OF THANATOLOGY SERIES

Teaching Psychosocial Aspects of Patient Care
Bernard Schoenberg, Helen F. Pettit, and Arthur C. Carr, editors

Loss and Grief: Psychological Management in Medical Practice
Bernard Schoenberg, Arthur C. Carr, David Peretz, and Austin H. Kutscher, editors

Psychosocial Aspects of Terminal Care
Bernard Schoenberg, Arthur C. Carr, David Peretz, and Austin H. Kutscher, editors

Psychosocial Aspects of Cystic Fibrosis: A Model for Chronic Lung Disease
Paul R. Patterson, Carolyn R. Denning, and Austin H. Kutscher, editors

The Terminal Patient: Oral Care
Austin H. Kutscher, Bernard Schoenberg, and Arthur C. Carr, editors

Psychopharmacologic Agents for the Terminally Ill and Bereaved
Ivan K. Goldberg, Sidney Malitz, and Austin H. Kutscher, editors

Anticipatory Grief
Bernard Schoenberg, Arthur C. Carr, Austin H. Kutscher, David Peretz, and Ivan K. Goldberg, editors

Bereavement: Its Psychosocial Aspects
Bernard Schoenberg, Irwin Gerber, Alfred Wiener, Austin H. Kutscher, David Peretz, and Arthur C. Carr, editors

The Nurse as Caregiver for the Terminal Patient and His Family
Ann M. Earle, Nina T. Argondizzo, and Austin H. Kutscher, editors

Social Work with the Dying Patient and the Family
Elizabeth R. Prichard, Jean Collard, Ben A. Orcutt, Austin H. Kutscher, Irene B. Seeland, and Nathan Lefkowitz, editors

Home Care: Living with Dying
Elizabeth R. Prichard, Jean Collard, Janet Starr, Josephine A. Lockwood, Austin H. Kutscher, and Irene B. Seeland, editors

Psychosocial Aspects of Cardiovascular Disease: The Life-Threatened Patient, the Family, and the Staff
James Reiffel, Robert DeBellis, Lester C. Mark, Austin H. Kutscher, Paul R. Patterson, and Bernard Schoenberg, editors

Acute Grief: Counseling the Bereaved
Otto S. Margolis, Howard C. Raether, Austin H. Kutscher, J, Bruce Powers, Irene B. Seeland, Robert DeBellis, and Daniel J. Cherico, editors

The Human Side of Homicide
Bruce L. Danto, John Bruhns, and Austin H. Kutscher, editors

Hospice U.S.A.
Austin H. Kutscher, Samuel C. Klagsbrun, Richard J. Torpie, Robert DeBellis, Mahlon S. Hale, and Margot Tallmer, editors

The Child and Death
John E. Schowalter, Paul R. Patterson, Margot Tallmer, Austin H. Kutscher, Stephen V. Gullo, and David Peretz, editors

The Life-Threatened Elderly
Margot Tallmer, Elizabeth R. Prichard, Austin H. Kutscher, Robert DeBellis, Mahlon S. Hale, and Ivan K. Goldberg, editors